MW01601066

A Place as Wild as The West Ever Was

Mesilla, New Mexico 1848-1872

Second Edition

Mary Daniels Taylor

assisted by Nona Barrick

Copyright © 2025 by Mesilla Publishing

All Rights Reserved

This book, or parts thereof, may not be reproduced in any form,
including information storage and retrieval systems,
without explicit permission from Mesilla Publishing,
except for brief quotations included in articles and reviews.

Front Cover Photograph:
Mesilla plaza with kiosko in early morning fog.
San Albino Church in the background,
circa 1979 by Mary Daniels Taylor.
Typeset by David G. Thomas

ISBN 979-8-9927568-0-7

Mesilla Publishing, Mesilla, N. M.

Contents

List of Illustrations

FOREWORD

In the Second Part of Shakespeare's King Henry the Fourth (Act III, Scene 1), the Earl of Warwick counsels the King that "There is a history in all men's lives..." At that moment King Henry is having trouble sleeping because he is worried about war and revolution and the other great events that impact on his royal life. Warwick's advice nevertheless rings true. History is more than the trials and tribulations of great men.

Today a growing number of historians and other scholars appreciate Warwick's words. This was not always the case. We doubt that Shakespeare could have appreciated the greater significance, and truth, of Warwick's point. And early historians were similarly narrow-minded in their conceptualizations of history. But today we appreciate that history is not merely the trials and tribulations of great men. Indeed, the truly important patterns and processes of history, those most responsible for making the world what it is today, are those that can best be described as "common." What matters are the thoughts, actions, and experiences of common people. What matters are the relations and associations among common events and trends.

Mary Daniels Taylor's *A Place as Wild as The West Ever Was: Mesilla, New Mexico 1848-1872* is a landmark publication, because it epitomizes the modern movement among historians to focus on the common and routine. By including the rhythms of daily life as a major focus of her work, Mary breathes life into the pre-railroad village of Mesilla more than many other authors and historians have done before. We can feel the heat of a July afternoon, for example; she spells it out in so many words, and by doing so gives it substance. We can feel the ways in which the oppressive weather worked upon people's moods and motivations, and sometimes their actions. Typical summer weather

is not a significant historic event or situation. But writing about it creates three-dimensional history; history with depth. It makes the past come alive. And while not strictly based on documentary, empirical evidence, it is nevertheless reasonable, holistic historical reconstruction. There are no accurate weather records for Mesilla in the 1850s-1870s, though we would wager that it was hot on most every July afternoon during these decades!

There is more to Mary Taylor's work, however. Writing the history of the common and the routine—doing good history—requires more painstaking, time-consuming empirical research than taking the traditional approach and limiting oneself to the famous (or the infamous) and the powerful. Researching the lives of most residents of Mesilla is harder work than researching the life of Billy the Kid. Data regarding the former are so much more difficult to find and interpret. Data on the latter, even accurate data sometimes overwhelm us in their volume.

Mary Taylor provides us with both three-dimensional and carefully documented history, the former being the result of her uncanny ability to bring history alive and the latter being the result of tireless, careful, study. This is a wonderful and important book, the product of many years of dedication, perseverance, and skilled archival research. It is also, quite simply and not insignificantly, a good read. The New Mexico State University Museum staff is pleased to have played a small role in seeing this notable work to fruition.

A number of people helped transform this work from author's manuscript to finished publication. Their contributions to the finished book have been many and greatly appreciated. New Mexico State University English student Jeff Becker did some of the initial editing of the manuscript. New Mexico State University Museum volunteer George Herman picked up where Jeff left off (upon graduation), and worked tirelessly over many months to help edit and format the text. Bonnie Newman helped prepare the manuscript. Another volunteer, Terry L. Corbett assisted with footnote editing. Dennis P. Daily of the Archives and Special Collections Department, New Mexico State University Library helped get the images ready for printing. Ray Gonzalez, Harry Myers, and Kaisa Barthuli assisted in preparing maps to orient the reader. Ray Gonzalez designed the book's cover. Helen Pustmueller introduced John Duane Rice, whose technical expertise was critical to the recovery and formatting of the electronic manuscript. Michael and Melody Sumner of Burning Books provided the expertise needed for the final production of the book.

Finally, Mary, J. Paul and Michael Taylor gave generously of their time to consult with Terry Reynolds regarding the editorial and production processes and decisions.

Terry Reynolds, Curator
Edward Staski, Director
New Mexico State University Museum
Las Cruces, New Mexico

Note to Second Edition

The first edition of *A Place as Wild as the West Ever Was - Mesilla, New Mexico: 1848-1872* was printed in 2004 by New Mexico State University Museum, Las Cruces, New Mexico. The book has since sold out and because of popular demand, it has been reprinted in this second edition. This reprint also coincides with the opening of the Taylor-Mesilla Historic Site owned and managed by New Mexico Historic Sites, Department of Cultural Affairs. The historic Taylor property facing the plaza in Mesilla, New Mexico, and its extensive collection, were deeded to the State of New Mexico through a generous donation by the Mary Helen Daniels and J. Paul Taylor Family in 2003.

INTRODUCTION

This book is about the history of Mesilla, New Mexico, a place as wild as the west ever was. Located 35 miles north of the Mexican border, its history has never been told in the fascinating way that is presented in the following pages. Mesilla was an anchor for European and Mestizo settlement in southern New Mexico and was a focal point of commercial, religious and military activity in the American Southwest. Its strategic geographic location made it the hub of transportation routes for the region from the early 1850's until the 1880's with the arrival of the railroad, which was routed a few miles to the east in Las Cruces. Its pivotal role as a center of commerce on the Chihuahua Trail running north and south, and on the various mail and stage lines running east and west, made it a crossroads of traditions and ideas. Mesilla continues to be a place where diverse traditions and ethnic backgrounds form an eclectic way of life in the region.

This publication is unique in that it presents the Mexican and early Territorial history of Mesilla from not only the Anglo, but also the Mexican perspective. Much of the information presented in these pages is gleaned from research into primary records that have been buried for the last 150 years in the collections of the Durango, Chihuahua and Juárez diocesan archives in Mexico.

Our mother, Mary Daniels Taylor, is the author of this publication. She was assisted for many years by Mrs. Nona Barrick, a long-time friend of our family. As the seven children of Mary and Paul Taylor, we grew up watching our mother and Nona Barrick working on this book in our Mesilla family home. With the expert help of Mrs. Margaret Mestas during the 1960s and 70s in reading the Spanish paleography of the mid 19th century, the information presented is as precise as it can be in its interpretation of what the Mexican archives tell

us of mid 19th century Mesilla. As children we all remember the great times Mrs. Barrick, Mrs. Mestas, and our mother had in translating these vivid accounts of the town's rich history. Their work also included scores of trips to the microfilm collections at New Mexico State University in Las Cruces and to the Juárez Archives in Juárez, Mexico. The research for this publication began in the 1950s, and half a century later the benefits of the thousands of hours of work are finally available to the public through this publication.

Our mother was born Mary Helen Daniels in 1922 in El Paso, Texas. She was the only child of Albert and Mamie Daniels. She grew up as a youngster within a few blocks of the Mexican border at Smeltertown (on the north edge of El Paso) where her father was foreman of the cement plant. The daily life along the border, with its inherent intrigue and social/racial discrimination, had a profound influence on her future work as a respected scholar of border studies. Mary Helen Daniels graduated from El Paso High School in 1940 and from the University of Texas at El Paso in 1943. She taught 2nd grade at White School and history at Bowie High School in El Paso. She later became an English instructor with the English Department at New Mexico State University in Las Cruces in 1946 and 1947. Our mother married J. Paul Taylor in 1945.

When our mother and father were younger, and before they knew each other, they each had visited Mesilla and liked the small-town atmosphere. So, after they were married they decided to move to Mesilla in 1947 and raise their family. In 1951, they purchased property on the west side of the plaza where they still live today. Our parents quickly became a part of the community, being deeply involved in the church and local politics. The property they bought was thought by most to be a dilapidated old adobe, which it was. But they had the vision to make it their home and commenced to raise seven children within its walls, renovating storage rooms and old barn areas and building additions as the number of children grew. The property is representative of the classic architecture of its day and has appeared in numerous articles and books over the years. Its role in the history of Mesilla figures prominently as part of the 19th century backdrop for much of what is talked about in this book. The property is on the National Register of Historic Places, and also listed as part of the Mesilla Plaza National Historic Landmark, the highest historic distinction a property can be given in the United States.

Our mother's contributions to the region as an historian, paleographer, and former archivist for the Diocese of Las Cruces have made her a leading authority on the history of southern New Mexico. Her perspective on the history is invaluable in that she has researched primary documents from Mexican archives for the last 40 years that provide previously unknown information on the Mesilla Valley and New Mexico. Recent fruits of her labor, with our father's assistance as a state legislator, have enabled the microfilming of the Durango archives pertaining to this region. Copies of the microfilm have been placed at the Rio Grande Historical Collections at New Mexico State University in Las Cruces for researchers. This accomplishment is truly monumental.

Mrs. Nona Barrick was our mother's partner in writing many of the chapters of this book during the 1960s and 1970s. Mrs. Barrick was born in 1915 in Hoosick, New York. She received her B.S. from Northwestern University at Evanston, Illinois in 1938, and also received her Registered Nurse certificate from Evanston Hospital. She married Professor Kenneth Barrick in 1938 and in 1949 they moved to Las Cruces, New Mexico. Kenneth Barrick is an accomplished artist who has painted many scenes of Mesilla's history, including some presented in this book. The Barrick and Taylor families spent many weekends together exploring the heritage of southern New Mexico at historic

military forts, along trails and at ruins of old settlements. Their shared love of history prompted Mary Taylor and Nona Barrick to embark on writing the fascinating history that is told in these pages.

The book has been added to and revised through the years, as new information from the archives emerged. Most of the collaborative work between Mrs. Barrick, Mrs. Mestas and our mother was done from the 1960s through the 1970s. Since then, our mother has added more information from the research gleaned in the archives. She edited and put final touches on the manuscript, with the valued assistance of Ester Geck (whose ancestors were prominent inhabitants of the Mesilla Valley). The task of preparing the final manuscript for publication has fallen in the very capable hands of Dr. Terry Reynolds, Curator of the University Museum at New Mexico State University in Las Cruces. Dr. Reynolds and our mother worked together in the early 1980s researching archives pertaining to the early history of Tortugas, a village located just a few miles from Mesilla.

As children in Mesilla we were privileged to have been brought up in an atmosphere of history. The celebrations and village events that we witnessed and were a part of with the other *Mesilleros* in the 1950s, were the traditions of Mesilla from 100 years earlier, ones that evolved from the traditions that the founders of the village had brought with them from deep in Mexico, and the Indian pueblos and Spanish towns of the north. We were witnessing the passage of time, the normal cycle of history, experiencing time-honored traditions mixed with new adaptations and ideas. The continued traditions of faith and family are still very much in evidence in many of the families of the Mesilla Valley today.

Our mother wrote about Mesilla's history in a way that is much more than just a scholarly assessment of what transpired in the past; she wrote about it from a deeply passionate point of view, having been accepted by the town elders who were always anxious to share their personal family stories of Mesilla. Many who she interviewed were second generation *Mesilleros* whose parents had been born in Mesilla shortly after its settlement in the 1850s. These people shared their personal stories of what transpired on feast days, on historical days such as the raising of the flag over the plaza ratifying the Gadsden Purchase, of the political riot of the 1870s that left many dead, of the floods, of the depredations by Apache avenging injustices that had been committed against them, and about daily life.

We are very proud to introduce this publication to you. We know you will find it enjoyable.

Mary and J. Paul Taylor's children:
Robert, Dolores, Mike, Mary Helen,
John, Pat, and Rosemary
December 2002

Chapter 1 | THE SOURCE

The captains of Francisco Vásques de Coronado, after a hard march of eighty leagues down the Río de Tigues,[1] the Río Grande del Norte del Bravo, dismounted and looked out over what is today known as the Valley of La Mesilla. They stood opposite the foot of the Sierra del Robledo and removed their helmets. The tallest officer had red hair, and it was wet with sweat which ran down into his beard.

It was the year 1541, and Vásques de Coronado had sent his soldiers down the River of the North, to look for possible habitation. Now that the eighty leagues had been counted out meticulously by the turning of the supply cart's wheel, they could begin the return the next morning to the north, to their headquarters at Tiguex. This evening, then, was one of relief—the journey was done.

In the green band of the Río Grande Valley winding its way southward toward what was to be known as El Paso del Norte, The Pass of the North,[2] the soldiers could see no living soul. The little plateau where the Spaniards stood was covered with green mesquite, and after the evening shower, the air was fragrant. Down by the willowed banks of the river, ravens called one to another; a blue lizard ran across the stones below. There in the Mesilla Valley, the Spanish soldiers made their evening fires. In the morning, they were gone, and the land returned to the indifference of sun and sand and sky.

Forty-one years after the conquistador captains of Coronado held their solitary watch on the mesa overlooking the river, Captain Don Antonio de Espejo, wealthy Spanish gentleman from Cordova, accompanied an expedition into Nueva Andalucia, as he called New Mexico. Since the avowed purpose of Spanish exploration was to Christianize, these soldiers and their captain who sought the Seven Cities of Cibola, accompanied Fray Bernardino Beltrán on the trail northward. For the first time, life in the Mesilla valley was recorded: a band of Indians which Espejo called "Tobosas" wandered the valley floor searching for meat and herbs and locusts to eat. They wondered at the fire from Spanish guns, the glistening amour, and the beasts which carried both Spaniard and his burden to the northern portion of the Kingdom of New Mexico.

When Don Juan de Oñate came through the Mesilla Valley in 1598 from Zacatecas with colonists and Indians to till the rich earth of Northern New Mexico and to build herds with the cattle they brought, he encountered the Manso and Suma Indians. Further to the south, their kin had watched as Oñate thrust the Spanish standard, the banner of the King, into the earth as he stood on the bank of the Río Grande del Bravo del Norte at San Lorenzo de la Toma.[3] In a loud voice he claimed all the territory for his king; a Mass was said. The Indians were astonished when the Spaniards knelt before the Crucifix, the symbol of their God—even he knelt who was most important of all, Captain Don Juan de Oñate.[4]

At the Pass of the North in 1630, the Franciscan Superior of the Conversion of New Mexico, Custos Benavides, recorded Indian life there as Suma and Manso. He set Franciscans to the task of Europeanizing—they baptized, taught the Indians Spanish and the sedentary art of farming. These Franciscans failed at first and abandoned their task, but in 1659 Fray García de San Francisco added Piros to the Manso population at the Pass, establishing the mission of Nuestra Señora de Guadalupe del Norte y los Mansos, Our Lady of Guadalupe of The Pass of the North and the Manso Indians.

The settlement, El Paso del Norte, was on the west bank of the Río Grande. It was originally a paraje or camping place at a natural ford of the

2 ~ Chapter 1

river. It straddled the early trail, El Camino Real, as it led circuitously northward on the river's other bank through rough and rocky mountain terrain. Even though hazardous at times, this natural ford made the river passable for wagons and travelers at low water.[5]

These Indians then, together with other Piros, Tompiros, the Pueblos and the Spaniards who fled northern New Mexico with Governor Antonio de Otermín after the northern pueblos revolted against Spanish authority in 1680, peopled the cluster of villages and missions around the Mission of Guadalupe. The Spanish governor of the Province of New Mexico, in exile at the Pass, planned to settle Indians and Spaniards into pueblos near the original settlement in an orderly manner, below and along the river. El Real de San Lorenzo was to be the crown colony, the center of Spanish government; Socorro del Sur, Ysleta del Sur, and Senecú del Sur were to be settled with proportionate numbers of Spaniards and Indians.

Twelve years after Otermín's flight downriver, another Spanish governor, Don Diego de Vargas, marched his army of reconquest back to Santa Fe. In spite of orders for all refugees to proceed with him, muster rolls and church records reveal that some families, Spaniards—Gamboa, Alderete, Tapia—remained at the Pass, and in a few years the population became, for the most part, one of mestizos, those individuals of mixed Spanish, Indian, and other blood. This mestizo population at Paso became diffused to an even greater degree by the practice adopted by Spanish officers as they pursued hostile Indians: officers on campaign often took women and children prisoners, and these were awarded to Spanish households at the Pass and to Indian scouts from pueblos below the Pass. These prisoners were to be settled "into the Bosom of the Holy Faith" and were noted in church records as *genízaros*.[6]

After almost one hundred and fifty years of European influx and influence, at the beginning of the eighteenth century, the settlement of Paso del Norte sprawled over the valley floor at the centuries-old crossing of the river. Here, after years of intermarriage and cohabitation, the circumstances of history had created a unique type of individual—a mixture of Piro, Tompiro, Tiwa, Tewa, Manso, Suma, Apache, genízaro,[7] mulato, and Spaniard. These mestizos were among the forefathers of the colonists who were to colonize the village of La Mesilla and the Mesilla Valley.

When one civilization imposes itself upon another, as the Spanish culture threw its shadow across that of the Indian at the Pass, only the excesses are remembered and chronicled. The aggression of the Spanish occupation all but eclipsed the beauty which the Spaniard added to the indigenous population—the Castilian tongue; the multihued heritage of the Spanish provinces of Castile, Aragon and Santander; and the richness of song went almost unnoticed in the wake of appropriation of lands, enslavement, and the attempted suffocation of the Indian religion. The severity and persistence with which the Spaniards subdued the Indian religion finally became the near nemesis of Christianity at the Pass of the North. The Mansos who lived at Spanish contact in shadowed canyons and on heights and parajes near the Pass grew restless under imposed Christianity as did the Piros and Tompiros there, and as did the Sumas who were, not unlike their Apache relatives, nomads. The struggle of cultures—Indian against Spaniard—became a catalyst for brewing storms of rebellion. The Manso with his religious rites and gods, hid away from the Spaniards in caves in the mountains near Paso del Norte. In the early 1700's they rose against the oppression of the Spaniard and his Christian God as the Indians had in northern New Mexico. Missions were burned; obscenities voiced and carried out against the material symbols of Catholicism. In turn, Franciscan friars fell upon images and instruments essential to Indian worship, burned and destroyed them. For the most part, these priests replied to the hostile rejection of Christianity only with punishment and threats, and these were only partially understood because many of the Franciscans were unable to, or felt no need to, learn the Indian tongues.[8]

Plate 1: The town of Paso del Norte (current day Ciudad Juárez) in its early years was small in comparison to the metropolis it is today. In the beginning it was the main paraje straddling the Río Grande before the trail went north to the Province of New Mexico. El Paso as seen by A.B. Grey of Bartlett's Boundary survey in 1854. Carl Schuchard Lithograph Collection, MS 0339, Rio Grande Historical Collections, New Mexico State University Library, Las Cruces, New Mexico.

But, finally, through necessity, and from the tireless devotion of a few dedicated Franciscans among whom was Fray García de San Francisco, the intensity of Indian devotion to their gods began to give way and to blend with homage to Nuestra Señora de Guadalupe, the Virgin Mother of God who appeared to the Indian Juan Diego on the hill of Tepeyac near Mexico City in 1531. Her image on his cloak, his tilma, today is venerated throughout Latin America. She became the special patroness of the Indian and his half-brother, the mestizo; Her intercession was, and is still, felt the length of the river valley. The friars who were most successful in teaching Christianity to the Indians allowed these religions to overlap, bargaining wisely that one day the beloved Guadalupe would triumph.[9]

As the centuries passed, the Indian matachínes continued to dance in the Virgin's honor before the mission of Guadalupe at the Pass. Even now, every December 12, the drums beat there and in pueblos along the valley from Tortugas, forty miles upriver from Paso, to that city itself, today known as Juárez. The dances of the Indian and the mestizo blend with kindred immigrant cultures of northern Mexico, and with those far to the south. The rhythm of drums and ankle shells, the sound of small bells suspended from shirts and aprons, purple, green, and blue peacock feathers, headdresses brilliant with inlaid mirrors and tinsel—this is the ritual from many sources performed each year. On this December day, the Indian peoples of the Río Grande once again reaffirm their claim to the heritage of Nuestra Señora de Guadalupe, Our Lady of Guadalupe, the unifying force for the people of the Pass to the Valley of the Mesilla.[10]

Traveling upriver on the sandy heights of the east bank, along the trail which would be known as the Camino Real de Tierra Adentro (Royal Road to the Interior Lands), Spanish chroniclers of the sixteenth and seventeenth centuries made no reference to any habitation, permanent or temporary, called "Mesilla" on the west side of the river. In those early years, the only designation for this spot was "paraje," campground, and this lay below a lonely, windswept western plateau where Indians sometimes left the framework of temporary dwellings and small rows of corn planted with the hope of enough rain for a harvest on their return.

On that western bank of the Río Grande, there were brambles and thickets of thorned bosque which discouraged travel, and knowledge of that side was scant, early cartographers concentrating on the east bank. Brigadier Don Pedro Rivera, in 1726 in his journal noted the mountains to the east of the Camino Real, those mountains which he called Sierra de Manso and which included the small range to be known as the Organ Mountains. In 1771 Nicolas LaFora of the Royal Spanish Engineers undertook a journey of presidial inspection along the Camino Real to the north. He noted only sandy places—llanos arenosos—to the west which ascended into mesas across the river. His cartographer Don Bernardo Miera y Pacheco at the same time recommended locations for the establishment of presidios in New Mexico, marking these sites on opposite sides of the great river as Mesilla and Ranchería. Now, on that solitary trail, the Royal Road to the north along the Jornada del Muerto, pieces of a Spanish olive jar and the rusted lock from a flint gun have emerged from sand ripples[11]—remnants of the journeys of early Spanish travelers.

Until the nineteenth century, then, Mesilla was an imprecise place name on the western bank of the river.

In 1810, in the little Mexican village of Dolores in the state of Hidalgo, Father Miguel Hidalgo y Costilla precipitated into full insurrection the quarrels between Peninsular Spaniards—gachupines—and the Mexican-born Spaniards, criollos. As the church bell at Dolores rang for early Mass on September 16, the Grito—the cry which began the revolution which eventually would free Mexico from Spanish rule—broke the silence of dawn: "Viva independencia! Viva Nuestra Señora de Guadalupe! Death to bad government!" Spanish patrols in the Mesilla Valley who now rode the trails after 1800 in pursuit of the Apache, including a new path on the west of the river, were only vaguely aware of this action to the south which had precipitated the conflict between Spain and her Mexican colony. The captain of one of these patrols, José Manrique, in reports sent back to headquarters, frequently mentioned the place of La Mesilla.

Before the struggle to throw off Spanish rule ended in 1821 and even after the collapse of Agustín de Iturbide's empire, officials of that government considered the establishment of a separate bishopric in New Mexico.[12] From reports of pastoral *visitas*—tours of inspection—as the bishops of Durango, Mexico, traveled through the vast bishopric of *Nuevo Méjico*, and from military explorations, much of the northern frontier along the Río Grande appeared ready for settlement. Along the river between the Pass and the paraje fifty miles to the north called Ancón de Doña Ana, there had been attempts to establish ranchos in the expanse of desert grasses; a few brave families tried to make homes at the alluvial mouths of canyons and in small river valleys. Thin chimney smokes were the only signs of the few who hung on while annihilation was a constant threat and often a reality when, from sentinel mountain peaks, the Apache, the Comanche, the Navajo and the Kiowa attacked at will.

Along the dusty mail route from Chihuahua through the Mesilla Valley the stops were for the most part abandoned ranchos: Rancho de Canutillo which had been settled in 1823 and Rancho de Brazito where Don Juan Antonio García y Noriega had made a brave attempt to settle in 1805, appeasing the Apache by planting corn for his use. Farther north, in the shadow of a mighty mountain rock was the deserted paraje and abandoned rancho of Robledillo.[13]

After the first hundred years, the mission settlements below the Pass, and the Pass itself, began to feel the cumulate effects of flood, drought, and famine. The vagaries of the river swept away the livelihood of the inhabitants, and inside the district of Paso, within the barrios or districts where the lesser farmers and day laborers lived,

the inhabitants were almost destitute. But in spite of the want brought about by the alternate flooding and drought of the quixotic river, the Indian and the mestizo persisted in seeding the land according to the cycles of the moon and petitioning both patron saints and ancient gods for good harvests. And on the twelfth of December each year bonfires—luminarias—brightened the night and drumbeats matched ancient dance steps in honor of Our Lady, Nuestra Señora de Guadalupe.

As early as 1827 the government at Chihuahua recognized the advantages of establishing a colony fifty miles upriver from Paso del Norte at the Ancón de Doña Ana.[14] The need for protection for wagon trains, and the establishment and extension of territorial claims of Chihuahua resulted in an insistence that such a colony be established. A few entrepreneurs were chosen—empresarios— important and wealthy men who would send their indentured servants, their *peónes*, to dig the acequia necessary to bring water from the river to the fields. It was essential that the ditches, acequias, be dug first; it was work made dangerous by the constant threat of Apache attack. The Mexican government, preoccupied by Texas troubles,[15] offered them scant protection.

On the rough, uncertain journey from Paso to Doña Ana, an escort of three soldiers had come with the colonists, bringing a few old muskets and a little ammunition, traveling at night to avoid attack. There on the trail at evening when there was no Indian sign, they would huddle together around the campfire singing melancholy, nostalgic songs as they thought of the uncertain future and the terror of the Apache arrow:

> Paso del Norte, how far behind you remain
> Bright haven, from you I am departing;
> There my parents are thinking of me
> Only God knows if I will return to see them.
> Oh, what hardships assail the absent man
> When he is away from his family and homeland;
> He sighs for his family and for his sweetheart.
> He is not far from giving way to tears.[16]

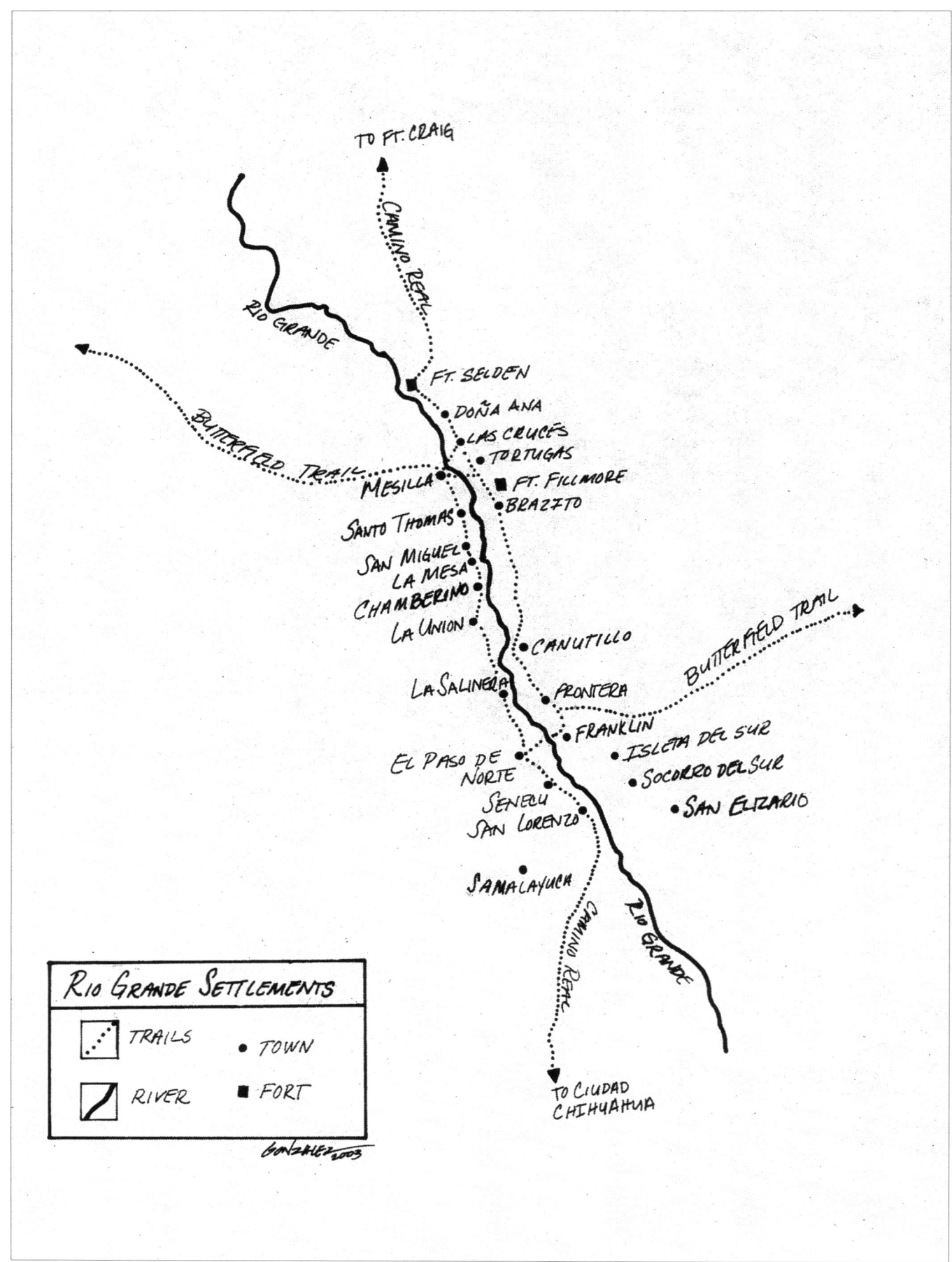

Mexican Colonel and Inspector of Frontier Forces, Don Mauricio Ugarte, on his way upriver to battle Texans occupying New Mexico in August, 1843, saw four colonists in the fields of Doña Ana. They were clothed in ragged fashion and tried to hide themselves from him. When he caught up to them, they told him that there were more settlers in caves in nearby hills who had seen the force coming—they ran to hide because they were nearly naked. Ugarte left them food, some ammunition against the Apaches, and uniforms to clothe themselves with. And he sent Lt. Ollaca back to the Pass to bring them additional provisions and necessary armament.[17]

But by 1844, the colony of Doña Ana was well established. Along the Camino Real in October, 1845, Father Eligio Tobar rode muleback—the secretary of the visita which Bishop José Antonio Zubiría was making to the Department of New Mexico and to the northern limits of the Diocese of Durango. He rode silently behind the bishop watching the heights rise before him and the river below shimmering in the noon of early Fall. The little parish ahead was Nuestra Señora de Candelaria at Doña Ana,[18] and the oratorio—the room in the Abeyta home set aside for bestowing of Sacraments and the celebration of Mass—was sometimes noted in the bishop's book as "Santa María de Candelaria." [19] It was here where Bishop Zubiría would now bestow the sacrament of Confirmation and say Mass. As they neared the village, Father Tobar could see the adobe elevation above that room, a *torreón*, a circular parapet which served as a lookout to detect movement of the Apaches. To the southwest across the river the expanse of thick bosque and desert mesquite, which in a few years would be cultivated into the new fields of La Mesilla, lay undisturbed in the sunlight. For the little village of Doña Ana it was a memorable day—the day when the Bishop of Durango celebrated the first Mass said in the village.

Chapter 2 | FROM BREAK OF DAY

From the break of day until eight o'clock in the morning of September 13, 1847, the fortified castle on the high rock of Chapultepec near the City of Mexico had been bombarded by United States artillery. After heroic resistance by young Mexican cadet defenders, Chapultepec fell, and shortly afterwards, the Zócalo, the central plaza with its Catedral Metropolitana,[20] was overcome. That night General Santa Ana and his forces left Mexico City and retired to Guadalupe Hidalgo[21] where he renounced the Presidency, and where later the Treaty of Guadalupe Hidalgo ending the war was to be negotiated. General Winfield Scott then marched the American forces up the avenue, later to be called Paseo de la Reforma in the Mexican capital where Aztec monarchs in a prior age had been transported on thrones borne in grandeur.

Six months after General Scott's entry into Mexico City, the Treaty of Guadalupe Hidalgo was signed by both nations on February 2, 1848. It was not to be ratified by both nations until May 30, 1848. In the United States on July 4, 1848, President James Polk proclaimed the treaty in effect.[22]

As regards any treaty between or among nations, the one most crucial instrument to the treaty's implementation is a good and accurate map of the territory involved. The definition of boundaries between the United States and Mexico during the process of negotiating the provisions of the treaty was complicated by the availability and accuracy of maps of the area. In those, terrain detail and spelling were often incorrect. The map Henry Disturnell drew in 1846 was the official treaty map. However, he authored more than twenty-two versions of this map, all different in detail regarding some degree or minute in latitude. Each one was used by a different agency or committee of the two countries, and hence there were many misunderstandings regarding the new boundary between the United States and Mexico.[23]

Eventually, the lands above El Paso between Hart's Mill in Texas and San Diego Mountain, north of Doña Ana in New Mexico and across the river to the west, measuring a full eight degrees in latitude, were to be a matter of disputed sovereignty between the United States and Mexico. This dispute was settled by the Gadsden Purchase, but not before the settlement of people at Mesilla in the disputed territory.

The course of the Río Grande added to the confusion and misunderstandings brought about by the Treaty of Guadalupe Hidalgo. The flooding in recent years of the Río Grande had swept its main channel further south. The boundary between Mexico and the United States, according to the treaty, was to be established at "the deepest channel": this phrase in the treaty, setting the boundary line in the center of the deepest, now newest, channel of the Río Grande, was to become the driving force for the initial flood of settlers from the Pass to the Mesilla Valley.

To the villagers at Paso del Norte and the nearby pueblos, the deepest channel had always been the old, the original channel; they knew no other until the river flung itself farther south. And they were naively convinced that the water would flow again into its former still damp course. The old channel of the river was to them since the beginning of memory, the only channel of the Río Grande. To the United States and its authorities the deepest channel meant the new channel which had recently cut farther south into Mexican territory by the relentless force of the mighty river itself. By 1848, the new channel was, by far, the deepest channel.[24] Consequently, American authorities ignored or did not understand the needs and the reasoning behind the desperation of the inhabitants of the pueblos whose properties and livelihood there would be forever affected.

The pueblos of San Elizario, Socorro, and Ysleta, all south of Paso del Norte, found themselves at the time of the American invasion in 1847-1848 on an island between two channels of the river. The island was considered as American territory as written by negotiators of the Treaty of Guadalupe. It was certainly within the boundary, the "deepest channel of the river," and locally, this interpretation was the source of bitter debate.

The pueblos of Senecú and San Lorenzo lay on the Mexican side, but to their anguish, their common pasture lands—their ejidos—and some of their cultivated lands, *terrenos de labor*, were on the American side across a river which had capriciously cut between their villages and their fields, leaving the inhabitants on the opposite side of the river from those lands. The American invaders had made it plain to these villagers that their rights to their ancestral lands, some of which now lay across the Río Grande, were to be ignored and defied. Many of them fled south toward the old paraje, the Ancón de Guadalupe.[25] Here was fertile land, and as the planting season was fast approaching, they needed fields to sow to provide food for their families.

The right of Mexican people in the conquered territory to retain their homes and fields had been guaranteed by the terms of the treaty. But by those same terms, the provision for the right to that property did not consider the plight of these farmers whose pueblos and working lands lay now on opposite sides of the river. The harvest and seed for next year's planting, the very lifeblood of the pueblos, seemed justly to belong, as it always had, to the families of Maese, Trujillo, Guerra, Madrid and others from those pueblos. To the Mexican, his grant which implied ownership of planting land was understood to be inseparable from his house lot, his *solar de casa*, in his village. The Americans, new to the territory, considered all this land ceded territory, not realizing nor thinking it important enough to consider.

But those who peopled Paso del Norte and the pueblos to the south on the Río Grande had a champion, a man with clerical collar and an unquenchable spirit and an always ready voice for justice. There were very many who loved him and a few shrill voiced well-to-do who hated him. He was a priest, a man with the wits and reputation for protecting the lower classes from those who would abuse and exploit them. In those years of the American conquest of Mexico, these unfortunate people had no rights or any voice except in him.

He was the Cura Ramón Ortiz, pastor of the mission of Nuestra Señora de Gaudalupe at Paso del Norte. It was said of Cura Ramón Ortiz that he "exerts a greater influence than any man in the state of Chihuahua."[26]

José Ramón Ortiz was born in 1814 in Santa Fe, New Mexico, of Spanish heritage with such illustrious forebears as Don Bernardo Mier y Pacheco, cartographer, soldier, and carver of saint images, a santero. Ramón was descended also from Nicolás Ortiz Niño Ladrón de Guevara, one of the Spaniards who first colonized New Mexico, and the first in that land of the numerous and powerful family of Ortiz. Ramón's mother Teresa Mier had many children, ten of whom survived. As she grew frail and weak, and as his father was a soldier and constantly off on Indian campaigns, the boy was sent to live with his grandparents Antonio José Ortiz and Rosa Bustamante. As part of a military family, it early became his dream to be a soldier, and when his widowed sister married again, her second husband, Don José Antonio Vizcarra, was Ramón's hero. Vizcarra, an officer in the Spanish army and governor of the Province of New Mexico in 1829, was a magnificent horseman, and from him Ramón learned horsemanship and military spirit very early.[27]

When Juan Rafael Rascón arrived in Santa Fe from Paso del Norte in 1829 as Vicar General, and Vicario General Visitador y Gobierno Eclesiastico,[28] Ecclesiastical Inspector and Ecclesiastical Governor of New Mexico for the Bishopric of Durango, he immediately saw the need for more

Plate 3: Church of Nuestra Señora de Guadalupe in Paso del Norte (current day Ciudad Juarez) originally built in 1659. Now the church is dwarfed by an adjacent construction of a newer church for the much larger congregation. Photo courtesy Museum of New Mexico, neg. no. 15671.

Plate 4: The funeral of Cura José Ramón Ortiz in 1896 was held at the church of Nuestra Señora de Guadalupe in Paso del Norte (Ciudad Juarez). So great was the number attending on that Holy Saturday that some sought a place to see in the bell tower of the church. Mary D. Taylor collection.

priests in this vast land and for a school where boys could prepare for the seminary by studying Castilian grammar and Latin. He set up such a school in his home with Guadalupe Miranda as teacher,[29] and here José Ramón began his studies. He exhibited such application and intelligence that the Vicario urged him to consider a vocation to the priesthood. Even though a military persuasion lingered in his heart, he was drawn to the idea of becoming a priest. And so when Juan Rafael Rascón began his return journey to Durango in 1832, José Ramón rode in the long caravan towards that city.

As the train of carriages, wagons, and horsemen neared the city of Durango, at the mining town of Cuencamé in October, 1833, Colonel Vizcarra, Ramón's beloved step-uncle and head of the military escort, died of cholera. Many members of the Vizcarra and Ortiz families died there, also, and it was here that Ramón learned from the native inhabitants to administer peyote and mariola to alleviate the symptoms of that dread disease.[30] It was with heavy heart that the young Ortiz arrived at the city of Durango and entered the seminary to begin his studies.

The revolutionary spirit of rebellion has always been spawned in the northern states of Mexico, and it was in the seminary of Durango, the principal educational institution in all of northern Mexico and New Mexico, that the foundation of resistance against tyrannical government was laid. In addition to theological and moral studies these young men, being concerned with basic rights of man, debated issues concerning the Mexican government in relation to the Catholic Mexican church. The ambience at the seminary was both conservative and liberal, and with fellow students and future rebels Diego Archuleta, José Antonio Martinez, and José Manuel Gallegos,[31] Ramón Ortiz became knowledgeable and astute in political thought. Their teachers were clergy who were among the most verbal opponents of Mexican government under the dictatorship of Antonio López de Santa Ana: Luis Rubio, Juan Rafael Rascón, and the bishop himself, Don José Antonio Zubiria y Escalante.[32] From this point on, Ortiz' vocation as a priest and

his dedication to political morality never separated. He remained a soldier all his life, a soldier of the Cross and a soldier in political strife. He was to become the gentle shepherd of the poor and the oppressed, and also a fiery patriot and opponent of centralized government in Mexico and of Santa Ana himself.

His curacy began in 1838 upon the death of Father Maximo de Jesús Yrigoyen at Paso del Norte, and his jurisdiction, his curato, extended from that villa north on the Río Bravo through the area of Doña Ana. On that desolate distance of river, the reputation of the young priest became one of preoccupation with the poor, the humble, the oppressed—those with few individual rights under the Mexican government. He cared for them during disasters of flood, famine, cholera, and he defended them in the despair brought on by centuries of despotism in Spanish and Mexican government—his courage brought new hope to those who had never known such a man as this. As pastor, he expected much from them; that their work be perfectly carried out, that the repairs and upkeep of the mission church be done in like manner, that they live and die as Christian law required. During his tenure as cura of Nuestra Señora de Guadalupe, and at the cost many times of his own safety, he served as buffer between residents of the Pass and tyranny. Self doubt assailed him constantly regarding his priestly vows of humility and obedience which, more often than not, conflicted with his passionate defense of justice and an eloquent spirit quick to defend his people.

In 1841, the expedition mounted in Texas to exert the new republic's jurisdiction over New Mexico ended in total defeat and disaster for the Texans.[33] As a victorious Manuel Armijo, governor and military comandante of New Mexico, sent Damacio Salazar south along the Camino Real towards Mexico City with the ragged and captive survivors of that expedition, the news of the officer's barbaric and savage treatment of the prisoners preceded him. At Paso del Norte, Salazar on horseback led the faltering column down the

Plate 5: No photograph or painting exists of Father Ramón Ortiz except for a photograph taken when he was very old. Ken Barrick made this sketch of him which relied on contemporary description and on certain resemblances common in his family. Painted in the 1980s. Mary D. Taylor Collection.

avenue past the home of the young Cura then only three years into his curacy. The sight of the emaciated and maltreated men was more than the priest could endure; he immediately notified Comandante José María González of the brutality of the Mexican officer. The commander detained and reprimanded Salazar, and Ramón Ortiz took the weary, starving Texans into his home, directing and helping his household bathe them, feed them and give them clean clothing. The sympathetic but fearful residents of the Pass, seeing their cura take this action, boldly came with food and clothing for the men from Texas. These men slept that night in clean beds hastily improvised by the cura and his parishioners. As a result, the would-be conquerors became respectful friends of the priest and his people. This was the first of many public and defiant acts on the part of the young priest in defense of those without hope.

During the War with Mexico, in December, 1846, when Colonel Alexander Doniphan's column of the Army of the West neared the villa of Paso del Norte, Ramón Ortiz was said to be the inspiration for resistance to the American invasion. After the defeat at the Battle of Bracito on Christmas Day, 1846, he was arrested at his home at the Pass and charged with sending information to the enemy at Chihuahua concerning the strength and destination of American troops as they moved South from Santa Fe.

Passionately Ortiz protested that it was not treachery to protect his country from an invader, and so eloquent were his words that Doniphan found himself admiring this young priest and his patriotism. On the road to the American conquest of Chihuahua as prisoner of war, he and the American colonel held long conversations regarding the future sovereignty of Mexico: Ortiz told Doniphan that it would be better for Mexico to become part of the United States than to fall under the power of any European authority. This sentiment was unfortunately revealed in the journal of a soldier in Doniphan's column, the special guard assigned to the priest, and it was later to be misinterpreted by his enemies as a declaration in favor of annexation of the Department of Chihuahua to the United States.[34]

When Father Ortiz was released by Doniphan in late January, 1847, after the Battle of Sacramento, he returned to his home at Paso Del Norte. But before the war had actually ended, he was called to Mexico City as representative from Paso del Norte, a *diputado*, to the Mexican national congress, and he was there in 1848 with the officials who drew up the Treaty of Guadalupe Hidalgo. Even though his voice rose in eloquent opposition to the adoption of that treaty,[35] it was ratified and signed by both nations. There he began to realize that his having American friends such as Colonel Doniphan, Hugh Stephenson, the wealthy Magoffin brothers with their in-laws, the family Verimendi from San Antonio[36]—that these friendships were to be a detriment to his concerns and plans for his parishioners and for his beloved country. And the specter of his statement on preferring American domination over foreign sovereignty was seized upon by his antagonists—his reputation for plain and direct words, truthful and patriotic as they might be, would be distorted at the Pass, at the City of Chihuahua, and even at the seat of national government in Mexico City.

The Chihuahua newspaper, *El Faro*, December 23, 1848, had reported that, along with annexation stories, there were the old rumors of a coalition of border states to form an independent republic— these rumors had begun as early as 1824, and were again being revived:

> So far Chihuahua had stayed loyal…but the ideas of annexation to the United States and of independence are floating about and might take hold because of the indolence of the federal government they pay very little attention to the frontier states.

Soon after the Treaty of Guadalupe Hidalgo was signed and ratified, Mexico recognized the need to secure her long new frontier by establishing both civil and military colonies, not only against further American encroachment, but for defense against constant Indian depredations. It was necessary also for Mexico to recognize the desire of some Mexican citizens in the conquered territories to return to territory within Chihuahua. A federal decree of August 19, 1848, which became part of the general organic law of Mexico, provided the funding for the founding and establishing of colonies in the State of Chihuahua. The articles of that decree provided for the emigration of those citizens from New Mexico who wished to maintain Mexican citizenship into territory generally considered Mexican. Twenty-five thousand pesos were allotted for transportation, for arms, and for seeds to plant in the new settlements. The Cura Ramón Ortiz was appointed Commissioner General of the Republic of Mexico to establish these colonies in the State of Chihuahua, to grant land[37] and place the colonists in possession of as much of that land as they were entitled to under Mexican law.

That the Mexican border states were eager to populate their new frontiers was published in a statement drawn up by an assembly representing the governor and commanding generals of these states regarding the handling of Indian incursions:

> In regard to the transfer of families who wish to emigrate from New Mexico and establish themselves in Chihuahua...this commission believes it to be very important, since this method will augment the population useful for the war [against the Indians]. They will populate in a permanent way, a portion of the points on the banks of the rivers and by springs and watering places.[38]

As Fall days shortened and brisk winter winds chilled the nights, American civil authorities displaced outraged Mexican officials. Joseph Francis White, appointed by the military governor of New Mexico, Colonel John Washington, as Prefect at La Frontera, was to be responsible for organizing the American government at the Pass. Former army Captain White wrote to Sebastian Bermudes, Prefect of Paso, November 18, 1848, from Frontera that he had received instructions to:

> ...extend my jurisdiction as magistrate of this territory over the towns situated on the eastside of the deepest channel of the Río-del-Norte below the towns of El Paso... I shall accordingly precede [sic] to extend my jurisdiction over the towns Ysleta, Socorro, and San Elizario—they belong on this east side of the deepest channel...and are therefore according to the late treaty... unquestionably within the limits of the United States of America.[39]

Angrily, José Manuel Villar of Ysleta wrote to the chief magistrate of the District of Bravos:

> I cannot be quiet about the account of today's occurrence at nine to twelve this morning in which Francisco White, employing armed force despoiled me...of my commission as the magistrate of this pueblo...[40]

By the time Father Ortiz could arrange to go to Santa Fe to begin to discharge his duty of Commissioner for Repatriation, winter had come to northern New Mexico, and being a native of that area and knowing first hand the difficulties of travel in the freezing cold of ice and snow, he decided to wait until Spring to go north, making the difficult arrangements for settlements while remaining in his curacy at Paso del Norte. In the very early spring of 1849, the remaining inhabitants of the pueblos were further intimidated by the Americans, and they were without fields to sow and little hope of a harvest to come. To the people at the Pass and below it—those who had not already fled the area, the winter months had been ones of despair. Famine was again a threat.

It was in January and February that a wave of the dispossessed cast hopeful eyes toward the Ancón de Guadalupe and even northward from the Ancón to the side of the river which the American forces had occupied. The President of the Mexican Republic received a letter sent on March 17, 1849, stressing the emergency at the frontier:

> The very illustrious President of the Republic will learn of the grave danger from which the Frontier of the State is suffering... [and] it will only be a matter of time until

the project of the American Governor will be accomplished, which seems to be to compel our border villages to solicit annexation to those states, persuaded by the misery to which they intend to subject them.[41]

Ramón Ortiz, *Comisionado de Emigrados* for Mexico, wrote to the Secretary to the Governor of the State of Chihuahua, that although he did not consider it right, that the Americans had occupied the pueblos of Ysleta, Socorro and San Elceario. Yet it was a fact. He asked the governor for direction in considering these Chihuahua citizens near the Pass emigrants under the same decree of August 19, 1848, which had made him commissioner. A reply written March 22, 1849, came but no concrete answer to the problem of title. And to make matters worse, in that reply there was a shadow of reproof toward Ramón Ortiz for having even considered the American occupation a fact.[42]

Complaints and pleas to both United States and Mexican authorities went on for months: Joseph Francis White meanwhile, continued dividing bosque lands among those who had crossed the river and among other Americans, his friends. Here they found wood in abundance to use in their various enterprises. But complaints reached him and other authorities from Mexicans who had cut and used this wood for years for fuel, for reducing fruit to liquor, and to repair the dam when high water washed away supports and the interwoven saplings.[43] This was only one of the many transgressions of the Americans against their new neighbors. And so the eyes of the dispossessed, and those of the more affluent empresarios,[44] too, were beginning to look further northward, upriver. This was now American territory—the people of Doña Ana had already taken the oath of allegiance in 1846. But here, north of Paso del Norte, lay hope. Fertile, unclaimed bottom land lay everywhere on both sides of the river. To an aspiring colonist, this great expanse of unbroken land took his breath away—the thought of opening rows of rich black loam to plant and then the harvest to feed his family—this revived hope and he was eager to begin.

After Commissioner Ortiz' fateful letter to the Secretary of State of Chihuahua, the idea that a few Mexican citizens favored annexation or at least citizenship on the American side, began to expand. The government of Chihuahua continued to voice its concern over the fact that two or three Mexican citizens had gone over to the other side of the river and had induced the unhappy people of the pueblos to request annexation or at least to go over to the other (U.S.) side where they were made to believe they would better their situation.[45]

From out of these urgencies, came a response. For those who were still left at the Pass in April, Secretary Joaquin Ygnacio de Arrellano published a new decree on the twentieth of that month, 1849, to the effect that those Mexican citizens of Chihuahua who requested new lands because they were deprived of their lands which "they possessed in the towns of Senecú, Ysleta, and San Elceario…" and because the government of Chihuahua considered these people as *vecinos* having equal rights as the Mexican citizens who wanted to emigrate from New Mexico, they should be granted free lands in order to form officially the colony of Guadalupe in Mexican territory. Some fields of the Ancón were already planted, and as the time to finish planting would soon be past, this exigency made the matter of apportioning terrenos urgent. Don Genaro Artalejo of Chihuahua was named in the decree to measure and mark off available lands at Guadalupe, and the colonists were instructed to ask Ramón Ortiz for funds to begin the new settlement and the sowing of fields.[46] By December, 1849, the Cura Ortiz reported 1800 persons at Guadalupe, and he requested a license for a temporary chapel there until he could build a parroquia, a larger church, and assign them a priest. But at the same time, he answered a charge made against him that he was bringing too many colonists from New Mexico. He said that if the government didn't provide him with the necessary funds, he could bring only a few anyway—"Far from working for their emigration, I am doing all I can to limit it for lack of funds to establish them." [47]

Subsequent disagreements between the emigrados verdaderos, the "true" emigrants who had first been designated in the decree of 1848 from New Mexico, and the newly classified colonists who were already at Guadalupe below the Pass, led to disillusionment and disappointment for those who wanted legitimate title to their lands. When Ramón Ortiz and Genaro Artalejo, escorted by a detachment under Comandante de la Frontera Emilio Langberg, appeared at that place for the official measurement of lands, the feeling there between the two groups was so hostile that the effort dissolved and Artalejo withdrew to Chihuahua to clarify the project undertaken for the survey.[48]

As Tiburcio Cuevas of Senecú had complained in March, 1849, many vecinos had already gone north to Doña Ana and Las Cruces[49] on the American side of the river. But many colonists, desperate in the face of quarrels over lands at Guadalupe, over floods in the partidos of Charco and Chibato at the Pass, over uncertainty as to titles for lands they had already planted—many of these preferred to look to the new villages upriver in hope of stability and the certainty of crops to feed their families. And their beloved Cura Ramón Ortiz was now the commissioner for new colonies to be created on the west bank, and in him they had always had faith. Here lay hope. Fertile, unclaimed bottom land lay everywhere on both sides of the river.

The uncertainty of possession of lands they had planted before did not deter them—these lands upriver and faith in Father Ortiz' ability to lead and protect them gave them courage to try again. Besides, spring was almost upon them; and as they had done so many times in the past, they hurried to arrive in time to sow fields once more.

Most of the settlers who came—ragged, cold and wet from fording the river—were the poorest residents at the Pass and at the villages around that Villa. Others were advised by the American military at the settlement of Doña Ana to cross the river to the west side and dig an acequia through the bottom lands.[50] At the foot of the peak called Picacho, close to the ford in the river used by the Apaches and across from Doña Ana, the new ditch was begun.[51] Ultimately, it would carry water from the Río Grande to the fields across from Doña Ana and southward to La Mesilla.

The settlers came with pretensions to no more than a piece of land to plant for the subsistence of their families; for this they were willing to dig the acequias under the direction of their empresarios and to do whatever kind of work they had to do. Pedro López declared in a deposition in later years that he had been born at El Paso, Mexico, and that he had come to Mesilla with the first settlers; he came with Don Juan Guerra. He had lived in El Paso with José María Moraga who worked as a slave "as we all were." Pedro Melenudo testified in like manner; he had come to Mesilla in 1848 and "helped build the first ditch and also the *contraacequia*, the cross-ditch.(52)

These were the first; the courageous few who came and worked, digging the acequia, the ditch, in order to earn their measures of ground. Then the first breaking of ground was done, the fields planted, shelters, *jacales*, built along the valley on both sides of the river, but the main force of migration was yet to come.

RAMÓN ORTIZ AND COLONIZATION

By late April, the Santa Fe River flowed with wisps of cotton caught in its waters and dropped from the cottonwood trees above.

Thus far, Ramón Ortiz had restrained his anger and frustration at the limits put upon him by the American governor, but as he traveled down river, his resentment grew. By the time he arrived at Doña Ana on May 18, 1849, he was so angry that Lieutenant Delos B. Sacket,[53] fearing a riot at the place, addressed a letter to the Adjutant General of the Army of Santa Fe:

> Don Ramón Ortis (Padre of El Paso) passed through this town a few days ago and since that time the people have been nearly frightened to death. I have since learned that he had told, he intended to revolutionize the lower pueblos on the Presidio and then his intention is to come to Doña Ana and treat them all as he would Americans. I have not the least faith that anything will take place, but the Padre has set an inducement of some kind at work which does not look the most flattering in the world…

In his great love of Mexico, it is likely that the Commissioner had threatened the people at Doña Ana because many of them who had come upriver from the Pass to that place, finding themselves in territory taken by American conquest, had sworn an oath of allegiance to the United States.[54] Furthermore, they were secure with the American garrison near to protect the village against the Indians. Even though most Doña Anans had felt the oath not binding because it was taken under duress, there was the threat within the text of Sacket's communication that Ortiz intended to "treat them all as he would Americans." That he, on the other hand, had offered them double lands as an inducement to return to Chihuahua from Doña Ana is probable—the inducement which Sacket remarked "did not look the most flattering

in the world." *El Faro* printed an article of a decree meant for these people:

> To the neighboring Chihuahuenses of Doña Ana, Isleta, Socorro, and San Elizario the government will allot lands of double the extension from the public lands on the right bank of the Bravo that [sic] those which shall be given to the Mexicans who will come from New Mexico…according to the decree of the 17th of January, 1849…

In the summer of 1849, as a result of the Decree of August 19, 1848, colonists had begun to arrive in the area of La Mesilla from northern New Mexico and from the Pass—ethnically different Indian, mestizo, Spaniard—all of them Mexican citizens. The partidos of Barreal, Chibato, and Charco in the Villa del Paso itself were flooded and crops ruined. Those who remained in the little village of Senecú petitioned the Jefe of Cantón Bravos, requesting that the punto de Mesilla be pointed out to them and permission given so that they could move their people to that place which lay forty miles to the north. The Jefe informed them that the land they asked for, in "public opinion," was in United States territory, and on August 15, 1849, from his office at El Paso, he referred the matter to the Governor:

> I enclose for Your Excellency a petition that three individuals of Senecú village and in the name of 15 more have placed before this judgeship asking that the site of La [line through] Mecia be pointed out to them in order that they may move their people, and that they may know under which country's law they must make their petition. This judgeship finds itself obliged to inform them that the land they are asking for is located at a distance from this municipality of 15 leagues and according to the agreement that accords with Disturney's [sic] map, the boundary line should pass at a

Plate 6: Ken Barrick's painting of Ramón Ortiz on horseback. Mary D. Taylor Collection.

distance of about 5 leagues...[55]

The Mexican authorities at the Pass, undoubtedly Commissioner Ortiz, along with the general public, understood that boundary line to be a few miles north of the Vado de Muleros, the ford above the Pass. The settlement established by Joseph Francis White[56] marked that border, and a customs house and trading post were established nearby.

With the presence along the river of a flood of emigrants from the north and those frantic, displaced inhabitants from the pueblos below the Pass, the need to survey officially and apportion lands at the new colonies of Guadalupe de los Nobles, San Ignacio, Nuestra Señora del Refugio, and La Mesilla on the left bank of the Río Grande preoccupied the Commissioner Cura Ramón Ortiz. On September 11, 1849, Don Genaro Artalejo, apprehensive about the scope of his duties as official surveyor for the state government, left El Paso for Ciudad Chihuahua "with the purpose of settling some doubts about this mission, and for this reason, it was not possible to obtain from him the report on the topography of the place called Mecia." [57] Actually, Artalejo had certain knowledge, as did Ramón Ortiz and others, of the sovereignty of the lands to be surveyed at La Mesilla. To him it was very clear that Mesilla lay within the territorial limits of the United States by the terms of the Treaty of Guadalupe Hidalgo. While Artalejo began his journey southward, serious problems assailed Ramón Ortiz as Commissioner of Emigration: the colonists he had brought from northern New Mexico voiced their resentment that the sought-after lands near Guadalupe were to be divided among those residents of San Elizario and the pueblos under its jurisdiction.[58] And, as compassionate shepherd of his river people, the cura was saddened by the spread of cholera morbus, by the ever present famine, and by the despair of families without crops. And in mid-summer, he heard the drum beat, *tocando la caja*, and the frightened cries of his parishioners as the earthen dams which held back surging flood waters from the Río Grande threatened to break.[59] For the Cura Ortiz, it was clearly time to get his weary people settled upriver.

But by the winter of 1849, unauthorized and desperate emigrating and immigrating, coming and going over the as yet undefined border, was clearly getting out of hand. Peónes and *deudores*—indentured servants and debtors, army deserters from both countries—these crossed and recrossed, settling and establishing homesites without consulting any authority. The peónes in Paso and in the pueblos below hurried northward toward new lands; the earth must be broken before planting time. Their *amo's* (master's) papers were carried

Plate 7: This vara was historically used in Mesilla to measure land allotments. It is now in the collection of the Museum of New Mexico. Sketch by Wendy Taylor, 1980s. Mary D. Taylor Collection.

with the colonists; the days they had worked were marked with strokes of five. Their indenture and indebtedness had been carefully calculated. Some were still bound on these papers to the masters they had served in Paso del Norte and the pueblos below. But, for the most part, these men were meted out their own terrenos by Commissioner Ortiz, and they hoped they could get far enough away from the masters so the debts would not apply. Some were to remain in the valley of Mesilla to open fields or to begin commercial enterprises. And in the resulting misunderstandings and struggles over lands, Father Ortiz tried desperately to organize colonies where all the expatriate refugees could settle.

The commissioner began to direct the stream of dispossessed and hopeful colonists northward to the new lands along the river. Empresarios, under the commissioner's direction, brought their peónes north along the river to develop large grants, sometimes double or triple allotments; from these, the peón settlers received their own smaller tracts of land. It was here that the peón, the *jornalero*, the day laborer found his place. He called himself and his relatives and friends "slaves," "esclavos," and he was bound through debt to his master, his *patron*, many times for life.[60] It was he who dug the ditches and plowed the fields, did the backbreaking work; and it was he whom the Apache bullet and arrow killed or wounded when he violated the land which the *indio barbaro* considered his own. He did all this willingly for his own piece of land, his suerte.[61] Along loamy river bottoms in 1850 near the place called "La Mesilla," small grey bears roamed the dense bosque growth of mesquite, and cottonwood.[62] The river silt was moist and rich, and to the desperate new settlers it offered a means of survival.

To those who came to La Mesilla in 1849 from Paso del Norte, to those who came from Doña Ana in 1850, and to others who received lands from the Cura Ortiz in 1851, the land lay before them in promising suertes bounded in possibility only by the power of the water of the river and by the labor of their hands.

Espiridiona, a daughter, born to Mateo and Eulalia Saenz, was said to be the first child born at Mesilla, although she was baptized in Doña Ana, the home of her grandparents, Juan Guerra and Macedonia Estrada, who had come from Socorro at the Pass.[63]

It is said by some of the oldest residents of La Mesilla, those directly descended from the first colonists, that Mateo Guerra was the first permanent resident on the plaza at La Mesilla. He was a merchant who periodically traveled on the long road from Chihuahua to Santa Fe, braving Apache attack on the desolate Camino Real. He and other colonists, for the most part brothers, cousins and *compadres*[64] settled in jacales on *placitas*, smaller plazas of those closely related, forming a contiguous, fortified square—a plaza. There are other records of early dwellings in Mesilla: Yrinea Lujan lived in *"un jacal de palos un tapeste y enceres,"* a shelter of slender poles covered with skin, not unlike the Indian tipi.[65]

Ramón González, fifteen years old, had traveled and worked on a wagon train with Feliz Guerra. He had been a member of the Guardia Nacional in 1846 at Senecú. To him is attributed the first adobe house, other than a jacal, in Mesilla. It was distinguished by a high *pretil*, a cantera stone coping, in this case of tall proportions, which served as a parapet behind which Ramón and his neighbors fought off Apaches. There were other early adobe houses built along the acequia close to precious, running water as it flowed towards the fields.[66] Thick *adobones*, sun-dried earthen bricks of great size, were formed as foundations for adobe homes thwarting the Apache who tried to saw through walls with wet rawhide.[67]

Among the first Americans to establish themselves on the Mesilla side of the river was Louis William Geck, a private honorably discharged at Doña Ana from Company H, First Regiment United States Dragoons. Don Luis, as he came to be known, was born in Poland. As an emigrant to the United States he did service in the War with Mexico and received 160 A. (acres) as bounty land.[68] Henry Cuniffe, who had come in 1846 with Doniphan's Expedition as a merchant with a wagon train, remained to claim lands on the Mesilla river bottoms. Sam Bean was with Doniphan, too, and he returned to settle there. There were others on both sides of the river: George Ackenback, Adolph Lea, Charles Coleman and George Fulton.

So it was at first, as the colonists came into La Mesilla—legends, half-facts, an endearing mixture of the real and the wished-for, a blending of fact and fancy which gave a heroic history meaning.

Chapter 4 | EL TRATADO DE MESILLA

When the American and Mexican people of Doña Ana received lands in Mesilla in 1850, the number of Americans among them had increased—discharged soldiers, traders, and teamsters—and they joined some of the others in sending a petition to the governor at Santa Fe in 1851. They stated flatly that it was their understanding when they moved to Mesilla that it was under the jurisdiction of the United States.

...The town of La Mesilla was settled some time in the early part of 1850 by Americans and New Mexicans citizens under the conviction that it was N. Mexican Territory and subject to its laws. Consequently, the town has flourished...

Some of the signers were Thomas Page, Henry Cuniffe, Pinckney Tully, Charley Fog, Thomas Bull, P.G. Cochran, J.R. Granjean, and William Geck. But more significant is the fact that Mexicans, too, signed the petition—José Moreno, Antonio Constante, José Francisco Cháves, José María Cháves, and others. These Mexicans may or may not have been the dupes of shrewd Anglos, but it is probable that there were those Mexicans who left Doña Ana for Mesilla certain that they were returning to their native Land—that by wading across the ford, goods floating behind them, they became once again citizens of Mexico.

And so the stage was set for the boundary dispute which did not end until after the signing of the Gadsden Purchase Treaty. Mesilla was so involved—hostilities so centered here—that the treaty was always referred to in the Mexican press as El Tratado de Mesilla.

General Pedro García Conde, the commissioner appointed by the Mexican government, and John Russell Bartlett, the commissioner for the United States, met in El Paso in 1850. Disturnell's map of the United Mexican States, published in 1847, was the official map for the Treaty of Guadalupe Hidalgo and the errors in it became the basis for almost endless trouble. Astronomical observations made on the ground confirmed suspicions that the latitudes on this particular part of Disturnell's map were too high by 30 minutes and too low by nearly two degrees. The south boundary of New Mexico on Disturnell's map is about eight miles north of Paso, but in latitude 32°52'; the true latitude eight miles north of El Paso is 31°52'. Conde insisted on placing the boundary line at 32°22' where it fell on the corrected maps—thus placing the line near Doña Ana. Bartlett argued for the true latitude, but eventually a compromise was effected and in the spring of 1851, he yielded on the latitude and Conde on the longitude. The longitude affected only the far western boundary of the territory and had little significance for the people in the Mesilla Valley. But the concession in latitude put Mesilla definitely, if temporarily, in Mexico.

On the west bank of the Río Grande the boundary Commission erected a monument in latitude 32°22', and from this point the surveying began. This one act, this pile of stones that marked the initial point, set up a whirlwind of Mexican colonization.

Even before it seemed certain that La Mesilla was to be in Mexico, Father Ortiz began to grant land in Mesilla to his returning Mexicans. Among the first of these were Esmeregildo Guerra; then Juan Ortega and Teodoso Dominguez, Miguel Ortega, and Agaton Avalos received lands. They came ready to do what Mexico demanded:

The state guarantees your property and always the free use of it as a citizen of the frontier...you will always be quick to defend the country against enemies who are hostile and who persecute you. You will take care always to be provided with arms and a horse...

Ramón Ortiz not only granted terreno baldio —uncultivated lands—but in a fever of patriotic zeal, he took away lands from Americans in Mesilla. A customs house was set up near the Río Grande and duties were levied on goods "coming across the border." Some of the American landowners in Mesilla moved back across the river to the east bank where they settled in the more peaceable and sympathetic towns of Las Cruces and the now quiet Doña Ana.

Events developed quickly. The time of the railroad was approaching, and the government in Washington had become painfully aware that it had now territory in the southwest upon which it could lay a road to the Pacific coast. Then in January, 1853 news came to Doña Ana of revolution in Chihuahua. And in New Mexico there was a change in governmental administration. The effects of all three of these events seemed to converge ominously on the border between Chihuahua and New Mexico—and the focal point was Mesilla.

Governor James Calhoun died on the way to his home in the states. Sixty-three-year-old William Carr Lane arrived in New Mexico in the summer of 1852 to take over a government almost in a state of anarchy. He had expected the support of the military, but Colonel Edwin U. Sumner, in charge of the Ninth Military Department, apparently in a sulky mood[69] retired with the troops from Santa Fe to Albuquerque.

The border dispute seemed to Lane one of the most pressing problems awaiting his attention. Furthermore, General Richard Weightman, New Mexico's delegate to Congress, repeatedly urged him to take possession of La Mesilla by force. After having consulted the best legal authorities available, Governor Lane moved down to Doña Ana where on March 13, 1853, he issued a proclamation so explosive that it resulted in panicky activity on both sides of the border. A Mexican garrison of thirty soldiers was sent to Mesilla and there were rumors that one thousand more were marching from the City of Chihuahua. Article 7

of his proclamation states that the "United States has been unjustly dispossessed of the portion of the territory in question...and the United States has a just right to exercise jurisdiction over it and protect its inhabitants..." The governor planned to use force if necessary.

In northern Mexico, in the meantime, in January, 1855, General Angel Trias had effected a coup, overturning Governor Cordero of Chihuahua. He made himself governor and military of the state of Chihuahua; and in the general convulsive condition of Mexican politics, Santa Ana was once again in control of Mexico. The American troops stationed across the river from Mesilla at Fort Fillmore[70] had been alerted but cautioned not to interfere with the internal writhing and strife in Mexico. However, there was a courteous exchange of pleasantries between the military establishment of Fort Fillmore and the new forces which held Chihuahua. On February 14, the Swedish Colonel Emil Langberg's colorful Mexican lancers came up from El Paso to dance at the birthday of Lieutenant McFerran's daughter. Colonel Dixon Miles, Commander of Fort Fillmore, made an official visit to Paso del Norte on May 11 to interview Trias. On May 13, Trias made an official visit to Fort Fillmore and in a howling spring windstorm the American troops were drawn up in full dress to parade for the Mexican officers. These friendly exchanges led to dark hints of collaboration—that "certain officers" in the United States Army encouraged Mexico's claim to Mesilla and the disputed territory.

The voice crying in the wilderness during this same spring of 1853 was that of Governor Lane. After making his bold proclamation in which he stated that he would not only stand his ground in regard to Mesilla, but would occupy it by force, he found that he had nothing at all with which to implement his declaration. Lacking any authority from Washington, Colonel Sumner made it known at Fort Fillmore that Governor Lane was not to receive any aid from Colonel Miles. On March 3, Sumner wrote to Miles that he had received a letter from the governor asking that a "Company of horses, a piece of artillery and a Flag" from Fort

Plate 8: Amansador (Bronco rider) from the Mesilla Valley, circa 1850s, by Jose Cisneros. From the Mary D. Taylor Collection.

La Mesilla Leñador
c - 1850

Plate 9: Mesilla Leñador (firewood seller) circa 1850s, by Jose Cisneros for Mary D. Taylor. Mary D. Taylor Collection.

Fillmore be placed at his disposal.

I can only suppose [wrote Sumner] that he intends making some demonstration upon the Mexicans. You will please refuse, on my authority, to furnish any troops for any such purpose, and farther, I enjoin it upon you, not to permit any U.S. troops, whatever, to invade any part of Mexico, or what has hitherto been considered Mexico, until you receive order from myself or some higher Military authority...

Governor Lane proceeded from Doña Ana to Fort Fillmore where he angrily and pointedly made his headquarters not at the fort but at the rancho of Hugh Stevenson about one half mile to the west. There was a formal exchange of notes:

Col. Miles
Dear Sir:
Please excuse me for not waiting upon you, this evening. I am fatigued and covered with dust...As the Army is subordinate and auxiliary to the civil Authorities of the U. S. in all the States and Territories, the Governor of New Mexico is certainly not accountable to the Army for his acts...The government and the people of the United States, have disapproved and repudiated Mr. Bartlett's line;...The Executive Department of N.M., (in the exercise of an undoubted right and a plain duty), has asserted the rights of the U.S. and of her citizens and some 350 troops, who are unemployed and are within 5 miles of the scene of action, fold their arms, in frigid tranquility, and there sustain the enemies of their Country...

Wm. Carr Lane

And the answer:

Governor:
Yours of last night I this moment received, and hasten to request, you will please excuse me for not calling upon you: it was after dark before I ascertained you did not intend making my house your home...the lateness of the hour induced me to believe the fatigue of your long journey had made you retire.

I regret the introduction in your communication of the discussion in regard to the disputed territory west of the Río Grande... instructions positively prohibit my permitting any portion of my command crossing the Río Grande...

D.S. Miles

Colonel Miles remarked indignantly in a subsequent letter to headquarters in New Orleans:

...he [Lane] chose to issue the proclamation, without authority from Congress, or the chief executive of the United States. If either had asserted sovereignty over this disputed country, it would have been quietly acquiesced in by the people residing within it, without a murmur of disapprobation and with the hail of joy and gladness from many...

It was exactly at this time that the Cura Ortiz, riding mule-back, face swathed against the spring winds, entered Doña Ana and threatened the governor's safety if he dared enter Mesilla. From this point, Father Ortiz rode through Santo Tomàs to the mission at Guadalupe in Paso to report to Antonio Jaquez and Tomás de Zuloaga, Mexican commissioners of the State of Chihuahua. Bitterly he spoke of meetings in Mesilla where the colonists had gathered to determine what should be done in case the governor of New Mexico should attempt to take possession of the colony for the United States. Many patriots, Father Ortiz said, desired to resist the American attempt at occupation, but in the group was a "traitor"—Don Nicolas Varela— who "thinking about our little funds and our weakness" convinced the majority that no matter what happened they should manifest agreement.

Perhaps for his forceful manner in handling the Mesilla dispute, William Carr Lane was replaced in the summer of 1853 by David Merriwether. John Garland, Brevet Brigadier General, replaced Edwin Vose Sumner. And for the heated and threatening manner in which he had handled his part of the dispute, Ramón Ortiz was replaced by Guadalupe Miranda, who had been the Mexican Vice Consul at Franklin, Texas. Miranda immediately proceeded to La Mesilla where he divided the land "properly" among the settlers. They had been gratefully content with Ortiz' division of lands, but now, under threat of military coercion, they were forced to submit to Miranda's demands to run new property lines. In this arbitrary manner, he took away from one and gave to another, leaving part of one house on another's property, dividing adobe walls and ordering the removal of dwelling houses. For his unsolicited services in La Mesilla, he charged each colonist from one to four dollars, collecting almost twelve hundred dollars. In the meantime, the United States Minister Extraordinary James Gadsden was negotiating in Mexico with Santa Ana for the purchases of Arizona territory. The controversial Mesilla Valley was adjoined to the area to be purchased.

The Gadsden Purchase was effected in December, 1853, in Mexico City. For some months following the ratification of the Purchase by Congress, the jurisdiction of the Mesilla area remained in dispute. The news of the arrangement between the two countries had sifted through to the Mexican public, and there was a great restlessness and dissatisfaction at Santa Ana's course. The restlessness was felt in Mesilla itself—when its young men were conscripted into the Mexican army which might do battle in this very place, they fled at once to the other side of the Río Grande into that part of the United States which Mexico recognized as American territory. Furthermore, the rumored advance of Mexican troops toward the disputed area was taking form. Angel Trias was observed at the head of eight hundred men on a march to Mesilla. Within fifteen days two thousand men from Durango would join him, riding to garrison the frontier from Mesilla to San Ignacio, a line of resistance one hundred and twenty miles long.

In November, 1854 General Garland considered the situation serious enough to come from Santa Fe to Fort Fillmore. A courier met him on the road with a confidential dispatch from Dixon Miles saying that word had just been received at Mesilla that President Santa Ana had issued a proclamation "turning over the purchased country to the jurisdiction of the United States authorities."

General Garland apparently continued on to Fort Fillmore where, on November 14, he ordered Colonel Dixon Miles to proceed "to the town of Mesilla, with a part of the garrison of Fort Fillmore, and there hoist the National Flag at noon of this day." Following reveille on the fifteenth, Companies A and E and the Band of the third United States Infantry, Company B of the First Dragoons and a small detail with two mountain howitzers, all in full dress, marched from Fort Fillmore toward Mesilla. The cavalry forded the river; the infantry crossed by ferry.

Gathered in the plaza of La Mesilla on that day were a great many persons: jefes politicos, political chieftains from Mexico and New Mexico, officers and soldiers of both armies, and most of the people of Mesilla. Don Juan José Sanches, jefe politico of the Brazos district of Chihuahua, and according to local tradition, José Salazar y Larregui of the Mexican Boundary Commission, General Juan María Ponce de Leon, Tomás de Zuloaga, and General Angel Trias all were present for the transfer of power. Mexican troops lined the southwest side of the plaza. There were three thousand people living in the village at this time, and many of them were there quietly waiting for the ceremonies to begin. Some thought they were citizens of Mexico. All would become American citizens unless, before one year had passed, they departed into their Mexican homeland.

Business stopped; doorways were filled; vendors of wines and food in the plaza were still. The silence was broken by the sounds of the howitzers being unlimbered for the salute. General Garland rose from behind the treaty table to read his proclamation which concluded thus:

> For the information of all concerned, it is hereby made known that our national flag will give protection to all persons who properly seek it. Criminals and other evil disposed persons

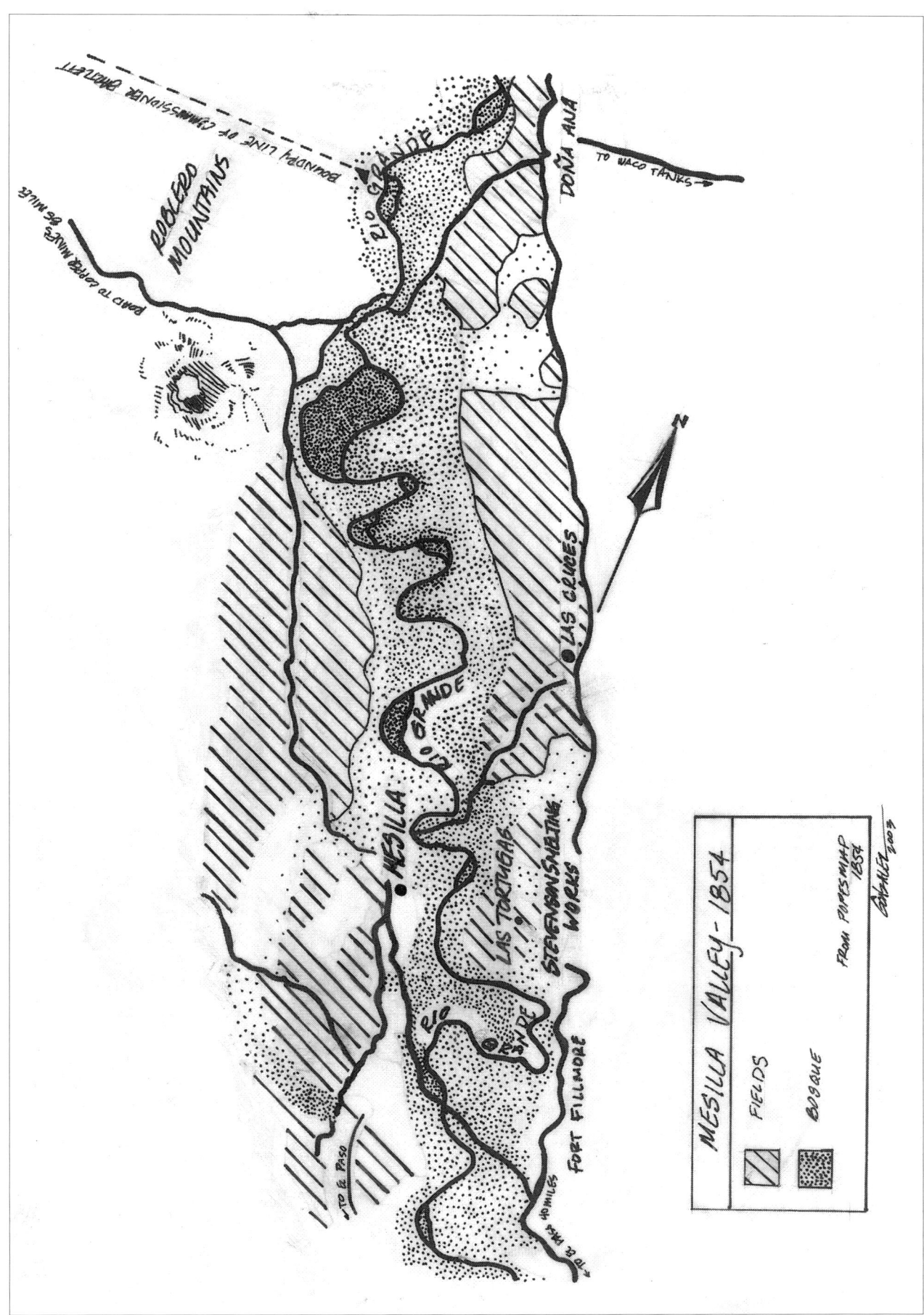

VALLEY AND TOWN OF MESILLA,
NEW - MEXICO.

Middleton, Wallace & C.º Cincinnati.

Plate 11: Early view of Mesilla, 1854, as A. B. Grey of Bartlett's Boundary Survey saw it. Carl Scuchard Lithograph Collection, MS 0339, Rio Grande Historical Collections, New Mexico State University Library, Las Cruces, New Mexico.

who seek to attain their ends by violent means and in violation of our known laws will find neither shelter nor protection under its ample folds.

A flutter of drums and the Mexican flag came down to be folded away by loving hands. The American standard was run up over the tops of the cottonwood trees—an event celebrated annually even today—"La Enaboración de la Bandera," the "Hoisting of the Flag."

The three years of colonization efforts leading up to this ceremony on the plaza in Mesilla were not without violence between Mesilla settlers and the Apaches who lay claim to this land. This strife was dealt with in large part by the colonists themselves. They formed a civil armed force that continued even after the United States took jurisdiction over Mesilla.

Chapter 5 | THE MESILLA GUARD

In the new colonies of the valley of the Mesilla—the civil colony of La Mesilla, the Bend of Doña Ana, Santo Tomás de Iturbide, and the Merced de Refugio—the young men learned what the old men knew: that a farmer's life is made up of labor and patience.[71] The wooden plow bit into the virgin earth, then the water, then the seed sown carefully, frugally, and again water. The glistening fields of wheat and corn, the vineyards like small vegetable gardens in their newness, were reward enough those first few years as the cycles of the seasons brought the fruits of persistence and patience.

Rafael Ruelas, the justice of the peace of the new settlement of Mesilla, in July, 1851, reported to the officials at the Pass that what he saw was very good:

> Tillable Lands: About 200 fanegas of crops have been gleaned and abundant harvests are expected in spite of the great drought which was experienced.

> Schools: Already there are established at this place such schools as you would find in an organized state.

> Troubles: None.

> Apaches: Since the founding of this village, to the present day, they have not committed any thefts, nor deaths, those wicked enemies.[72]

The next year in July, Ruelas reported that all was going well. Although there had been Apache harassment all around Mesilla, the alcalde noted that Mesilla itself was quiet. Good health was enjoyed by the people, and the harvest was abundant.

It was the last time for such a report—almost before the summary was filed at headquarters at the Pass, the discordant in the pastoral began. Ruelas knew from agonizing experience in Senecú del Sur and San Lorenzo what devastation those "wicked enemies" could bring to the new colony. The colonists were vigilant, mindful of the cry used throughout the frontier in those years and used even today in painful circumstances: *Ay, Chihuahua, cuánto Apache!*—Ay, Chihuahua, what a lot of Apaches!

In the pueblos below the Pass, the inhabitants relied upon the Guardia Móvil, cavalrymen, almost all of them kindred—compadres, brothers, fathers. In the new colony of Mesilla, the *Guardia Móvil* became the Mesilla Guard. The Guerras were there led by Esmeregildo,[73] who because of his Pueblo descent, was respected and feared by the Apache. He was aided by the sons-in-law of Simon Guerra, Juan Mirabal, and Jesús Belarde; by Juan Ortega, Cosme Ríos, Rafael Bermudes, and Silvestre Maese. The husband of Bernardina Cubero was Narciso Galván and he followed the Guard; Silvestre Jurado also rode with them. They were clansmen and primos hermanos (first cousins), colonists of La Mesilla, ready to defend it in the new settlement along the river.[74]

The Apache himself considered his pillage a natural return for the *rancherías*[75] usurped by the colonizing movement along the Río Grande. The settlers cultivated the very sites of his small fields and used his game for sustenance. And when he saw the new acequia cut from the river to the fields, he began his attack, plundering goods, crops, and animals.

In order to complete the ditch in each frontier colony, part of every settler's working time was devoted to digging. Two groups of men worked— one with wooden spades and, perhaps, a precious piece of iron forged into a pick. The others watched—muskets ready—atop the pile of earth, for the Apaches might at any moment appear from the west or from the hills to the east. From behind the earthen barrier one group of colonists fired at the Apaches. The others below dug with wooden spades. And then there was the gentle, small joke which made a laughable thing of a great fear. The muskets had fired once; the barrels were reloaded with powder and ball; the heavy hammers were brought back. Across to the men who had quickly thrown tools aside for muskets, they called *"Espérate tantito!"* Wait a little bit! Wait so the Apache would receive full force of the second volley, and one day the musket itself was affectionately called "Espérate Tantito."

Almost overtaking Ruelas' report of July, 1852, came news of violence in the fields near Mesilla. At Bosque Seco, Rafael Provencio fell at the hands of the Apache. Rafael had come to Doña Ana from Senecú del Sur, and then to the Merced de La Mesilla. It was his voice shouting the war cry from the fields that signaled the raid. From the animal *corrales* his wife could see him as men ran to aid him—saw him encircled by a ring of Indians, saw him grasp the end of the *lanza* wedged in his chest and draw it out while a bloody stain spread on the woven straw of his *jerga*, slipped on that morning against a cold summer rain. With another great effort, he flung the lance, speared a warrior from his horse, rose from his knees and held his hand over the hole in his chest. His kinsmen surrounded him and carried him to shelter.[76]

Some of the relatives and neighbors of Rafael Provencio had been scouts in the Guardia Móvil.

Traditionally they were enemies of the Apache—and now they heard the beat of the drum called La Coronela, the hollow piece of giant cottonwood tied tight across the top with cowhide. In the sandy, ragged plaza of the village, the drum beat out the agony of an Apache lance. They ran toward their houses, hearing the heartbeat of La Coronela—their throats felt it; under their feet the ground trembled with it.[77]

The Apache nation now became aware of a coordinated guard. These men of Mesilla had promised to "always be quick to defend the country against enemies..." and "always to be provided with arms and a horse..." This they had pledged when they were allotted their lands. That they had the "manliness to defend themselves" was evident, for when La Coronela sounded, family after family was called upon to give up one male member to ride resolutely and swiftly into the terrifying world of the Apache.[78] Equipped with a musket, a lance, a leather bag of parched corn, pinole, and one of water, the Guard sometimes traveled for three days, following and recapturing prisoners and cattle. It was then that, finding the raiding Indians disappearing into México, and from accounts given by traders on their way up from Chihuahua, they knew they must reckon with the Apache working from one country to another. After striking deep into the ranchos of Chihuahua, the warriors lashed back into American territory, left tranquil and off guard by their absence of several months. This then became their habit: to make a treaty in one nation and strike the other. Not many of the citizens on either side of the border realized that a treaty made by one chieftain was not binding upon any other part of that tribe or any other head man.[79]

Even when confronted by an organized Mesilla Guard, the Apaches rode hard against the Mesilleros. Gregorio Aranda was ambushed and murdered by Apaches in the summer of 1852. The Indians who killed him were those who had just stolen ninety head of cattle and horses from Paso del Norte. The men of the Guard who rode in pursuit turned back—their horses could not keep up with the Indian ponies. These same guardsmen found an abandoned captive "cristiano"— wearing Castilian shoes. He was unable to speak, but as the squad tied him to a horse, the captive broke a small branch in two, made a cross and placed it on the spot where Aranda fell.[80]

At Paso del Norte in November, Marcial Padilla was commissioned by a reluctant *ayuntamiento* to make a punitive expedition against the Apache. He recruited eighty men in that villa, and on the road to Mesilla, he added sixty-four from Mesilla, where there was difficulty in mobilizing men for the

Plate 12: Irrigating fields in La Mesilla in the 1940's. Like early settlers, this man was assigned certain hours for watering his crops. To miss was to endanger his harvest. Photograph by Mary D. Taylor.

campaign. Few of them had horses—the Apaches had stolen nearly all of them. Marching northward he passed the paraje of Robledo by December, paused at San Diego ford, leaving his wagons there so the rumble of wheels would not alert the enemy. At Santa Bárbara, Padilla had recognized mustang and moccasin tracks leading west toward the Florida Mountains. Moving in forced marches, the company camped at Arroyo Perrillo about the halfway mark on the Jornada del Muerto. Scouts met him at Ojo Caliente and reported that the trail led to the Magdalenas, toward a stream there called La Monica. These found a wounded horse belonging to Ramón Sanches of Mesilla and several enemy rancherías. It appeared that their journey was done, for it was plain that part of the Indians had gone into the centers of towns on pretext of trading and could not be apprehended without danger to the inhabitants. The remainder had fled into the Mogollon mountains. And the most recent tracks had become obliterated in the falling snow. In addition, the growing hunger of the men turned the force toward Mesilla by way of the mountain trail from El Cobre. Heavy snows slowed the return home, and the sick were left in Mesilla with villagers while the unsuccessful divisions returned to El Paso.[81]

In the middle of December, 1852, Rafael Ruelas reported with alarm that a messenger had arrived from New Mexico bringing news of a great gathering of Apaches for the purpose of invading Mesilla. He promised to put up notices in all the settled points on this side of the Río Grande.[82]

In the early part of 1853, Domingo Cubero wrote to the Jefe Político of Cantón Bravos that twenty-six Apaches had crept into the common lands, ejidos, of Mesilla. Early morning light revealed them leading away fourteen head of cattle. Three sub chieftains led the Indians—the very three who had been living in apparent contentment at their rancherías near Doña Ana and Fort Fillmore. The *comandante de armas*, Cesario Durán, could not find any of the culprits, only faint hoof prints on the trail east to the mountains revealed that two warriors rode a horse and a mule.

Domingo Cubero complained bitterly to Cantón Bravos at the Pass that the Mescaleros could go back and forth over the river with perfect impunity while pretending to be at peace. He also stated that neither the military nor the political authorities would do anything about it—that they always replied to his reports with evasion.

There was good reason for evasion on either side of the river. The boundary commissioners from Mexico and the United States, following the Mexican War, still disagreed on the initial point from which the line was to be surveyed. Jurisdiction of the Mesilla Valley was in dispute, and neither country was willing to precipitate military action by sending troops into the town of Mesilla. Civil authorities were equally reluctant to effect apprehensions. The settlers themselves seemed to think that the area was "independent." It was a time of waiting in the disputed area—malcontents, debtors, deserters from the army, smugglers, and fugitives of all kinds crowded into that area taking every possible advantage of the reluctance for decisive action on the part of either country.

Whisky and lead were smuggled and sold to Apache and settler alike by those who counted the harvest by the dollar. Anastacio Barela traded whiskey for fine buckskins; Loreto Griego was the subject of a territorial suit for selling liquor to the Apaches near Fort Thorn.[83] Wild and unrestrained were the brutalities, and the revenge for brutalities—wound for wound, lash for lash, life for life. There were no conquering heroes, no victors, and no vanquished. The yield was made up of widows and orphans and much suffering.

A letter from Cubero to the Cantón in February enclosed the ugly news from the Prefect of Doña Ana to the *juez* at Mesilla that Mesilleros had attacked a band of Indians. The little company had left Doña Ana about vesper time on February 4, driving ahead of them their horses and cattle. When they did not arrive at their destination, a scout was sent after them. Only one Indian was found on that road, a woman dead from a heavy blow to the head. On the way to Mesilla, the scout and his men

Plate 13: Sketch of drum possibly used by the Mesilla Guard to sound the call to arms, by Ken Barrick. Mary D. Taylor Collection.

arrested members of the Mesilla Guard: Felipe Saiz, Juan Arroyo, Victor Baca, and Juan Mirabal. The cattle taken from the Indians were seized from them, and at Las Cruces they were turned over to Richard Campbell. The prefect warned the citizenry that abuses and outrages would surely follow the death of the Indian woman.[84]

Again an Apache raid—young Valentín Varela ran to advise the prefect that Indians were destroying crops on the terrenos. The prefect wrote his report to Cantón Bravos:

> Instantly I ordered the commander to go, accompanied by the town defenders down by the lower end of the fields, and I went to the other end of the village accompanied by residents... At the same time the Santo Tomàs colony was assaulted by nineteen Indians, capturing and carrying off a six-year-old boy and twelve horses. We lost three men, killed by the Apaches, two on top of the plain because they persisted in following the Indians too closely... [85]

While the treaty of 1853 offered the Apache food, breeding stock, protection against illegal traders, defense against enemy tribes, and farm instruction, he was emphatically warned against thrusting his spear into the heart of Mexico.[86] All of the advantages, except for the proviso on farming, were only promises on paper, for the traders continued to take advantage of the government and of the Indian, and the protection against enemies was nonexistent. As for the farming, the Mescalero was afraid to plant "lest their Tata Dios would destroy game, mescal, and take their arms from them and make them as effeminate as women." [87]

The Apaches tried to sue for peace with Mesilla on three separate occasions. Alone, or sometimes with other head men, the chieftains came over the sandy trails, crossed the Río Grande, and approached the sentinels of the cautious town. Josecito came with five warriors and sixteen Indian women, saying that he had come in peace from the fort on the Mimbres. Mesilla's prefect claimed that the *capitancillo* had no proof of his friendly

intentions, and when Josecito asked to stay in the neighborhood of Mesilla for ten days, the request was abruptly refused. The prefect, moreover, posted notice that a twenty-five peso fine would be levied against anyone who sold liquor to an Apache. Nor could any transaction take place between villager and Indian.[88]

Once again Josecito, this time with Cuchillo Negro, tried to enter Mesilla with manifestations of peace. When the juez beseeched headquarters for a directive, headquarters replied by enclosing a letter from the governor himself which reminded Domingo Cubero of the latest depredation that had been committed at Mesilla. A handsome stallion had been stolen from Mateo Guerra, and members of the Guard found it later in the caballado of Delgadito. His Excellency recalled for the Mesilleros that the Indians always came in peace and the Mesilleros believed them—and then committed crimes among them.[89]

The third attempt was made one morning early, when Cuchillo Negro rode through Mesilla over the Río Grande to the east side of the river. Here he met Pancho el Francés, Francis Fletcher, a French-Canadian, interpreter in three tongues. They plotted to dupe the Mesilleros into a trade agreement favorable to the Indians and the Frenchman. Fording the river, they headed into Mesilla. Before the prefect, Domingo Cubero, they swore by the God of the Mexicans and by their own sons that they had come in peace and wished only to trade in a friendly fashion. Cuchillo Negro, speaking through Fletcher the interpreter, raised his arm in a sweep toward the south. The Apaches would harm nothing, raid nowhere, he said, up to the town of Guadalupe. The disturbing future status of the area past that town and the fact that Francis Fletcher was part of the bargain, alerted Cubero and his townsmen, and he turned them away.[90]

On the fourth day of November, 1853, Cuentas Azules, a Mescalero chief and former bandit,[91] rode with fifteen of his tribe to Fort Fillmore. Since the Mescaleros were suspect in the murder of ten Californians on the Chihuahua trail, and since Major Electus Backus had threatened vengeance on the whole band, it was the chief's purpose to present himself at the fort and disclaim responsibility. His wife, his mother, and his infant daughter, and a few warriors rode in the shadows of the Organ mountains toward Fort Fillmore.[92] The Mescalero was confident that the Major would deal fairly with him.

Major Backus received the chief's peaceful declaration with appreciation and allowed the little band to camp just outside the military reservation. On the first of December, Cuentas Azules sat at his campfire completely delighted by a spirited horse which Pedro José Borule, a resident of Mesilla from northern New Mexico, had sold to a recently discharged dragoon. The Indian approached the exsoldier; he and the chief bargained together, and the horse was sold to the Indian.

Having been dismissed and sent on their way to the mountains by Major Backus, the chief and his little family and his few warriors approached Doña Ana and encountered on the road Pedro José Borule, the former owner of the horse. He, apparently surprised at seeing the Indians with the horse, angrily claimed it of the chief as his property. Cuentas Azules refused to surrender it. He appealed to the prefect of Las Cruces, Richard Campbell, who ruled that the horse legally belonged to the Indian, Borule having sold it to the soldier.

Toward evening the chief and his company approached Doña Ana and camped near the town. Before he went into Doña Ana he drew a mark across the road and warned his warriors not to cross it.

In town after the Apache chief had become intoxicated, he allowed himself to be drawn into an argument and lured by friends of Borule to a secluded spot where Borule set upon him with a club.[93] Leaving the chief for dead, they rode away with the horse. The *Santa Fe Gazette* reported on November 19, that, as of two o'clock in the afternoon, Cuentas Azules was not yet dead, but would perish shortly, as his brains were literally beaten from his head.

The *New York Times* for February 2, 1854, gave an account of the incident as reported by a correspondent from Albuquerque:

The court having exhausted its resources, the affair now rests for the action of the Government. The Indians of three different bands of Apaches had assembled within a short distance of Doña Ana, and watched the proceedings of the court (which was explained to them) with great interest. In an interview with Judge Benedict, they stated that their chief had come in at the invitation of the whites, that they were peaceable; that they had received from the President of the United States a medal, upon which his image was impressed; that he had called them his red children; and that they had looked to him for protection and justice; that they would not act hastily, but wait [ten days] and see how we administered our laws...and if we did not give them justice, they had laws of their own, and knew how to get satisfaction; that they had lost their Chief, a man they loved and respected. He was wise and they obeyed him...and if the Americans did not give them justice, they could not say what their young men might do.

In a bill found against Pedro José Borule, Sydney A. Hubbell, District Attorney, described the club used and the wound: "...the length of four feet and of the breadth of two inches and in the value of one Penny...Pedro Borule ...held in both his hands...upon the right side of the head near the right temple...did hit..." By the time of the issuance of the true bill, Borule and his friends were across the river in Mesilla.

The United States Marshal, Charles S. Rumley, tried to serve a warrant for the arrest of Borule and reported: "I hereby certify I cannot apprehend Pedro Jesús Borule, he being secreted in the disputed territory of Mesilla. Dated this 25th day of November AD 1853." [94]

Remiglo Hernández, Borule's servant, Gorgonio Vigil, and Miguel Torres were indicted for murder in the May term of court, 1854. Attempts

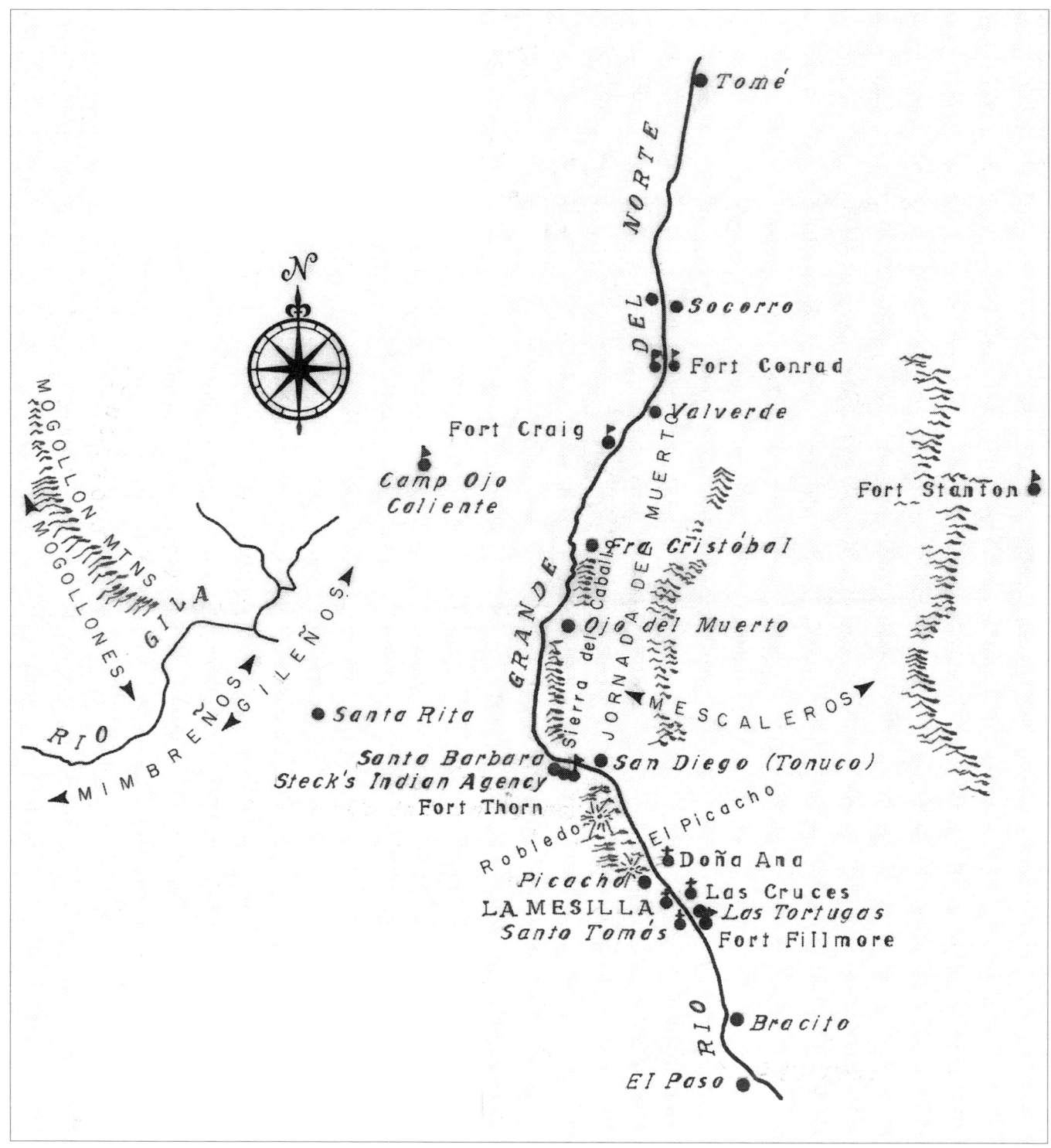

Plate 14: Forts and Apaches 1850-1854.

were made to subpoena witnesses to testify: José Moreno, Antonio Moreno, and Rafael Rivas. They could not be found in Marshal Rumley's district.[95]

In a letter from Governor David Meriwether to Major Backus on November 14, 1853, the governor declared that if force were used to extradite the fugitives from the Mesilla area, the United States would admit to México's jurisdiction there.[96]

News was slow to reach the frontier, and the decision on the jurisdiction of the disputed territory did not reach the officials in Doña Ana County until the fall of 1854. The United States flag was raised on the plaza of La Mesilla on November 16, 1854.

The Doña Ana District Court immediately exercised its authority and Benjamin F. Read, Deputy United States Marshal, arrested Borule in Mesilla and committed him to the county jail. He pleaded Not Guilty, and in November, 1854, a jury acquitted Pedro José Borule.

Dr. Michael Steck, a former surgeon with the Army of the West in New Mexico, became Indian agent on May 9, 1854, at the newly created agency near Ft. Thorn, forty miles north of Mesilla. The fort had been established in December, 1853, to protect the dangerous crossing at San Diego alongside Tonuco Mountain, and to provide escorts for California-bound emigrants. Dr. Steck, on arriving in New Mexico with David Meriwether, the new governor, viewed with concern the uneasy situation between the Apache Nation and the settlers. He saw hate grow and fester, and for those colonists who were descendants of Pueblo Indians from the Pass, he deplored an anger grown tribal.

It has from time immemorial been the custom for the Indian to steal from the New Mexicans and then the Mexicans to steal from them—this system of thieving and retaliation has been kept up under the Mexican rule organized parties were permitted to make campaigns for the avowed purpose of stealing Indian stock and prisoners and dividing it among the captors.[97]

One half-mile to the east of Ft. Thorn along the bank of the Río Grande lay the little town of Santa Bárbara—on its adobe outskirts the Apache Indian agency lay, its buildings and warehouse rented from Pinckney A. Tully. From here Dr. Steck waged continuous war with officials of the Indian Bureau in Washington. His pleas for help were ignored; requisitions returned. "...The game was scant and during summer and early fall they resorted to mescal, acorns, juniper berries, and when these were exhausted, devoured their horses and mules. When the animals were consumed, they must steal or starve...and they would not starve willingly." Chiefs and head men in desperation began to lead their people into the agency at Fort Thorn, and the warriors began breaking the ground for planting.[98]

In their new-turned fields at the agency, the Apaches worked, clad in loin cloths of scarlet and blue-printed material, caught around the waist with a strip of leather, the cloth ends extending, in front and in back, down to their knees.[99] To ward off the chill of spring plowing, they wore blue frock coats brought in from the east; hickory shirts and red blankets were issued them. Dr. Steck was able to supply them occasionally with needles, thread, axes, a little tobacco and very little beef. He continually repaired rifles for them—those of Cuchillo Negro, Pajarito Negro, Rincón, Delgadito, and Loco. His wards, in exchange for these issues and services, brought into Dr. Steck's agency soft dressed deer skins and bags of piñones.[100] But often, he complained to Washington, the primary staples of existence had to be denied—the soft goods they delighted in receiving never filled their hungry stomachs.

Indian attacks from all directions still beat the Mesilleros back to their adobe walls and found them increasingly short of supplies. Offers to strengthen a native militia, a guardia civil, only heightened Dr. Steck's suspicions that this volunteering was only part of a plan to steal animals from the Apache, or to recapture beasts and captives. The Mesilla Guard was born not of cupidity, but of necessity—the necessity to survive.

When the Mesilla Guard rode out in pursuit of the Apache, they had, perhaps, each one, three or four cartridges apiece—some men in desperation left their muskets behind and carried clubs. On May 8, Domingo Cubero wrote desperately and hastily to El Paso for powder, one hundred sixty flints, and a ream of paper for cartridges. Indians stole Mexican children from the cornfields; the Mesilla Guard trailed Indian bands and captured Apache children. Two Mexican boys, fourteen and sixteen years old, escaped their captors and came into Fort Fillmore. One of them couldn't remember who his parents were. The other was returned to his father in Mesilla.

In the face of these exigencies, Richard Campbell on December 10, 1854 ordered a mobilization of fifteen men from each of the towns of Las Cruces, Doña Ana, and Mesilla. They were to be held in readiness to defend the property of the citizens of the county in the event of continued Indian depredations.[101]

The ferocity of the war between the Mesilla Guard and the Indians reached such a point in 1855 that Michael Steck sent word for the Mescalero chiefs and captains under Balanquito[102] to come in and talk. A little distance from the mouth of Dog Cañon the ten head men were mounted in a line—Balanquito sat a little ahead of the others. He wore wide cotton drawers, settler-fashion, and his rigid leather leggings carried a knife on the right side. The Indian chieftain vowed that he and his tribe would fight and kill and steal no more.

The treaty of 1855, containing severe and impractical provisions for the Apaches, provided that the tribe should surrender those who wronged white men—that the whole tribe would be held responsible otherwise, and if they were not surrendered, soldiers would come among them. The treaty was marked with an "H", by almost all the chieftains and head men including Gomez and Mateo who were among the worst offenders against the colonists. Dr. Steck, his knowledge gained through dependable informants, declared that these two properly belonged to the state of Chihuahua.

Gomez, the chief renegade, had gone into Mesilla soon after the treaty, inciting the residents there to rebel against the Americans and kill them or drive them out of the territory. Gomez had provocation. His father had been killed by an American near Agua Nueva in Mexico.[103]

In October, Lieutenant Colonel Miles wrote to Dr. Steck[104] that Francis Fletcher had accused the Mescaleros of stealing his mules. Balanquito and Marcos came to Miles at Fort Fillmore on the twenty-eighth, protesting their innocence, and offering to track and find the thieves: Negrito at San Agustín and Janeiro at San Nicolas. The colonel believed that the Indians had never stolen the mules—he suspected more of Fletcher's treachery. Furthermore, he reflected the opinion that the Frenchman was behind every outrage inflicted on the Apache by enraged citizens of Las Cruces and Mesilla. Not caring to accuse Fletcher without proof, Colonel Miles accepted Balanquito's offer to track the mules and return them to the owner. If he did not, he would be considered guilty of breaking the treaty. The chieftain replied with melancholy dignity:

Since I formed and signed the Treaty, I have had my horses stolen by the Mexicans, bridles and saddles taken off of my horses... also blankets and other things—some of them before my face and in disregard of my remonstrances—I have complained to you and [the] alcaldies [sic] of these outrages—but you have not made these Mexicans give up my horses, bridles or saddles—they have also with impunity, outraged my women and beat my men and children the U. S. Government has given me or my people no redress—have you not broken the Treaty? But I want peace and not war—I have borne all these wrongs patiently and now that someone, you don't know who, has stolen a few mules, you charge my people and say I must and shall return them... I'll obey your orders, I'll hunt up the mountains and through the valleys and if I can find them I will bring them to you, if I can't find them and you make war, I will bow with submission to whatever you direct. I will not, nor shall my band fight.[105]

Balanquito, chief of the Mescaleros, the shrunken old one, died in September, 1856. Cadete was natural heir to the leader but he refused, reasoning that the Mescaleros were troublemakers and would make all the Apache Nation responsible for their deeds.[106]

Late in December of 1856 La Mesilla lost one man killed, and two were wounded in an early morning raid. Apaches cut into adobe corrales by quietly sawing with a strip of wet rawhide, and fifteen good horses were led away—animals silent—Apache hands over their muzzles. Colonel Miles from Fort Fillmore and Colonel J. H. Eaton from Ft. Thorn were convinced that the Mimbres band had carried out the sortie, and Dr. Steck dispatched an express to the head men of that band to discover exactly who was responsible. Before the messengers arrived at the Mimbres, Delgadito had heard the news and had sent Dr. Steck's interpreter and scout, Costales, to the agency with the names of the guilty ones. The doctor was away from the agency but had left word with Colonel Eaton to do nothing until he returned. But the officer, having received certain information and believing he could overtake the Indians, fitted up an expedition, and moved out immediately. The chase was a failure—the thieves were not overtaken and the Indians of the agency, alarmed at the sudden and unannounced movement of the troops, left to watch from higher ground.

When Dr. Steck returned, he again made an appointment to meet with the chiefs and head men, this time at Sierra Blanca, fifty miles west of the fort. Delgadito, Itán, Riñón, Lucero, José Nuevo, and Pajarito came to the agent with Mónica and Costales as interpreters. As they knew the Indians who had committed the crime, they denied that their own band was guilty. Retaliation was instantaneous. On December 29, two Mexicans took sixteen horses from Delgadito's camp. The half-Mexican, Costales, a price on his scalp, with Ratton trailed them to Mesilla the next day, but the

thieves escaped with the five finest animals. The two headed northwest again for the agency and vanished.

On New Year's Day, Second Lieutenant Alexander Steen, with Amon Barnes and a military detail, entered the boat house at San Diego ferry and discovered evidence of murder. The earthen floor was covered with a butcher's gore; there were two stained knives, some bloody manta and Costales' hat lying in disorder. Outside, the trail led to the river, and the soldiers drew from the water the body of Costales. He had been scalped and mutilated. The reward offered in Chihuahua for the scalp had no doubt already been claimed. They never found Ratton.[107]

On three separate occasions scouting detachments of the Regiment of Mounted Rifles from Fort Fillmore spurred after the Apache. Thomas G. Rhett and twenty-five men rode down the El Paso road on February 7, 1857, pursuing renegades. Later in the month, citizens reported more forays, more animals taken, more murders, more captives seized. On the twenty-second, Bvt. Captain Alfred Gibbs, of the same regiment, followed Apache sign to Los Amoles where he lost the trail.

On the twenty-fourth, the Mesilla Guard sent a messenger to Fort Fillmore asking help in capturing or killing fourteen Gileños hemmed in among the high rocks twenty-five miles northwest of Mesilla. The Indians escaped again.

The third incident occurred in March at Robledo where J. W. Garretson, Deputy United States Surveyor, was camped. The Apaches quietly ran off his remuda of horses at first light. Captain Gibbs again rode in pursuit of the seven Mimbres Indians, with Garretson and a man named Dickens as guides. They followed the horsemen into the rocky depths of Robledo's high-walled arroyos. At noon at a water hole the silent men came upon the Indians so engrossed in stuffing raw meat into their hungry mouths that they did not hear the soldiers. Gibbs attacked, slashing and firing into the bloody handed Apaches until six were dead. They

Plate 15: Mesilla Guard by Ken Barrick. Painted after listening to his wife, Nona, and Mary Taylor talk about their research. Mary D. Taylor Collection.

followed the seventh, crawling among stones and desert willows, and killed him. But before the six were dead, one of them threw a lance into Captain Gibbs' stomach, stretching him helpless on the ground. An express brought Dr. J. Cooper McKee the next morning from the fort with an ambulance and Captain Gibbs was in the garrison hospital by sundown.[108]

Once more a patient Dr. Steck rebuked the Indians who sought revenge. From notes for his talk, he reminded them of their alternatives to peace:

...you have paid well for your bad conduct—and if you wish we will commence anew—the road to war is rough, etc.—Peace smothe [sic]—every night you hear your children & wives crying for some one lost and if you wish to prevent this you must act like honest men & friends...Bad men among us all—we will try to control ours & you must yours—if robberies committed you must report &c.c.—will expect you to live at peace—I can make no promises now but will try to inform Sup. &c. of your wish for peace—assure you that something will be done for you...Go to your friends in the White Mts. & tell them how you have been received—that they have peace in their own hands & If depredations continue war will be the consequence & God know where it will stop. You can go home & sleep without a sentinel &c. &c.—In war you cannot run—Navajo North—Mimbres E—Mex S &c.—your corn will again be destroyed & your children will cry for bread—They have given you back your captains—we are sorry they are not all here...Those that are here take them to their friends & God be with them.[109]

While a Fort Fillmore detachment rode south on the seventh of February in 1857 looking for renegades, at the north end of the plaza in Mesilla, just as the bell of San Albino's rang for the first Mass, thirty horsemen drew up in rough rows. Juan Ortega led that day; Meregildo Guerra was not among them. Across the nose of each man a line of

red ochre was drawn from ear to ear; many of them wore chamois or hickory shirts and high-leggined moccasins; around each forehead a bright-colored band held back the hair, ready for battle. Slung at the point of each saddle was a wine flask.

Down alongside the plaza on the road that led to Rancho de Tortugas rode the Mesilla Guard—La Coronela's beat followed the dirt-thud of hooves. The posse of thirty men, drinking steadily from wine flasks, rode through Tortugas, through a startled Las Cruces, and on toward the Apache camp on the hills behind Doña Ana. Before long they could see the smoke of the campfires along the mesa where the then-peaceful Apaches had gathered for the week of the fair at Doña Ana. Just east of the town the horsemen entered a small camp of renegade Indians, murdered and scalped three of them. Then the line of mounted Mesilleros suddenly appeared before the main camp, howling, brandishing on their lances the bloody scalps. The noise and force of it stunned the Apaches momentarily—until the Guard was almost upon them. Then suddenly the peaceful camp became one of disorder—men and women caught up the little children and they all began to run toward Doña Ana.

The massacre was vividly sketched in a hurried note from the lawyer John Watts at Doña Ana to Dr. Steck at Santa Barbara:

I have been this afternoon an unwilling and helpless witness of one of the most uncalled for murders, atrocities that has been committed in our government...they, [the Apaches] were throughout the week perfectly sober and well-behaved, more so than I have ever witnessed them before, on yesterday I heard it said that two of these Indians had been quietly killed a little distance below town, but I did not believe it. I went yesterday to Las Cruces, and spent the night there, on returning here this afternoon with Mr. Davis and Murick I was astonished at the sight of from 30-50 well armed and mounted men charging into town painted and dressed as Indians. They surrounded and broke into several houses, dragged helpless Indian women out in the street and murdered them in cold blood, committing such atrocities that I am not willing to describe it on paper. They killed 3 men about 2 miles out of town and 4 women and boys in town, there were but 4 Americans of us in town, we three that came up from Las Cruces were unarmed and by the time we could understand what was going on, it was too late for us to prevent any part of the unfortunate affair, the other American (George Ackenback) I am sorry to say, appears to sympathize with the murderers...This party are all from Mesilla, except the goldsmith from Las Cruces who was the only one I knew. An old Mexican living opposite Davis had several Indians in his house and like a man faced the murderers with his gun in hand until joined by some of us unarmed when they withdrew, but you come and get all the particulars and find the dead Indians unburied and hear worse descriptions of the affairs than I have given you, some children were killed.[110]

In his report to the Superintendent of Indian Affairs, Steck said that the first group of Indians that the Guard had killed were renegades who had arrived there an hour before the attack, after hiding booty in the Organ Mountains, and did not belong to the peaceful camp. Furthermore, those peaceful Indians who were camped outside Doña Ana had for the past six months helped the villagers with the corn harvest; some of the farmers had gathered their entire crop with no other than Indian help.

Among those renegades who were killed, wrote Steck, was the chief "…Showa'no, the terror of the territory for the past three years. If they had only stopped there, good."

There will be no peace this way, Steck wrote. "Mesilla complains, but brings it on itself...It would be useless to attempt to bring the perpetrators of the outrages to justice as vast majority of the people and the officers of justice sympathize with the murderers..."

Miguel Montoya, Justice of the Peace, Precinct of Doña Ana, having received the official protest from Dr. Steck about the behavior of the Mesilleros, in turn protested to Rafael Ruelas, Prefect and Probate Judge of Doña Ana County who lived in Mesilla. Don Rafael replied:

> ...it seems very strange that the Indians are at peace with the people of Doña Ana and of other places in the county, yet they are stealing from the inhabitants of La Mesilla. In other words, they are at peace with one side of the river and war with the other...on the 7th of the current month at dawn we were awakened by the sound of the drum [La Coronela] and then we knew that the Indians had stolen some animals from a poor soul...volunteers assembled, and following the bellows of the animals, found that the Indians (thieves) had crossed the river near Tortugas and from there they went in the direction of their ranchería in the little hills near Doña Ana where they were attacked by our troops. Then the Indians came fleeing from the 'ranchería' and came straight toward the pueblo of Doña Ana where they sought protection within the houses where some of them were killed. Now if you in Doña Ana begin to protect the thieving Indians when they have broken every peace treaty they have made…and I think there is no section in any treaty which gives them permission to steal… they do wrong. The 'Mesilleros' have punished them and they are responsible for having made the raid. We do not esteem you in Doña Ana [for] treating us as savages and barbarians for having done our duty. It is the first law of nature to protect oneself and one's property.[111]

It was at Doña Ana on the fifteenth of February that Dr. Steck showed that special courage and determination which made him respected by all who knew him. One hundred Mescaleros lined up on the sandy mesa above Doña Ana. They were dressed for battle—warriors with hair caught back with cloths, faces painted in the familiar red line across the nose. The chief sat mounted in front of the file of Apaches. It was their sworn purpose to avenge the massacre; Dr. Steck was all that stood between them and Mesilla. Quietly and forcefully he spoke to them. The words were bitter, but they heard the truth. It was time for the Apache to go home.

A petition was sent to Brigadier General John Garland and signed by several hundred citizens of Mesilla and La Mesa. The petitioners ask that Fort Fillmore not be evacuated as planned.

The statements of barbarous atrocities committed...in Doña Ana as published in the *Santa Fe Gazette* are grossly exaggerated and false," reported a petition sent to Brigadier General John Garland and signed by several hundred citizens of Mesilla and La Mesa. The petitioners ask that Fort Fillmore not be evacuated as planned. The continued depredations upon our property particularly on the western side of the Río Grande by the Gila Apaches and those residing in the Florida Mountains and near the Mexican line keep us in a state of excitement and alarm.

Our losses are numerous and serious, for most of those who lose their animals, lose that upon which they principally rely for support... although we may have in our country a mounted force of minute men to pursue our enemies, it is the presence and certainty of aid from the United States forces which gives us confidence in our ability to sustain ourselves...

We submit an incomplete list of names of persons residing on the western side of the Río Grande in this county who have lost property by Indians within the last 6 or 8 months, some of the property has been recovered but, most of it is irrecoverably lost; this list numbering nearly 200 head of horses, cattle could be largely increased and verified by ample testimony of its truth, but even this list will suffice to convince you that we are seriously depredated upon by the Apache tribes...

We are convinced that if you will station a company of mounted troops here, there will be but little occasion for the services of the volunteers... [112]

General Garland denied the request, and upbraided the petitioners: "Those who perpetrate acts of violence have no claim to the protection of the military..." Within two months came the second of the attacks on peaceful Indians.

On the rain-washed plain before the village of Santa Barbara on the seventeenth of April, desert willows lined the shallow arroyos; the bosque before Fort Thorn was full green. Covering the ground near the Indian Agency were regular rows of small plants: corn, pumpkins, and squash. It was the day for the distribution of rations, and Indians on horse and on foot approached the quadrangle and lingered about the doorways of the buildings.

An Apache warrior strained at a horse-drawn plow. He turned to the south breeze and the whole line of the plain came into view. There, mounted and silent, sat a group of men watching him. Each carried a rifle in his hand. A little to the advance of the line sat the leader, straw sombrero shading his face from the sun. Instinctively the Apache dropped his plow and began to run for the agency. The next day a grieving Michael Steck again made a report:

It becomes my duty to report another disgraceful and wanton attack upon the Indians of my agency. On my return from a visit to the Mescaleros on the 18th of April, I was informed that the day previous an attack was made upon peaceable Indians at the agency by an armed party of 36 men from the town of Mesilla. After careful enquiry into the facts I am informed that on the morning of the 17th the people living at the agency were aroused by the screams of Indians and upon going to the door saw the party above referred to indiscrimantly butchering Indians ...After the first attack the Indians probably 30 in number ran for the woods nearby and were followed by the assassins... Information of the brutal attack was at once sent to Lieutenant Wood, commander of Fort Thorn who immediately ordered out the troops under his command and took the whole party prisoners, thirty six in number...In fifteen minutes from the time he received information of what was doing, he rushed into the midst of the outlaws drew his pistol and demanded of the leader an immediate surrender...Immediately after the fray, seven dead bodies were picked up and buried by order of Lieutent. Wood and it is thought that others have been killed in the woods that have not yet been found...So far as I can learn there has been no cause given on the part of the Indians for this cowardly and murderous attack...

This is the same party of men who committed the outrageous murders in Doña Ana on the 7th of February, 1858...They are now prisoners of Ft. Thorn...It would in my opinion be useless to attempt to execute the laws upon these men in this county. I hope therefore that the list of offenders will be placed in the hands of the United States District Court... [113]

To the Honorable Judge Kirby Benedict, United States Judge for New Mexico, General John Garland lamented:

Another outrage has been perpetrated by some lawless men purporting to be residents of Mesilla...The case is a grave and important one, new to me, being somewhat at a loss as to the proper course to be pursued, I desire your opinion upon the subject; we have neither a U. S. Judge, District Att'y, or Governor in Santa Fe at this time with whom to consult.

Will you do me the favor to send instructions to the District Att'y who is said to reside somewhere in the vicinity of Mesilla. It would not surprise me to hear that he was the chief counsellor in these acts of violence. [114]

Judge Benedict immediately issued a federal warrant for the arrest of the entire Guard. [115] A messenger carried it to the sheriff who was to remove the thirty-six men to Socorro; they were to be accompanied by a heavily armed military escort. The Guard was to remain at Socorro until the commitment or discharge of the prisoners.

In the third Judicial District on July 3, 1858, their bond was set at five thousand dollars, which was secured by seventeen Mesilla friends. The defendants were ordered to appear at the fall term of court in Socorro.

The case was presented on October 12, 1858, at Socorro in the United States District Court as the United States vs. Juan Ortega, et al. Lieutenant W. H. Wood, Michael Steck, Cleto Trujillo, and Adolph Beck witnessed to the murder of three Indian men, three Indian women and one boy. "... the said Indian woman... [they did strike]...in and upon the head...did shoot...with leaden bullets... numerous mortal wounds...said Indian woman instantly died."

Public sentiment was with the highly respected Mesilla Guard, and they were never convicted of the crimes.

Federal records show: October, 1862, the United States vs. Juan Ortega, et al., a continuance; in October, 1863, the United States vs. Juan Ortega, et al., forfeiture of recognizance. [116]

However, in a letter to President Abraham Lincoln, June 2, 1861, Judge Kirby Benedict reinforced his remarks about the respectable behavior of the Mexican citizens of the state: "I tried thirty-six men for murder for the same indictment but I met no uncommon trouble and no resistance." [117]

Before they were acquitted, and before any more unauthorized attempts by individuals to redress their own wrongs, Governor Abraham Rencher wisely appointed and commissioned Meregildo Guerra captain of the company of the Mesilla and Mesa Mounted Volunteers of the Militia of the Territory of New Mexico. Juan Ortega received a commission as lieutenant, as did Cayetano Domínguez—two of the original thirty-six. [118] These men were now responsible to Meregildo Guerra; the whole Mesilla Guard answered to the state militia—should there ever be another such occurrence, the Guard would stand before a stern and impartial court.

Chapter 6 | CALLE DEL CORREO

When the moon is in its first quarter, there are those in Mesilla who can hear the lonely sound of a conch shell; then quickly, the clatter of hooves against a dry and dirt packed trail. When the moon is bright enough the outline of a rider appears, buckskins dark and wet from the river. Behind the rider in the saddle he carries two mailbags; from the pommel hangs a leather pouch of water and within easy reach, his musket. These viejitos, the old people, never see his face, but moonlight outlines his hands on the reins. And when at last the sweating horse turns north along the street called San Albino, the rider reins west onto Calle del Correo, called such because there was a time when mail did come this way. Stopping there, he abruptly tosses the reins into a mesquite bush and disappears.

Even before Mesilla was settled, up on the road from Chihuahua to Santa Fe, mail arrived in two wheeled carretas, carts drawn by one or two animals. In Spanish times, and when Mexico controlled the Mesilla Valley, there were orders from Mexico City to be delivered, there was news from both the New and the Old Worlds, and there were letters from families separated, lonely for one another. Men risked their lives to bring the written word from one end of that long trail to the other.

The Spanish set up a regular mail to Santa Fe. Twice monthly it left Mexico City, but it was often delayed en route. After the Mexican republic was established a tri-monthly mail from El Paso to Santa Fe[119] was carried by authorized postal officials.[120]

When the first settlers came to La Mesilla, the mail was brought by a lone horseman who would bring it across the river to Mesilla from the caravans going north or south along the east side of the river. In 1849, Captain Henry Skillman, guide and frontiersman, carried the United States mail on horseback between San Antonio and Santa Fe.[121] At least a decade before the great overland Pony Express carried the mail on more northern trails, these men defied danger and death to reach lonely habitations along the river.

Early Mesilla depended on its farmer merchants and its wagon trains for transportation not only of produce but of people. Blas Duran was one of the first merchants. He grew his own wheat, ran his own mill and transported his own products. His *terreno de labor*, his grant of land to be worked, lay just north of the village, and was bounded on the west by the acequia madre and to the east by the Camino Nacional. Here, in between the mother ditch and the road, lay a small empire. There were ten acres of land fenced in with adobe, the timbered gate mortised and pinned so that it swung open and shut. Luxuriant wheat fields made a golden sea waving along the green, tree-lined acequia.

The L-shaped main building was made of thick adobe and was heated by a fireplace in each room. There was the large waiting room, rooms for cooking and others for sleeping, and cool, cavernous rooms for storage. There was one room, with light only from small, high windows, where oxhide pouches dripped the juice of the grape into wine casks four feet in diameter. From the storage rooms, flour was loaded onto carts. Great wooden yokes held the teams of oxen close to the carretas; the trip to the new forts of Fillmore and Conrad was ready to begin.

Always there were passengers, sometimes a family or two, who rode along to make the first lap of a journey to Santa Fe or perhaps southward to Chihuahua. The returning carts would bring travelers from the north to the first unofficial "stage stop" of Mesilla.[122]

There were many such merchants who sent out great numbers of wagons loaded with corn, wheat, or wine vinegar. In addition, precious metals began to be carried from the mountains to the east and west. To Port Lavaca on the Gulf of Mexico would go, at one time, 25,000 pounds of copper to be shipped to Marseilles, France, or other foreign ports. Silver, too, was shipped from six fine veins of silver in the Organ Mountains[123]—the rough ore smelted at Stephenson's *"hacienda de beneficiar metales,"* the adobe smelting furnace not far from Fort Fillmore. From the new mining regions of Pino Alto to the northwest came gold, and sometimes as much as $1200 in gold dust, to be sent out under heavy guard.[124]

One crowded, long, and uneven block directly south of the plaza, gradually became the center of the wagon train business. On these *solares*, on this piece of ground bounded by the Street of Parián to the north, the Street of San Albino[125] to the east, were the storerooms of the Armijo brothers, Rafael and Manuel; the corral and office of the very successful firm of Leonart & Maurin; Vincent St. Vrain's corral, home, and business occupied space here, too. The partners, Hoppin and Appel, carried on their merchandising business in this long block.

For the refreshment and amusement of the men who came and went with the incoming and outgoing trains, Joshua Sledd had in his large adobe "hollow-square" house in the center of the block,[126] its prosperous billiard room and bar which was stocked with wines, liquors, oysters, lobsters, salmon, pineapples and sardines.[127] These buildings in the fore part of the block had common walls, so that a solid front presented itself to the Calle Principal.

In 1857 Guadalupe Miranda was proprietor of a dramshop in La Mesilla—a small business on the south end of the plaza. From the portal in front of his establishment he could see up and down the street. Behind him in the shadows of his shop were the casks of wine and the bottles—translucent, precious glass bottles of *vino del pais*. The new church was being built on land which he had given

in exchange for an equal piece at the southern end of the plaza which was irregular and bordered with little sand hills. Gusty winds blew the sand back and forth. On the southeast corner, at the intersection of Guadalupe and Parián, stood Nestor Varela's store. Juan José Duran's tiny jacal—la casa de mi morada—his dwelling place had in former years stood near this corner.

Varela had been a business partner of Nepomuceno Ancheta who had fled the Mexican Revolution of 1856. Partnerships dissolved twice before this property on the southeast corner became the celebrated stopping place known as Bean's Hotel and Bar. Its cool rooms surrounded a patio with fig trees and green plants, and to the east of the building a large wall enclosed corrals, one for wagons and one for carriages.

First had come the pony expressman down the little pathway, the Calle del Correo, and then the wagon trains, and in 1857, came the stagecoach. Before long, the concentration of mercantile businesses included the offices and stopping places of the three great stage lines that were to come through Mesilla: The San Antonio and San Diego mail line, the Butterfield, and much later, the National Mail and Transportation Company. David Wasson contracted to carry a monthly mail from San Antonio to Santa Fe in 1854 with stops at Fort Fillmore and Las Cruces. George Giddings of San Antonio took over the franchise in 1855. The next change was to a weekly mail when Giddings and Thomas Bowler of Santa Fe obtained a mail contract. There were four post coaches: The "Phelps," the "Beale," the "Otero," and the "Neosha" carrying the mail between San Antonio and San Diego. They did not stop at Mesilla. But a contract was signed in Washington on June 22, 1857 with James E. Birch which was to bring a regular mail to Mesilla at last.

Now over the shimmering stillness of the Camino Real, through the ascending waves of heat, came the first Celerity Wagon, James Birch's San Antonio and San Diego Mail, the "Jackass Line." For the first time Mesilla was connected with the

SILVER MINES OF THE ORGAN MOUNTAINS.
New-Mexico.

Plate 16: The mines in the Organ Mountains were rich in silver and other metals. Suppling mining operations added to the economic vitality of Mesilla. A. B. Grey of Bartlett's Boundary Survey in 1854. Carl Schuchard Lithograph Collection MS 0339, Rio Grande Historical Collections, New Mexico State University Library, Las Cruces, New Mexico.

Plate 17: La Mesilla Plaza in the latter part of the 19th century. On the right can be seen equipment for a traveling circus that periodically came to town. Photo courtesy Museum of New Mexico, negative number 37917. Editor's note: recent research has suggested that the scene depicts Las Cruces, not Mesilla.

west coast.

James Birch, a former stage driver from Massachusetts and a brilliant organizer, had recently built up a California stage company into a million-dollar corporation. George Giddings became the proprietor at the eastern end of the line, and Robert E. Doyle managed the California end. Isaiah Churchill Woods was made general superintendent.[128]

The Celerity Wagon was a light, trim vehicle with a superstructure of duck, with roller flaps for protection at the sides. Interlacing leather straps took the place of springs. The coach was loaded with baggage, mail, and passengers. To guard against the Indians, there was an escort of six to eight men; the stage itself bristled with Colt revolvers and rifles. At first, a relay of mules went along—to be fresh when switched for the weary animals pulling the wagons. When regular stations were established with corrals of fresh animals, the relay was no longer needed. Often *ramudas*, or herds of mules or horses, were kept at watering and grazing places near the rivers, and were exchanged here for fresh ones.

There were no way or swing stations for rest and refreshment at first. Two meals were cooked each day—over an open fire—breakfast at eight or nine o'clock—supper at five or six. Passengers sat on the ground in a circle and ate "their provender out of pewter plates." [129] Sometimes all the mules would give out and the passengers had to walk, and sometimes the road would be lost in the blackness of a moonless night and there would be an urgent striking of matches as the travelers tried to locate the ruts of the road again.[130]

In 1857, after the stop at Franklin, Texas, the first San Antonio & San Diego (SA & SD) Coach made its way to the Río Grande where the passengers enjoyed the beauty along the river—the fields of tall green sugarcane, yellow sunflowers, the wild geese and great blue cranes that fed along the river.[131] About ten o'clock in the morning, a stop was made at Skillman's ranch at Willow Bar about halfway to Mesilla. Breakfast was served by a native-born woman, and the coach proceeded to Fort Fillmore.

From the fort, it was about five miles to the ford over the Río Grande. Here two strong Mexican men took lariats in their hands and after fastening the lassos to two of the mule's necks, the men plunged into the swift, muddy river pulling the animals after them. The other mules followed, frightened, thrashing in the water. The stage was floated across the 300 yard ford, its wheels resting on rafts.[132]

The first stage rolled onto the plaza at La Mesilla on the thirty-first of August, 1857. The driver on the box was Henry Skillman. He held a twelve-foot lash of buckskin, but he never touched the backs of the mules as he cracked the whip in the air. Signaled by the sudden explosions of leather, the animals brought the coach around the corner to the mail headquarters.

The first begrimed passenger alighted—it was Superintendent Woods himself. Stepping down onto the hot street, he entered a cool adobe building for a very brief rest.[133] A cloud of fine dust had accompanied the passengers almost all the way from San Antonio; no article of clothing was protection—it crept under a man's collar; he could taste it, gritty between his teeth.

After the brief refreshment at Mesilla, the stage headed on towards the western mesas.[134] After Tucson, the exhausted travelers would climb onto mules for a punishing ride over the desert—the advertisement of the Jackass Line reported a 108-mile stretch by muleback—the passengers reported a 500-mile trip.

James Birch did not live to know that the first coach arrived safely and on time in San Diego. After setting his line in operation, he boarded the ship, the "Central America," in California to return to his young wife and new son in Swansea, Massachusetts. He was drowned when the ship sank off Cape Hatteras on September 11, 1857.[135]

Woods did not learn of Birch's death until he arrived in San Diego after his thirty-eight day trip from San Antonio, which he confided to friends, "nearly killed me." [136] Mrs. Birch turned the line over to Otis Kelton, her stepfather and an old "stager," but there was so much opposition to his appointment by stockholders that she returned the line to Giddings and Doyle.[137]

In the meantime, the need for funds for the line was immediate and pressing. In December, Woods was able to negotiate a mortgage on the stock in use and Simeon Hart of El Paso loaned the line $10,125.61 on nine celerity wagons, complete harness for each wagon, and 152 mules branded with a "B". Woods was able to keep his schedule; Giddings and Doyle continued to maintain business at the respective ends of the line and not a single mail was missed.

By 1857, La Mesilla was flourishing in spite of Indian troubles. Into the little town of 1500 inhabitants came traffic from north, south, east, and west. Where the first colonists had received their solares de casa, their lots for homes around the plaza, (for it was much too dangerous to live across the acequia madre where most of the farmland lay) there were the beginnings of shops, hotels, salons and gaming houses. Incoming stage passengers from the East found it "singular and picturesque." [138]

Overlooking the plaza on the north was the completed Church of San Albino which had replaced the little jacal church. Around the square Mexicans dressed in broad trousers and the colorful garment, the serape. Vendors' baskets were filled with grapes and figs, or peaches, apples, melons or candies. Mexican women, shawls almost hiding their faces, passed an American on the streets and there would be only a flash of dark eyes.[139]

Some passengers found Mesilla a town of drinking shops, where 104 proof grape and 83 proof peach brandies were specialties. Behind the dram-shops were the ever-present games of chance: *cinquian*, a type of five-handed poker, *jipon*: monte. John McGran and Thomas Massie kept the best monte houses in the territory. Between the dram-shops and the gambling and the trouble over

the beautiful *señoritas*, Joshua Sledd, who was the jailer as well as a shopkeeper, found his frail, small jail continually full.

There were those travelers, too, who came riding into Mesilla on a chilly December evening to find their hearts stirred by the beauty of the great bonfires built on the mesas behind the village. The hillsides were set aglow by miners who were not too rough to herald the coming of the Christ Child to signal by these great *candelas* the approach of La Noche Buena—Christmas Eve.

The rough ride from Mesilla to Yuma was almost beyond endurance; the road had hardly been broken through this wild country. The Secretary of Interior to Washington, Jacob Thompson, had been aware of the need for a good wagon road through the Gadsden Purchase even before the mail contract was signed and the stagecoaches began to go through. An appropriation of $200,000 had been made in the spring of 1857 for improving the road from El Paso to Yuma. The road from San Antonio to El Paso had long ago been beaten down by government wagon trains and the mail coaches from San Antonio to Santa Fe.

In May, about three months before James Birch first began his SA & SD, James B. Leach, who had been quartermaster on Doniphan's expedition during the Mexican War, and who had been assisting in the transportation of U. S. mails between Salt Lake and California, was appointed superintendent of the project. He was to locate and construct where necessary or improve the roads between El Paso and Fort Fillmore, and also from Mesilla to Yuma. N. Henry Hutton was chief engineer and his assistant was N. P. Cook. M. A. McKinnon was appointed disbursing agent; Dr. J. R. McCay was the medical officer.

Leach chose as his assistant, Isaiah Churchill Woods, the same Woods who became superintendent of the SA & SD. With Woods masterminding manipulation of funds, far too many people benefited from the resulting collusion of the mail line and the wagon road project. Among them were Woods himself, Leach, and others who did not hesitate to close their eyes to fraud.

Isaiah Woods had been well chosen. He arrived in California in 1848 on a trader which had come from New Bedford, Massachusetts, and he immediately became involved in money-making schemes. Within seven years after his arrival on the west coast—he was still a young man not much more than thirty years old—he had accumulated assets amounting to $256,997 which included more than 2000 acres of land in San Mateo County, California. His home, "Woodside," was the scene of lavish weekend parties, but his residence in California was abruptly terminated when the Adams & Co. Bank, of which he was a co-partner, failed in February, 1855. Litigation followed and Woods and his associate, A. A. Cohen, were accused of embezzling large sums of money. Just before the failure of the company, Woods wrote to Cohen instructing him to make "entries to cover the deficiencies existing...in such a manner that no person but yourself or I would be enabled to unravel them and find out where it is or what it was or anything about it." In the midst of legal proceedings, Woods left for Australia. From there he went to London, then Boston, and in the spring of '57 Leach appointed him his assistant.

Now it was May, 1858, and James Leach sat in a straight-backed chair in his office in Mesilla while a spring rain fell steadily. Across the street, the adobe walls were ribboned a darker brown where the wind had cast the rain in great strokes. Mr. Leach was in an embarrassing position.

There was one deepset window to his left, looking out on Calle Principal—the El Paso-Fort Yuma branch of the Pacific Wagon Road projects had, in addition to purchasing supplies and borrowing to the extent of $20,000 from the firm of Leonart & Maurin, set up offices in their building. No one had passed the door within the last two hours—the rain had filled the street to the foundation of the long, low adobe building; the solitude gave Colonel Leach opportunity to reflect upon the occurrences of the past year.

In May, 1857, just a year ago from that rainy day Leach and his friend, Woods, had assembled forty wagons, provisions, and a staff of assistants at Memphis, Tennessee. The caravan was to proceed to DesArc, Arkansas, where they hoped to purchase more oxen—the supply in Memphis had been scanty. The train arrived at DesArc about the second week in July and the assistant engineer, Cook, set about looking for more oxen to buy. Supt. Leach became anxious because of the delay and with Hutton the engineer, proceeded to El Paso with fifteen wagons drawn by mules. He left the oxwagons and a portion of the hands under the charge of Capt. D. C. Woods—a seaman from Massachusetts—who was probably kin to Isaiah Woods. McKinnon, the disbursing agent, also stayed at DesArc. There they awaited the arrival of oxen from Ft. Smith, Arkansas.

The ox train was delayed in Arkansas for two months—a delay which McKinnon said was "never satisfactorily accounted for." It finally arrived at Fort Belknap, to winter the stock rather than expose animals and men to a long, cold trip over the Texas plains to El Paso.

Meanwhile, Isaiah Woods was busy with SA & SD business—well-mixed with wagon road business. It was reported from San Antonio that wagon road equipment and supplies had been useful in getting the mail line under way. Woods also made a fraudulent contract with Berford and Company of New York, a transportation company, in the name of the wagon road project. He made that first stagecoach trip, officiously insisted on assisting in making up the accounts for the wagon road commission for the quarter ending Sept. 30, 1857—substituting false vouchers for the originals. By his systematic use of forgery and fraud, he cleared over $3000.

Leach, in the meantime, as he sat in his office that day in Mesilla, visualized his most immediate needs.

When he had arrived in El Paso in October of '57, he had added Mexican laborers to the one hundred easterners he had brought along. He made up working parties consisting of fifty men. Each party included a carpenter, a cook, a blacksmith, a herdsman and a watchman. Now the road from El Paso to Mesilla was finished and Leach was desperately in need of money. It was time to pay off these men, and there were other unpaid bills that were growing old. Although it was May, the oxtrain had not yet arrived from Ft. Belknap. There had been no word from McKinnon, the disbursing agent, for two months.

The Pacific Wagon Roads office in Washington had been instructed that all vouchers be signed by McKinnon, by Leach, and by the producer, seller or laborer. To make contact with McKinnon as he was en route to Texas and at Belknap had been difficult or impossible. Leach had had to plead, beg, borrow, and almost steal to keep the roadwork going. He had at last signed the vouchers himself, and without McKinnon's signature, sent them directly to Albert Campbell, head of the Wagon Road office in Washington. This was irregular and he knew it—and displeasure was apparent in the letters from Washington.

The answer of the authorities in Washington was to send a special investigator, Welcome B. Sayles, to Mesilla to look into the affairs of the wagon road project. He arrived in El Paso on June 4, 1858. On June 20, the long-awaited ox train finally arrived—eleven of the wagons having been abandoned on the road from Belknap.

As he checked into accounts, Sayles found many things irregular and unsatisfactory and Leach's explanations just as unsatisfactory. Furthermore, Sayles found Leach's personal habits were such that they brought discredit upon the Department of the Interior. At the laborers' camp just three miles south of Mesilla, there was so much drinking and gambling that it was disgusting to Sayles.

Accusations against the ubiquitous Isaiah Woods began pouring in. When he and Leach had first begun in Concord to order the forty wagons from the celebrated coachmaker, Mr. Abbott, he met them at their hotel, and there Woods took him aside and told him to make up his full price for the forty wagons in vouchers with $25 added to each. This would amount to $1000 which would be shared by Woods, Leach, and Abbott. Mr. Abbott flatly refused the proposal.

Charles Whitcomb, who had been employed to purchase horses and mules for the project, reported that he had been instructed by Woods to get vouchers or receipts with signature only—the rest was to be left blank. Woods then filled in his own price.

Meanwhile in Mesilla, Welcome Sayles had to make a decision—whether or not to allow the expedition to go on and finish the road to Fort Yuma as was first intended. After consideration, but with doubts, he allowed the group to proceed.

The wagon road followed the valley out of Mesilla for six miles through low bottomland intersected frequently by acequias. For three miles of this "line" the roadbed had to be isolated by ditches which were dug on either side, and the surface of the road was raised with the excavated material. The workers found this mixture of loam and sand difficult to work with.

Sweating laborers built bridges over five of the acequias. These bridges, spanning eight to ten feet, were made of cottonwood logs which were cut along the riverbank. Large logs formed a base and smaller logs were used for cross-pieces, and the log bed was covered with a layer of earth about eight inches deep. A supervising engineer on this project recorded his observations of the valley of the Mesilla. Easterners were consistently critical of the customs and habits of the people, although now and then there were those who understood the philosophy of the Mexican who savored life in his own unhampered way.

The engineer wrote:

   ...these people are engaged in agricultural pursuits for which the bottom lands of the Río Grande are admirably adapted...Immense quantities of pumpkins, melons, and chile [sic]...are consumed...[There is] cultivation of

Plate 18: Mesilla streets in the 1880's. López Family Photographs, RG84-159a, Rio Grande Historical Collections, New Mexico State University Library, Las Cruces, New Mexico.

Plate 19: This property was originally the site of the Mesilla government building in the 1850s. In the 1930s it was the old Billy the Kid Museum owned by George Griggs. It now is the La Posta Parking lot, a block east of the plaza. Mary D. Taylor Collection.

the vine and fruit...The number of Americans at present residing in the valley of...Mesilla... is small, not yet sufficient to have succeeded to any perceptible degree in modifying the customs and habits of the mongrel race now occupying the soil...They have advanced in but a slight degree, beyond the use, if indeed not the knowledge of the most primitive methods of agriculture known to record. It is not less strange than true that they use nothing more than pointed sticks, clumsily attached to long wooden beams or levers, for the purpose of upturning the soil, which however with this imperfect care brings forth "a hundred fold." The corn crops are planted in such a manner as to leave five or six stalks standing in a hill... Equally shiftless and unprofitable is the manner of harvesting wheat...there are few finer sights than a field of wheat ready for the sickil on the Río Grande. Acre after acre stretches away before the pleased vision "as level as a barn floor." The heavy and bending ears of the grain seem ready to burst with the fatness of plenty. In some corner of one of these fields a circular enclosure of fifteen or twenty steps in diameter is "cleared off..."and fenced...with willow or cottonwood saplings. Into this enclosure is thrown bundle after bundle of wheat...a number of mustang ponies...are forced into a circular kind of a trot...The chaff is then separated from the wheat by hand farming...Pass by one of these threshing places, two weeks after the storing...where the wheat was thrashed out will be seen a dense growth of young wheat which speaks of bushel after bushel after bushel of grain wasted to no purpose...gamma [sic] grass of the hills is inexhaustible. Fear of the Apaches however keep the people at home, and until a war of extermination shall have driven these red devils out of their haunts...or a healthy influx of American blood shall have changed the character of the population...it will be nothing more than a lounging place for a degenerate, mixed race of people, who are content to take out an aimless existence on a few "tortillas..."(140)

Finally in August when this portion of the road work had been completed, Leach as charged had paid off the local workers: fifty-five of them were left, Mexicans and Germans.

From La Mesilla, Leach took the remainder of his road construction equipment on to Fort Yuma, building that section of the road in such a hurried fashion that parts of it were never used and weeds were growing in the faint tracks made by the expedition.

Leach was to sell off the stock and supplies when the work was finished. But Sayles, suspecting "that a plan was on foot to throw the stock into the hands of certain parties at prices far below its value" made Leach agree that no sale should be made unless it was approved by Hutton and Sayles' assistant, Austin.

Leach thereupon took most of the mules and wagons to San Diego and, disregarding his promise, sold them upon a "short and limited notice" for prices greatly below their value. Judge Hart of El Paso had guaranteed to buy the stock for $900 per team (a team consisting of six mules, harness and wagon) but Leach sold the teams at San Diego to H. E. Doyle for $600 apiece. By the same type of coincidence which "happened" to all the dealings of the wagon road project, it "happened" that Mr. Doyle was superintendent of the western division of the SA & SD mail line and the brother-in-law of Woods.

James B. Leach was indicted by the United States government and charged with forgery and falsification of vouchers to the amount of $10,000. The records of the Department of Justice, Case #208, U. S. vs. James B. Leach, report that he could not proceed to the trial until December, 1859 for want of witnesses "who reside outside the jurisdiction of the court." The trial was never held.

Isaiah Churchill Woods was indicted and returned to Texas for trial, but witnesses failed to appear against him, and he, too, escaped prosecution and punishment.

The SA & SD in the meantime had suffered a near-fatal blow. The big dream of a coast-to-coast mail and passenger line came true with the awarding of a contract not to the Giddings and Doyle line, but to John Butterfield and his company. They were to carry the mail from St. Louis to the west coast. On September 15, 1858, the Butterfield Overland Mail running handsome new coaches left east and west terminals simultaneously with little fanfare.

Since the Butterfield route duplicated the route of the SA & SD over a 600-mile stretch between El Paso and Fort Yuma, the postmaster general discontinued the Jackass Mail on that portion of the line; the little line continued operations along the rest of the route and held on until August, 1861.

With the coming of the great Butterfield, changes came to Mesilla. Captain Giles Hawley, a New Yorker, became superintendent and made his headquarters in Mesilla. In 1859, as agent of the Overland Mail Company, Hawley purchased Vincent St. Vrain's house and corral and the adjoining Leonart and Maurin property for the office and stage stop of the Butterfield line.

From New York came Frank DeRyther, too, to be local Butterfield agent, and agent for the Wells-Fargo company which connected with Catlett's Express, the fast little line which ran between Pino Alto, Mowry City, and Mesilla. It could make the trip in eighteen to twenty hours, depending upon water and animals. On one such trip Catlett carried to Pino Alto Judge McDowan, Colonel Thomas Martin, three other men and three "sinoritas." On the return trip, he carried fifty-five letters and messengers. Corlew, Bonneville, and MacWillie, brought back two "sinoritas" from the mines. St. Marmaduke and Mr. Dyer, who was sutler for Fort Webster, were picked up at Pachitiju Spring (later called Apache Tejo) where the fort was located.

Antonio Torres, former cook at a Butterfield station, and George Frazier took up Mr. Catlett's franchise when Catlett found himself beset with debts. Torres called the little line the Pino Alto and Mesilla Express. His stops were Picacho, Cook's Spring, Mowry City, Faywood (Hot Spring), Floyd, Agua Blanca (White Water Draw south of Santa Rita mine).

W. D. Skillman, Henry Skillman's brother, was postmaster of La Mesilla and also local agent for the remnant of the SA & SD. His post office consisted of a cozy corner fitted up in the SA & SD office.

About this time, the stage line employees forced a peculiar victory over the Apaches: There were two rival hotels on the plaza of La Mesilla. The proprietor of the hotel on the south side of the plaza had imported a huge Chinese gong to attract customers arriving at the stage station. The owner of the other hotel rang a big bell every time a stage drew up. The Overland employed C.W. Garner as guard on the route from Mesilla to Tucson, and, as Mr. Garner's sympathies were with the man who rang the bell, Garner stole the gong and hid it in a departing coach of which he was the conductor.

The route of the coach led through the treacherous Cooke's Canyon. About halfway through the canyon, Garner discovered Apaches lying in ambush. The coach hauled up and turned about preparing for a fight. Suddenly Garner remembered the gong. He stripped to the drawers and covered himself with flour. Then he advanced alone on the waiting Apaches, dancing about and screaming and wildly striking the gong. The blows upon the big brass disc reverberated in the canyon, echoing up and down the length of it, like the thunder of some ancient Apache god. The Indians fled in terror, Garner returned to the stage, and the party resumed its trip.

There were some mutterings in Mesilla about the number of "northerners coming in," but they were generally trusted and liked. Frank DeRyther lived out the rest of his life in Mesilla and his successes at beautifying the village by planting trees and shrubs and flowers became known throughout the territory.

When in the spring of 1860, Captain Giles Hawley planned to leave on the stage for the East for a short visit to the "folks at Home" a splendid farewell ball was given by the citizens of Mesilla. Dancing took place in Sledd's "commodious assembly room," and Saturnino Barrientos prepared and served supper in the patio which had been covered with canvas. One hundred twelve bottles of champagne were uncorked.

Inside the hall, the entire ceiling had been covered with the "Stars and Stripes" which had been loaned to the committee by the officers of Ft. Fillmore. Suspended in the center of the room was a portrait of Washington, and to his right and left were portraits of General Jackson and President Buchanan.

Two miniature stagecoaches had been put together expressly for the occasion. One of the coaches was followed by a hungry coyote, and the horses of the other were being attacked by a lion. On one coach was painted in white letters, "We are bound to run all day"; on the other, "We are bound to run all night." Two new and beautiful whips formed a star, and under the star was a magnificent set of harness which had never been in use. When the dance master called "Crack your whips," the band of six brass pieces, a harp, and a violin played "Wait for the wagon and we'll all take a ride."

Along with the superintendent and agent from the East came experienced station keepers and drivers for the Times Butterfield line. Between the Río Grande and Tucson seventy-five men were employed. Some of them were serious young men who became good citizens—John P. Walker, Charles Edwards, H. W. Lyons, and Eugene, Frank, and W. N. Van Patten, nephews of Colonel Butterfield. But too often in Mesilla there were bitter, senseless fights between the Mexicans, the employees of the stage line, and the soldiers from Fort Fillmore.

Early one morning on the rooftop of Bean's hotel, some Americans, including Jim Tevis and his friends, crouched under siege. The Overland Mail employees shared the rooftop with other Anglos helping to hold off the angry Mexicans below. In Sledd's "bily" dance room the night before, a dance had been violently interrupted by drawn knives and guns. All night long the Anglos and the Mexicans fought, and near morning the Americans disappeared out the back door and scrambled for the roof top. A rider had been sent to Fort Fillmore for help, and with early morning came dragoons riding under the command of a coldly angry Lieutenant Lord. The marooned Americans were rescued, and order was restored as the dragoons rode among the resentful townspeople. Alcalde Anastacio Barela agreed, under threat of artillery fire, not to let his citizens get out of hand again.

On October 6, 1859, Mat Mason and William Twilly of the Overland Mail squared off in Sledd's hall to decide their differences. In the brawl that followed Twilly was shot and died immediately.

James Ottoway, a former cook with the SR & SD line, met his death in a particularly bitter way— as a quiet bystander. In Sledd's hall another fracas involved Mexicans, Americans, Overland Mail employees, and soldiers. A Mr. Casson insulted a Mexican standing near the door. Captain John Phillips made a slurring remark to Casson. Casson swung and missed. The captain seized him around the neck and stabbed him in the back. When some of the crowd tried to separate them, the cocked pistol that the captain held was accidentally fired. The ball hit the twenty-four year old Ottoway directly in the forehead.

As the American Civil War drew near, southern sympathizers along the Butterfield route— especially in Texas—ravaged stock, coaches and supplies. There were other acts of vandalism. "The Butterfield route is cut up by the roots...cut right into at the center. It is stopped in all its stages through the state of Texas some 6 or 700 miles," said one United States Senator in agitating for better connections with the Pacific coast. In March, 1861, Butterfield employees received orders to transfer the line to a central route, but before the stock could be removed at either end of the line, there were a series of tragedies.

One warm evening in April as the locust blooms sent a faint, sweet breath out into the evening air, the eastbound coach rumbled in from

Plate 20: Butterfield Stage at Mesilla, painted by Bob Diven. Mary D. Taylor Collection.

Tucson. It was seven o'clock and the saloon on the corner of the plaza was beginning to fill with weary farmers. As always when the coach arrived, a little knot of men gathered about. This time there was bitter news. It had left its mark on the set face of Anthony Elders, the conductor, and on the shaken, tired passengers.

Although Elders' stage had been unmolested, he brought news of an Indian attack on a westbound coach. The attack took place about forty-five miles outside of Tucson. A party of forty or fifty Tonto Apaches had come swooping down out of the hills. Parks, the driver of the coach, had been shot through the loins and had fallen from the box in six or eight seconds. Twenty or thirty yelling Apaches surrounded him as he fell. William Willis, the conductor, had been asleep inside the coach, but upon awakening had been able to get out and up onto the box. Twelve or fifteen Indians armed with shotguns had followed the coach several miles, and had not the team been the fastest on the line and a station only a short distance away, they would have succeeded in overtaking it. When the stage arrived in Tucson, Elders, who was about to depart for Mesilla, counted sixteen ball holes in it besides a large number of arrowheads.

In spite of the news of Indian attacks, George Giddings and the Doyles, Robert and John, were determined to keep the southern mail and passenger service going. The three men purchased the Butterfield buildings in Mesilla and set about reviving the run of the old SA & SD—from San Antonio through to Los Angeles. Isaiah Woods was to be superintendent. Captain Henry Skillman accepted the management of the western division, and his brother, W. F. Skillman, was appointed local agent in Mesilla. But an express reached Mesilla on the evening of the 8th of May bringing news which almost ended the revival before it began.

On that 8th day of May, George Giddings in El Paso heard the news of the firing on Fort Sumter, and the news of the violent death of his brother, John James, at Stein's Peak, April 28, 1861, near Apache Pass in Arizona. Cochise, who had been

reportedly killed in Sonora, reappeared with his braves determined to wage war on the whites. The expressman, Mr. Price, brought the details of the series of killings.

A provision wagon left Tanks Station, (south of San Simon Station an alternate route) near Stein's Peak in Arizona on April 23, 1861. Edward Donnelly and Pat Donahue had been sent to get a load of flour at San Simon Station about fifteen miles west of the Tanks. They completed their errand, started on their return trip, but never reached the Tanks. The next day, two expressmen, Paige and O'Brien, left the Stein's Peak Tanks westward bound. They never reached San Simon Station.

In the meantime, Michael Neice, road agent of the Butterfield Overland Mail along with Anthony Elders, Samuel Neely, and a Mr. Briggs—all Overland Mail employees—set out from Mesilla to take in the Butterfield stock from the western division. Riding along in the six-mule coach was John James Giddings who intended to make an attempt to pacify Cochise and his warriors. The stage arrived safely at Tanks (Barney Station East of Lordsburg). On the 27th, the five men left in the coach for Tucson. Two of their six mules returned to Tanks Station (Stein Peak Station) badly bruised; to Expressman Price it was clear that there had been a severe struggle. He saddled up and rode northeastward to Fort McLane (Apache Tejo) for troops.

A lieutenant and sixteen rank-and-file were dispatched and with Price returned to Stein's Peak Station to investigate. At the Peak they encountered the train of William Grant, army contractor, which was coming east from Tucson. Grant and his party had had a fight with Cochise and his braves, but worse than that news was the confirmation of fears that the coach with the five men had been ambushed and captured by the Apaches at or near Doubtful Canyon—that dreaded canyon near Stein's Peak. Grant told them how his train had been attacked ten miles east of San Simon, the mules stampeded, and a running fight had occurred as the men pursued the Indians. One Apache had been killed, two mortally wounded. Grant's train went on and reached Stein's Peak Station at dusk. Here they found scattered along the ravine newspapers and other mail matter, pieces of harness, spokes, which had been chopped out of wheels, and shreds of the top of the coach. Nearby were the bodies of two men who had been tied to trees by the feet, heads eighteen inches above the ground. Their arms had been extended and fastened to pickets, their bodies pierced with arrows and lances. Beneath their heads were the evidences of slow fires. Recognition was impossible. Employees of the train quickly buried the men and fearing another attack, immediately pushed ahead into the night.

After receiving this information from Grant, Price rode with the news to Mesilla. The detachment of soldiers and an emigrant wagon train which had arrived at Stein's Peak from Mesilla hurried on westward. In the train from Mesilla were Hiram Stevens and his family, Jim Tevis, and Charlie Brown. They found the remains of the missing coach in the canyon. It was not hard to visualize the attack. The Apaches had hidden themselves in the heavy growth of skin oak which covered both sides of the gulch. They had surprised the stage as it descended into the canyon, the lead mules had been shot, the coach stopped, and not a man escaped. Three bodies were found near the stage. The other men were never found. Stevens, Tevis, and Brown quickly buried the men in shallow graves and when they were through, they proceeded westward to Dragoon Springs with the escort of soldiers.

When the news of the massacre came to George Giddings at El Paso, he hurried to Arizona where he gathered together twenty-five men to go out over the line. As he checked the stations along the line, he found buildings burned and coaches wrecked. Mules and horses had been stolen. Some of the stock herders had been killed. When all had been buried, Giddings returned to El Paso and went on to San Antonio.

Doggedly, the Doyles and Giddings went on with their plans for a revival of a through run of the SA & AD. On May 17, 1861, the plaza in Mesilla was lined with people watching the Butterfield Mail pull out. Equipment and stock had been gathered from Fort Davis, Texas, to Mesilla—100 men, 200 animals, twenty coaches, and many more pack wagons. The Butterfield employees of Mesilla joined the caravan and they all rode out together, heading for the stations on the central route. Behind them, following the dust of their exodus, came twenty-five men and a herd of stock for the reorganized SA & SD.

The next day the first through mail from San Antonio to Los Angeles under the control of the revived SA & SD was to leave Mesilla. An escort of six picked men prepared to accompany the coach. However, in June, Giddings was still trying to get the line in thorough working order and was waiting for Henry Skillman to get the western division organized.

As a through line, the old SA & SD never really got under way again. The mail coach continued to run between San Antonio and El Paso, but on August 12th, Henry Skillman left Mesilla to withdraw the stock on the western division. He was accompanied by a lieutenant and fifteen men since a brush with the Apaches was anticipated. He was successful in withdrawing the stock which he took to California with him and the old SA & SD was discontinued permanently. Mesilla was without regular mail or passenger service to the west coast until after the Civil War.

Chapter 7 | LA ENTRADA

La Mesilla in July, 1861, was a village lovely in the rich textures of rain-washed adobe and irrigated fields of chile, corn, and wheat. On the lonely trail from El Paso to Santa Fe and Tucson, it was an oasis for the wayfarer, a place of refreshment and of pleasure. But the tide of the Civil War would soon wash away this tranquility.

On the night of the 24th of July, 1861, Colonel John R. Baylor and the Confederate troops waiting before Fort Fillmore restlessly listened to the buzzing of mosquitoes sweeping up out of the bosques of the Río Grande. There was time to think now; time to be afraid. They had longed for action during the days of drill and confinement at Maggofin's Rancho in El Paso where they had arrived on Independence Day. The quadrangle at Fort Bliss—the new name for the Rancho—had been a pretty place; the adobe rooms were kept cool in the July heat by large-leafed, rustling cottonwoods. Spanish clover growing in nearby fields made fine pasture for horses spent by the long march from San Antonio. When, in the middle of July, George Buhl and the Mesilla Brass Band had made the journey to El Paso to enlist they had drilled and paraded to stirring military marches. But now, confronting the enemy, hands clenched and unclenched around rifles ready for use, Baylor's Babes[141] were awaiting daybreak.

Colonel Baylor moved among his men. He was in command of the two hundred twenty Texas Mounted Rifles, and was second in command of Brigadier General Henry Hopkins' Brigade which was to follow and sweep through the southwest and secure for Jefferson Davis the gold and the seaports of California. Baylor was a big man—six feet three—and he weighed almost two hundred fifty pounds. His size, his military carriage, his courage, together with a certain irresistible magnetism combined to give strength to the boys who waited with him that night. Even in the darkness his unusual clear, almost translucent, blue eyes seemed to shine in his bearded, ruddy face. He walked quietly as he reminded Captain Peter Hardeman commanding Company B, and Captain I. C. Stafford of Company E, and presently Captain Bethel Coopwood of the San Elzeario Spy[142] Company, of his plan. At dawn when the animals of the Union forces were taken to water, the Texans were to silently entrench themselves between the fort and the river. Colonel Baylor hoped that this would bring forth Major Isaac Lynde commanding the fort and his 7th Infantry, and that the Federals and the Secessionists would meet, with the advantage on Baylor's side in his secure position.

It was after midnight. Abruptly staccato notes of a bugle shattered the stillness. There was a moment of silence. The bugle notes echoed among the hills. Then the long roll of drums was heard from within the compound. Quickly came the noise and clatter of running, shouting men. Sympathy for the unsuspecting soldiers within the fort had overcome a former Union soldier who had joined Baylor's forces, and he had quietly warned the garrison.

Texan horses strained against reins. Men grunted and swore, whirled about by nervous animals. Colonel Baylor and his disappointed men moved half a mile downriver where they camped until daylight.

On the morning of the 25th of July, the hot sun already sending sweat running down their faces, the Confederates took up the march again and crossed the river to Santo Tomás. Two companies of United States troops had been stationed there, but they had been recalled so hastily by Lynde that lying about were clothing, pistols, ammunition, a gold watch lying right in the road, and food. Anxious Mexican farmers watched from within the walls of the little village—watched the Tejanos as they gathered up their first booty.

Ten miles to the north lay La Mesilla. A few brisk commands and the two hundred twenty men rode toward that town in the still, hammer-like heat. A sergeant in a handmade gray blouse led the horse of the picket who had informed the Federal forces at Fillmore. At the head of the column rode Colonel Baylor, a pistol thrust into his silver-buckled belt, the hem of his dark blue coat just touching the saddle.

Through the town from south to north ran the main street—Calle Principal. Long, continuous wooden portales shaded the store fronts on either side of the narrow dusty road. A block south of the Old Plaza was the headquarters of the Overland Mail where Frank DeRyther was in charge as Assistant Superintendent. To the north nearby was Joshua Sledd's Billiard Parlor. The adobe-walled Church of San Albino, doors and wooden gates closed, stood across the plaza which was now beginning to be lined with people. The white-aproned German bakers, opposite San Albino's, stood beneath their painted sign: "Frietze and Applezoller." Samuel Selles stood with them, withdrawn, wringing his fingers behind him. H. G. Hendrick, the photographer, having set up his camera outside Nester Varela's store, put his head under the black photographer's cloth and once again reset the focus.

On the east side of the plaza, the courthouse side, ran the Street of Guadalupe with its drug store and office. Outside Bean's Hotel and Bar, south of the courthouse, a number of business men stood together—Sam Bean, James Lucas, Joshua Sledd—Anglo men with Mexican wives. Their children spoke Spanish; their food was the zesty fare of the native New Mexican. They baptized their children in the Catholic church; they even thought in Spanish.

Just three streets to the east from the Old Plaza, a new world had begun. There was a new plaza—the Gran Plaza—and surrounding it were neat town blocks laid out ready for new businesses and new homes of Southern sympathizers. Settling in this Plaza was a nucleus of Missourians, Kansans, and Texans with Anglo wives and of the Protestant faith. Samuel Jones, the sutler at Fort Fillmore, who had at one time defended "southern rights" in Kansas, had a new residence on Capitol Avenue on the south side of the new square. L. S. Owings, Governor of the newly formed but yet unrecognized Arizona which included the Gadsden Purchase, was building a home across the plaza. The energetic, fiery Robert P. Kelley, in partnership with his brother-in-law D. W. Hughes, bought up lands in the new development, brought in a steam mill and put it to work on the acequia to the east. With Bredett C. Murray as publisher, *The Mesilla Times* was introduced, with Kelley as the editor. He encouraged the building of The Mesilla Academy which was being erected under the direction of the Methodist Episcopal chaplain at Fort Fillmore.

Forming the focal point of Secession activity were these Gran Plaza men along with Sam Bean, James Lucas, Charles Hoppin, the lawyer M. H. Macwillie, and DeRyther who commanded a regiment of Arizona militia. Joining them were the unexplainable Mexican rebels—Rafael Armijo, Ygnacio Orrantia, Marcial Padilla—literate and violent in their common bond and outdoing their Anglo brothers in Confederate passion. But all about them lay fields worked by these Mexican families who knew little else but the land—to whom the events and affairs of the nation seemed remote and incomprehensible—and who disliked Tejanos. These were the people who would have to be wooed and coerced to aid in the subsistence of the Brigade to come.

Every hot-blooded Secessionist was on the Old Plaza by ten o'clock on that 25th of July, 1861, waiting for his part in the American Civil War. The rooftops along the Calle Principal held spectators—the cottonwoods were alive with small boys; dogs ran criss-cross beneath, adding to the noise and confusion.

Suddenly Marcial Padilla stepped from the boardwalk in front of the courthouse and knelt on one knee. He put the palm of his hand on the ground. Talk ceased; men broke away from groups and watched him. He rose, white powdery dust on the knee of his tight dark trousers. "Hay vienen, compadres! They are coming, friends!" To the south a cloud of dust arose. The earth began to reverberate with the beating of hooves. Through the shouting and the noise came the thin sound of a fife; the steady roll of drums. On top of Thomas Bull's store people began to wave and cheer. Doors opened—the fife and drum an irresistible ally for the South.

Straight down Calle Principal they came, two by two, young heads held proudly, horses tight-reined and prancing—the Confederate boys from Texas. The horseman in front bore the flag of the Confederacy, the straps from the heavy pole digging into his collar. The pole was balanced precisely in the stirrup—a little dust wind sprang up and ruffled out the standard and the cheers and vivas ran all down Main Street. Colonel Baylor, riding between the columns touched his hat and smiled. The Stars and Bars fluttered above the courthouse, the Mesilla Brass Band swung into a Mexican doble, and La Mesilla was a part of the Confederate States of America.[143]

On August 1, Colonel Baylor proclaimed the Confederate Territory of Arizona. It included the vast region of all of southern New Mexico and southern Arizona. He declared Mesilla as its capital. A building was rented south of the plaza to contain the territorial headquarters. He appointed various persons in Mesilla to Confederate governmental posts including Robert P. Kelley as Surveyor-General for the Territory.

The enthusiasm for the Confederates waned as Kelley in his position as editor of *The Mesilla Times* pointed out various problems and Baylor's shortcomings in meeting them. Soldiers loyal to Baylor told him they would retaliate, but the Colonel took matters into his own hands. On the afternoon of December 12 as Kelley walked in the direction of the plaza on Calle Principal, Baylor stepped out of a doorway and hit him on the head with a musket dropping him to the ground. Baylor then shot him in the face with a revolver as Kelley tried to defend himself with a small knife. Kelley lingered for awhile and wrote about the incident for the newspaper several days later, but he died on January 1, 1862 from his wound.

This murder of a prominent citizen as well as other incidents left the people of Mesilla wary of Baylor and the Confederate occupation, but they would not remain long. When the Confederates learned of the large Union force formed in California and marching eastward toward Tucson and Mesilla, they considered their options and fled before the California Column reached either town. They were gone from Tucson in early May and from Mesilla in early July.

As they retreated south into Texas, they confiscated cattle, horses and food for their supply and to deny any to the Union troops and indeed to those left behind. People in Mesilla hid their property as the troops retreated. They had to take care of their families until the fall harvest. They cached goods from their businesses and food for themselves in their yards and waited for the men from California.

THE CALIFORNIA COLUMN

The summer of 1862 was a season of hot, languid days in Mesilla. Doors and windows opened early to let the freshness of the cooler night into adobe interiors. They closed again in mid-morning, keeping rooms cool and making thick clay walls a defense against the waves of heat. Shadows grew thinner toward noon; dogs lay in whatever scant shade they could find, along slender shadows of poles and under benches and along western walls. Earthen thresholds were swept and sprinkled, and this made the heat seem less. Late roses bloomed within inner patios, but the fluted and fragrant white blossoms of loco weed stayed closed until late afternoon.

Colonel Joseph Rodman West's forces, ten companies of the First California Infantry of the California Column[144] of the Union Army, arrived in Mesilla on August 15, 1862 amid cheering. People from Mesilla were exuberant and happy. A parade with flags and uniforms which were not Texan, gave them reason enough to rejoice. There were many among them who had a genuine affection for the Union, and they were almost unanimous in their aversion to the Stars and Bars.[145]

They watched the troops march onto the plaza, officers mounted, with regimental and troop flags flying. As the officers rode down to their quarters, the buildings of the Overland Mail where the Texans had been, residents gathered, small groups of them, to speak of this new influx into Mesilla. Some faces were serious, and enthusiasm dimmed as the regular business of the town began once more.

The soldiers began to accustom themselves to the rhythm of Mesilla life. They drilled at five o'clock in the morning,[146] on the plaza and in the streets beside their billets. The sweet, cool breeze of dawn in this strange land, the serenity of the still quiet valley, the sleeping town dimmed the memory of the long hot march from California.

The bells of San Albino's Church rang for Mass just before army breakfast—and then the town began to stir. The citizens of Mesilla began to feel secure now with soldiers about; the past Texan invasion and its memories began to fade. In those first months of occupation, Mesilla men hunted and fished with the soldiers in the evening after work in the fields or in town, and regular *bailes*, dances, were held where the Californians danced with those women they termed in letters back home "Castilian beauties."[147] The village was patrolled every two hours at night—Mesilleros loosened up and began to assume that life was back to normal.

With the advent of the Column, mail service was resumed through military express riders.[148] Newspapers began to arrive telling of the progress of war in other theatres. Knots of soldiers gathered around the rider as he threw down his leather pack and the mail was doled out. Any news from home was welcomed by all of them, no matter to whom it was directed.

The new flagpole on the plaza flew the Stars and Stripes—each morning reveille sounded, and the notes of the bugle had a reassuring sound for La Mesilla.

By September 1, General James H. Carleton, organizer and commander of the more than 2,300 man Union Army's California Column, was in Las Cruces. He assumed command of the Department of New Mexico and declared martial law in all of New Mexico. Colonel West and his troops were to remain in Mesilla for sometime to come.

On September 15, 1862, it had cooled a little—houses were left open to the air longer in the mornings and the troops marched drill in the early morning light. Young Mariano Barela and his mother Rafaela Garcia stood outside their store on the plaza's west side and watched the preparations for the fiesta celebrating Mexico's independence from Spain. Most of the plaza would be roped off and fenced tomorrow for the bull fight. But today stalls were beginning to do business with games of chance and tables of tacos, enchiladas, and sweets. Small cook fires sent up fragrant smoke; the aroma of hot tortillas filled the air from the Barela store south to the end of the block. Father José de Jesús stood in front of the business establishment at the far end, a brick building rising slowly to a two-storied structure. He smiled and nodded to his parishioners as they walked by.

Off-duty soldiers tentatively tried the Mexican foods, at first slowly and then with more gusto. There was bustling activity here, and good-humored anticipation.

In the evening of the fifteenth, benches were placed around the temporary bandstand for the listeners and those waiting to dance. Girls and young women sat here, accompanied by their mothers or aunts or by other responsible members of their families. They were eyed and admired by young Mexican men and soldiers who approached and, bowing, sought partners in the dance. The Californians knew some of the steps, and soon the whirling music had most of them quick-stepping with the most experienced Mesillero. Verses were sung by the crowd and the dancing couples, and once in a while some elder member of the community would compose a new couplet, singing to the beat of the music. For an angry suitor:

Si tu papa me diera
Los bueyes y la carreta
No me casara contigo
Pesqueso de gallareta!

If your father gave me
The oxen and the cart
I would not marry you
You crane's neck!

And the betrayer with a flit of skirt and a glance at the dancers:

Si tu papa me diera
Los bueyes y el arado
No me casara contigo
Pesqueso de gallo pelado.

If your father gave me
The oxen and the plow
I would not marry you
You molting cock's neck! [149]

When the card shark with the big hat and stained sash began to call for players, there was another song:

Habia un tal Pilar Membrilla
Hombre buen carcamenero
Que gritaba el dia entero.
Tan fino como una esquila
Quince versos a la fila
Decia de cuando en cuando
Hasta que se le seco el gosnate
Diciendo que el cacahuate era
El que estaba enfermando. [150]

There was a certain Pilar Membrilla,
A bloke well suited to barking
Who did endlessly daily shout
As clear as a cowbell calling
Fifteen verses in succession.
He said them often in progression
Till alas his throat went broke
A peanut, he explained,
Did make him choke. [151]

There were many Union soldiers in and around Mesilla by October 15, 1862, and a new contingent came marching in as Teresa Garcia[152] was being baptized in the church of San Albino. Military feet marked time on hard-packed earth; bells pealed as black Jean Baptiste Clotier, bell-ringer, made the bell ropes sing on their wooden pulleys by the force of his strong hands. Teresa's padrinos, her godparents, had brought her to the adobe church in the long white dress they had bought for her. Josefita Ortega Gonzáles held her while Father Baca anointed her with sacred oil, placed a tiny bit of salt on her tongue, and then carefully spilled water over the top of her head. Josefita wiped the water away gently and pulled the little cap closer around the small sleeping face. She and her husband, Ramón Gonzáles, turned and faced the guests and carried Teresa toward the door. Outside a wind had come up sweeping yellow leaves before it, and the column in blue had just turned the corner toward their station. Outside the church, Soledad Bermudes waited for her baby, and smiles became broader as the ancient verses were sung:

> Comadre, compadre,
> Aqui esta mi ahijada
> Que de la iglesia salió
> Con los santos sacramentos
> Y el agua que recibió.

> Comadre, compadre,
> Here is my godchild
> Who just came out from the church
> With the Holy Sacraments
> And the water she received.[153]

Soledad Bermudes took the baby in her arms and sang softly

> Recibate, prenda mia,
> Que de la iglesia saliste
> Con los Santo Sacramen
> Y el Agua que recibiste.

> My little jewel, you have received
> The Holy Sacraments and
> Water and now you
> Have come out from the Church.

Ramón and Soledad Gonzáles, and Antonio and Josefita Garcia gave each other abrazos, embraces, and then the families present embraced each other. The churchyard echoed with Spanish words of congratulation and greeting; joyous shouts of children playing eclipsed the sound of marching feet. The whole world outside the village of Mesilla was forgotten; soldiers, flags, and wars were no longer part of the life in this small village. For one joyous afternoon, there was nothing but song, the breaking of a piñata, good food and wine, and the contented reminiscences of old friends and relatives.

But some Mesilla townspeople by now were not so sure that this army wouldn't be like any of the others which had occupied Mesilla during its years of existence. There was a matter which occupied the thoughts of serious members of the community and which worried Father Baca—the number of illegitimate babies, hijos naturales, born to Mesilla girls. In town, it was considered to be the result of the Texan-Confederate occupation from July, 1861 until early July, 1862. Texans had rarely married local girls, and Mesilleros feared that the Californians' stay would have the same result. But soon the Californians were being registered in the marriage books of San Albino's and St. Genevieve's in Las Cruces with their Mexican brides. James Malone, first Battery, Veteran Infantry, Company D married Mariana Bernal on the twenty-fourth of December, 1862. Frederick Burkner, of service to the Union army as messenger and scout, married Anamaria Lueras in 1863. Patrick Helms and Perfeta Sanches were married on the tenth of December, 1864; John Ryan of the First Veteran Infantry married Juana María Chavez, December 25, 1864.[154]

At the first chill of fall, 1862, the air in Mesilla was fragrant with mesquite and pine smoke from outdoor fires where green chile roasted on racks. As the sun warmed the earth, women peeled the long pods and strung them on lines to dry for winter, spring and early summer months. But there was concern now over what was to be eaten with the chile. Usually there were corn or flour tortillas, beans—sometimes meat. But the military quartermaster at Mesilla was buying corn from Las Cruces, La Mesilla, Picacho and Doña Ana. The going rate was four dollars a fanega, a measure of a little more than a bushel. The army paid not in currency, but in military certificates. Some refused to sell, and their corn and wheat and flour were taken by force. Soldiers forced open warehouse doors and confiscated sacks of grain. Some tried to hide their supplies, but an order was issued making this a crime, and anyone caught hiding foodstuffs was to be treated as an enemy of the United States. Others tried to take their sacks of grain into Mexico, but military guards were posted along the border to prevent such passage. All the villages along the Middle river felt the sting of Union foraging: San Elizario, Ysleta, Socorro, Franklin, Amoles, La Mesa, Sanchez Ranch,[155] Santo Tomás, Mesilla, Las Cruces, and Doña Ana. Families were not allowed to keep more than the amount the military considered two months supply, and this was quickly used up.

One fall day, José María Aguirre stood sullenly before the military court over which Colonel West established himself as judge, and refused to receive payment for corn taken from him—ninety dollars in Treasury notes. To him these meant nothing—he did not even extend his hand to examine the bundle thrust at him. The commission handed down to Aguirre a fine of ninety dollars for refusing payment. Lawyers present remarked that he had always been a good citizen and deserved better treatment, but Colonel West bade them be quiet—it was none of their business, he said.

The citizens of Mesilla had friends among the Anglo-Americans of the town, and Joshua Sledd was one of them. On November 15, 1862 under martial law, Union soldiers broke into his warehouse and took his grain supply from which he had been feeding many of the families who had no food. When the detachment came, he was a few doors away tending to some business. When he approached the crowd gathering around the confiscation, the soldiers pushed him roughly aside and kept at their task of removing sacks of grain. Sledd went to Henry Jenkins, the lawyer who was recorder for the military commission; but upon Jenkins' applying to Colonel West for permission for Sledd to keep some of the grain for his family, he was told that West was having dinner and could not be disturbed. So Joshua Sledd found a hidden and undiscovered supply from which to buy flour at twelve dollars and fifty cents a hundred pounds, and he gave this and meat and beans to the hungry and served soup in his business location south of the plaza. Later the commissary officer, hearing what had happened, gave him ten sacks of grain to distribute to the poor. It lasted for several days.[156]

Cold and hunger stalked the people of Mesilla.[157] Luis Montes stole a soldier's overcoat, was caught with it on and confined by the officer of the day on orders of Colonel West. The colonel, even if his military rule was absolute, found his troops restless and the civilian population sullen and uncooperative. In the guardhouse from time to time were confined those whom the military accused as spies and collaborators during the Texan occupation.[158] The presence in Mesilla of individuals considered seditious and as having sympathy for the Confederate cause made escape for some of the suspects relatively easy. Colonel West was constantly beset by reports of escape, and he determined to arrest the whole guard on duty at the time of escape.

On the morning of November 26, Captain Pettis reported that the guard from Company K was in irons, including Sergeant Miller, for letting a prisoner escape. At drill on the plaza at five o'clock in the morning, Captain Pettis commanded Company K. Corporal Charles Smith stepped to the front, saluted and declared he would do no more duty until Sgt. Miller was released from irons. The captain admonished him, in view of his good record, to retract. Then, turning to the line of Company K, he inquired if there were others who felt the same way. All but three soldiers stepped up beside Corporal Smith. Pettis ordered the company to drop arms and retire to quarters.[159]

The mutiny was immediately communicated to Colonel West who ordered the "Long Roll." [160] As the rumble of drums rolled over the quiet plaza, a close thunder threatened, shutters opened slightly, and then quickly closed again. Even the thin chimney smokes were still.

The remaining infantry companies, armed, fell into line on the plaza; Company K formed without arms. The morning sunlight was still cold on the damp earth of the plaza when Colonel West rode up to Co. K and asked Corporal Smith to advance ten paces. The colonel asked the corporal if he was prepared to do his duty and take up arms again; the young soldier said he would after the irons were removed from Sgt. Miller. Corporal Smith and the rest of Co. K were about twelve paces in from of the wall around the church of San Albino. Col. West ordered Mitchell's Company D to wheel to the right, bringing them behind Co. K. Col. West reined his horse to the right and gave the command to fire at Corporal Smith. They fired, but Charles Smith only waved his cap in the air—the wind tossing his hair like a boy's. West, with his sword, pushed down some of the rifles pointed upwards and ordered the volley again. Smith still stood erect. Some at the balls this time thumped against the wall of the church. The third time the colonel offered to cut down the man who did not fire at Smith's heart; his drawn sword he held up and ready to carry out his threat. The volley sounded and the soldier fell on his back, but he was not yet dead. By this time, there were onlookers, saying nothing, standing quietly on the sides of the plaza. There were also parishioners just coming from church who stood and watched. When Charles Smith fell bleeding, someone put an anvil under his head; another brought him a cup of water. Col. West ignored the wounded man, rode up to Co. K again and asked man after man if he would do his duty, in each case pointing his sword directly at him. At the end of the Company line, he said, "Men, I intend to see you well treated and cared for, but the moment a man raises a finger to disobey an order of mine, that moment his death warrant is sealed."

With this, he rode off the plaza and the men were marched back to quarters. A stretcher was brought and Corporal Charles Smith was carried to hospital rooms. He died very soon and was buried without a public funeral on orders of Colonel West. Company K was marched again to the plaza with arms and drilled all day; the colonel had established absolute order at heavy cost. The company which fired and Company K developed a feud that endured until each company was ordered to other posts. The Mexican populace was uneasy, and they were angry, too. Dr. William Black's little son standing by the church had been shot and killed during the confrontation with Smith and a Mexican man had been wounded.[161]

The severity of military rule continued. Royal Yeamans ran the ferry across the Río Grande between Mesilla and Las Cruces—he did this through the Texan occupation and during that of the California Column. His bill to the federal officers was for one thousand dollars, and he was never paid. His ferry boat was confiscated, and he was imprisoned for forty-four days because he had taken a shotgun up on a roof during the shelling of Mesilla in July, 1861. He never fired the gun, but for this and because the Union officials could not find his corn supply, he was jailed. He was finally released on two thousand dollars bond.[162]

Isidro, "Cidro," Cháves was a merchant in a modest store on the Mesilla plaza, selling goods which the Mexican inhabitants needed: sugar, lard, candles. He was arrested and, although very ill, was forced to work under military guard on street repairs. When released, he also left for Chihuahua; he, too, said he could no longer live under the American flag.

Under martial law families grew thin and hungry. In Doña Ana, fifty fanegas of grain were taken from John McGran; one hundred from Pablo Melendres. The poor bought, when they could, an almud (about a quart) at a time for six bits or a dollar. There were men and families who went back into Mexico, loading their meager possessions and slipping over the river.[163]

From fifteen hundred to two thousand families left Doña Ana County, abandoning ranches, farms, homes. Some of them never returned.

In those bitter years of war, Mesilla was not spared recurrent epidemics of smallpox. During the Confederate occupation, it had claimed lives of inhabitants as well as soldiers, and in these times of cold and hunger, it struck again. From sturdy adobe homes, replacements of the earlier jacales, came a faint aroma of asafetida, a noxious mixture of herbs and resins blended to ward off infection. The odor of carbolic acid blended with chimney smoke as the people of Mesilla sought to escape the pox. Those who remained in Mesilla wrapped themselves in layers of clothing, drawing scarves and rebozos close around their throats where the asafetida bags were tied. It was a winter of silence, suspicion, and fear.

The military occupation was not all of Mesilla's troubles. In those years, Apache tribes were still capitalizing on the civil conflict between the white men. They continued to swoop down on haciendas, ranchos, and herds in Chihuahua, then fleeing to southern New Mexico and Arizona only to wreak the same havoc there. Lightning raids and ambushes caught the frontier on the American side preoccupied with war, and the Apaches were successful—then they rode swiftly back to Chihuahua. The four companies of Union infantry at Mesilla could not, and did not even attempt to cope with attacks on outlying fields and herds of the Mesilleros. Stationed at Fort Fillmore were a battery of light artillery, two companies of infantry, and, from time to time, up to four companies of cavalry.[164] It was useless to try to get word from Mesilla to the fort in time to retaliate, and the Mesilla Guard rode more than once in pursuit of stolen captives and cattle. *Cambalache*, barter, was resorted to sometimes to regain captives—a situation which did not exist previously. Boys brought more than women in trade; for them a mare, a rifle, underdrawers, powder, bullets, knives, tobacco. The price of a woman, more or less, was a blanket, a length of calico, some tobacco, and a little corn.

In November definite measures were finally taken by the Federal Union troops against attacks and raids by the Apaches. Captain William McCleave, camped south of Mesilla about twenty miles near the cottonwoods at Camp Johnson, was ordered by Colonel West to march against the Dog Cañon Apaches on November 14, 1862.[165] There were already settlers from Mesilla on the Ruidoso and Tularosa Rivers, settlers who hoped to plant wheat and other grain—and to avoid the effects of civil war. McCleave was ordered to take his force there together with twenty Mexican guides and Juan Arrollos, an old hand on the trail. With map and orders in his saddle bags, the captain sought out the Tularosa settlement of dugout huts,

or *chozas*,[166] where he was to operate against the Apaches and from where it might be possible to buy or requisition supplies. Colonel Christopher Carson, First Regiment New Mexico Volunteers, wrote from his post at Fort Stanton in December that there were Mexican settlers near the military reservation working in gold mines and planting. Somehow, somewhere, these transplanted Mesilleros hoped to live in peace, grow food for their families, and so survive.

Storms continued to lash Mesilla. The wet winds whipped through the bosques and made November and December dreary months without much sunlight. Now, there was a new threat of a Confederate invasion from north Texas. In the minds of most of the inhabitants of Mesilla, Doña Ana, and Las Cruces, all flags and uniforms were synonymous with misery. They remembered the wild cry of the Texan in battle, and the prospect of it again frightened them. Colonel West wrote to Captain Ben C. Cutler, Assistant Adjutant General, Santa Fe, on November 27 that the talk of this new invasion was in Franklin, Texas and he wanted orders to intercept the Rebels by marching further South. He had been ordered to inspire the Mexican population to defend their lands against the Texans, but he said it could not be done without putting arms into the hands of the Mexicans. He needed five hundred stands of arms, and he received none. He hoped the commander would not expect too much "of my exertion when he remembers that he had taken away every mounted man absent when most needed: that I have no arms for a New Mexican partisan warfare, and they have none: that I have no funds to purchase forage...no shoes for my men to wear...partially demoralized command from lack of efficient officers to command them...I have enough prisoners on my hands to occupy the attention of a full company." This letter, considered insubordinate, did not win favor for Colonel West with General Carleton.[167]

Colonel West's apprehension regarding a new Texan invasion began to have substance. At Hart's Mill above Franklin, Lt. Col. Edwin Rigg reported that in August Brig. Gen. John R. Baylor had arrived at San Antonio from Richmond with authority to raise six thousand troops. His instructions were to train them to take, and this time to hold, New Mexico. As grain was confiscated by Union troops in river towns, it was to be taken to Ft. Craig to be stored or to be destroyed.[168] And it was now decided that, rather than obstruct Mexican passage into Chihuahua, it would be better for the families to cross the river or to go northeast of the Jornada as settlers had already done, opening fields on the Ruidoso or the Tularosa. Partisan warfare was urged on a frightened and resentful people.[169]

Other precautions were taken: all suspicious Americans or foreigners were to be seized, taken to Fort Craig and given shovels to erect fortifications against the Texans. Secessionist homes and stores were to be burned; the roofs over the buildings at Fort Bliss were to be set ablaze. In case the oncoming Texans were to force the Californians and regular Army to retreat, Bull's grinding mill at Mesilla and Grandjean's at Las Cruces were to be destroyed—the Mexican population who remained could rely upon grinding corn on metates again. And, if the Texans came, cattle and horses were to be rounded up and driven North.

The tragic retreat of the Texans from New Mexico in 1862 did not dim the apprehension of a new invasion. There were rumors that Henry Skillman had "dropped from the clouds" and was recruiting a new Confederate army of invasion traveling north and south along the Río Grande.[170] It was known that he had a military organization at El Paso del Norte, and for several days had tried to kidnap and carry off into Texas men who persisted in their loyalty to the Union. As Federal forces reported on his activities and wrote warning reports, they remembered that at one time, in 1847, in another war, he had held the plaza at El Paso for two hours with just ten men.

Whispers that French designs on Mexico were being implemented by Rebel-Texan presence in Chihuahua and Sonora inspired even more anxiety among the inhabitants along the border. Once again along the arid, sandy trail past Samalayuca

to Chihuahua rumbled the wheels of cannon; the retreating Texans had sold the guns to Simeon Hart backed by notes from the Siqueiros Family of which Hart's wife was a member. It was a limping journey—the cannon rode unevenly, bent out of shape, wheels askew, trunnions shattered and scorched. The Texans had tried to render them useless, thought the better of it and needing money, sold them to Hart.[171] They lurched along now, some of the parts and the smaller howitzer pieces carried in wagons. Federal reports confirmed that they were of more danger to those who fired them than to the enemy.[172]

On January 1, 1863, President Abraham Lincoln issued a proclamation freeing slaves in the United States. They were to be freed completely in Arkansas, Texas, Mississippi, Alabama, Florida, Georgia, and South Carolina; in Louisiana and Virginia they would be free with certain exceptions. Missouri, Kentucky, Maryland and Tennessee were entirely excepted being border states. Lincoln pledged the Army and Navy to make good the proclamation.

For Mesilla, the new year, 1863, brought scarce good news. Colonel Joseph Rodman West was unpopular with the military and civilian population in Mesilla—he found fault with almost everything he saw or heard. Regarding the lands abandoned because of fear of the Texans, he wrote:

> The people of this Valley are assured of the ability of the United States government to fully protect them. They are advised to return to their homes and divest themselves of all apprehensions of danger, and to renew peacefully their agricultural labors, with the prospect of a bounteous harvest...a larger market for their products than has ever been offered on the Río Grande.[173]

He said nothing regarding those who had fled from hunger and fear after the confiscations of grain by the Union Army.

Rumors of the Texan invasion accelerated: Henry Skillman was indeed making lightning raids on the American side of the Río Grande, darting back and forth unhampered by any official. He appeared around the City of Chihuahua armed, claiming he was pursuing Indians. Presidio del Norte felt the lash of his renegade band more than once. On January 2, Colonel West instructed Captain David Fergusson, First Cavalry, California Volunteers to go to the capital of Chihuahua to confer with Governor Terrazas.[174] In addition to trying to dissuade the governor from selling any supplies to the Confederates or from buying anything from them, he was to arrange with persons in Chihuahua who had connections in San Antonio to transmit information regarding military movements of the Texans. As a result of Fergusson's efforts, Ruben Creel of that city became the confidential agent of the military authorities of the Department of New Mexico. Fergusson was empowered to pay hard American dollars for information regarding what supplies the Union Army might find in Chihuahua and Durango if it marched on Texas from that quarter. Before Fergusson left for Chihuahua, Henry Skillman was reported ten days away from headquarters of the Department of New Mexico.

While Col. West waited at Hart's Mill with Co. B, First Cavalry for the expected invasion, Carleton sent word to him that he could not spare the 2000 men requested. All he could afford to send was 1000, and he cautioned West not to be surprised by an alternate Texan route—that he was to stand between the Texans and Ft. Craig at all costs. He recommended partisan warfare again, counseling that he use as signals smoke in the daytime and fires at night. Guerilla groups might include such Union men as Henry Jenkins, John Lemon, and W.W. Mills to direct the Mexican scouts.[175] They were to lay the country in waste upon first word of a Texan invasion. Brigadier Gen. Carleton doubted that the Texans would come at all, and directed his energies to a more important and visible foe—the Apache. To Carleton, this threat was far more menacing than the illusory Texan advance. Indians swept back and forth over the swollen Río Grande, raiding on both sides of the river, seizing the opportunity which civil war afforded to attack wagon trains, to murder, and to seize prisoners.

General Carleton, commanding the California Column and the department of Arizona, deployed his regiments and companies to meet the Apache on his own ground and to pursue him into the deepest regions of the mountains. To this effect, Company G of the Fifth arrived in Mesilla in January together with a company of cavalry and five companies of infantry. Companies A and F were at Franklin; Company R of the Fifth came to Fort Craig and Company A to the Pino Alto mines. Most of the cavalry was kept on the trail of the Apache.

A young soldier, Albert Jennings Fountain stationed at Fort Craig, wrote his sister, Fannie, a letter which any soldier might have written home in 1863, but one which had unusual perception of affairs in New Mexico.

When I received your letter I had just got into camp at Crow Spring, Texas. We had made a forced march that day of 33 miles had suffered much for want of water, but as soon as we got into camp it commenced to rain and snow it was about 9 o'clock at night and so dark we had great difficulty in finding the spring which is nothing more than a small hole dug a short distance from the road in a hollow, the water is very bad being strongly impregnated with sulphur. The spring is on a barren desolate plain without a shrub or bush for miles around. We were forced to turn in supperless for want of a fire to cook, and rolling myself up in my blanket I lay shivering in the mud, now ankle deep, and thinking how much I would give for a cup of hot coffee...I stood the tramp very well and was only tired, but a number of the boys had very sore feet pains in the bones resembling Rheumatism, and bye the by I have often been kept awake after a long march by being too tired to sleep and hearing the groans of the poor fellows...and so we lay huddled together, horses, men, and mules; we were all soaked to the skin the rains and sleet would beat through our blankets. About 10 o'clock as I lay shivering I heard the approach of horses, and shortly after the hail of the sentinel Halt; who comes there? Friends was the answer. We had all turned out in hopes that it might be an enemy, it proved to be a scouting party just from 'Mesilla' with letters and papers for our command. I got one from Mother...your and Maggie's besides two from California by the light of a comrades pipe I made out to read... some wanted me to put my letters at auction the next day...After six weeks very hard times we returned to Franklin moving there on New Years Day. The next day we left for 'Mesilla', and laying there one day were ordered to this place which is now Regmtl head Quarters.[176] Coming to this place we crossed the Celebrated 'Jornada del Muerto' or journey of death... It was here a short time ago that one of our trains was attacked by 'Menges Colorados' (red sleeve) band of Apaches they killed one teamster and took 3 wagons loaded with clothing 4 companies have gone in pursuit... We found no great difficulty in crossing except that the nights were terrible cold and froze the water in our canteens causing them to burst... Fort Craig is situated on a high bank on the west side of the Río Grande is about 200 miles from nowhere...Since the war began the fort has been surrounded by a ditch and they are now at work throwing up the bastions one of which on the right lower corner is completed and the guns mounted...7 miles from the fort is the town of 'Fra Cristobal de Praqueja' [Fra Christobal de Paraje]...above the fort and this side of Santa Fe are several small towns... about 3 miles from here is the Battleground of 'Valverde' where 'Sibley' was defeated. Taken at the best the whole country so far as we have seen is a most miserable one affording but a scant subsistence to the few families who have the hardihood to live here exposed to continual attacks of the Apaches...The country is infested with numerous bands of hostile Indians who eternally on the watch to attack trains. Only two nights ago they came into the little town 7 miles from here killed two persons and run off a large amount of stock pursuit was next to useless for they made for the mountains where they know the watering places and

where soldiers would starve to death looking for them. The 'Río Grande' which runs within 100 yards from the Fort...from its source to its mouth nearly 2000 miles is not spanned by a single bridge, and in the summer season may be crossed by wading, at any point...The air here is remarkable pure. Objects can be distinguished at a great distance looking southeast from here may be distinguished 'Sierra de los Organes" or 'Organ Mountains' (so called from their resembling the pipes of an organ) over 100 in miles distant and yet they do not look as far as the hills of Staten Island do from the Battery. The Mexicans display much better taste in naming places then we do...On the 'Río Mimbris' a dried up apology for a creek, are some of the greatest natural curiosities ever witnessed among others are the 'Giantes de los Mimbris' or 'Giants of the mimbres' they are sandstone rocks standing about 60 feet high about 3 feet in diameter at the bottom and about 12 at the top they take their name from the startling resemblance the middle one bears to a human being when viewed from a distance. Here may also be seen ruins of what have been cities that would have surpassed New York in size... [177]

When early spring came again to La Mesilla, the earth opened again to seeding, and water trickled down the acequia madre, and then surged against the banks cutting away loose earth and exposing pale grass roots. On March 1, 1863, colonists who had been here for a dozen years, once again walked the fields, this time with a figure of San Albino, the French bishop of Brittany whose feast day it was. Mayordomos appointed for the year—those who would collect *diezmos*, tithers, in currency, corn, and wheat—carried the figure on a litter; other men dressed in black Sunday best and bareheaded fired rifles into the air. Again sparks and gunpowder did battle with any evil spirit who might affect the fields. Father José de Jesús Baca walked alongside blessing the earth and its seeds with sprinkled holy water.

In Spring, 1863 the Río Grande forever shrugged aside its traditional course in the valley of Mesilla and flung itself far to the West, washing away towns and roads and fields with equal abandon. In the aftermath of the flood, the area from Las Cruces south changed its character geographically. The river at its highest swept south across the valley taking with it the little towns of Santo Tomás and Los Pencos near the foot of the western mesas, adobe walls crumbling as their inhabitants fled to higher ground. The settlers of those two towns, their acequias ripped apart and great masses of earth tumbling before the rushing waters completely changing topography, found all the familiar landmarks buried. At the same time, the river scooped out walls of towns, corral timbers and outbuildings; fields and beginning crops were buried in silt or completely washed away. Some of these families resettled in a new Santo Tomàs to the South;[178] others created the new community of Bosque Seco to the East, not far from Fort Fillmore and Tortugas.[179]

The Mestas settled at Bosque Seco as well as branches of the Garcia family. There were Benavides and Delfin. From Tortugas also and from the ranch extensions of the Ascarate empire south along the edge of the sandy mesas came people to fringe the settlement and intermarry with those already there. A small chapel was built dedicated to San Eugenio.[180]

In April, the interim governor of New Mexico, W.F.M. Arny arrived in Mesilla and on the sixth directed a letter to Governor Terrazas of Chihuahua seeking to establish an appointment with him regarding cooperative action by the governments of Mexico and the United States against the Apache.[181] Colonel West had already conferred in January with José María Uranga, prefect of El Paso del Norte, concerning the Apache. General Carleton on the East, West, and North of the border moved his forces against the Indians, and, as usual, when the Apache felt himself hard pressed in the United States, he fled across the border into Mexico. Janos, in northwestern Chihuahua, accepted the warriors after such raids and bought plunder from them, paying in powder and lead. Gov. Arny had communicated with Terrazas in blunt military fashion, and the governor of Chihuahua refused to meet with him. Between the lines of his reply, it was evident that he considered the request too peremptory and on too short notice. For the time being, plans for cooperative military action against the Apache failed.

S. M. Baird in San Antonio still contemplated a Texan expedition to New Mexico; he reported late in April that 30,000 Texans were ready to arm themselves for invasion. Supplies were arriving every day to support it; from Chihuahua more than thirty wagons and carts loaded with flour, shoes, and blankets had come into San Antonio by way of Presidio del Norte and Ft. Lancaster.

On May 5, in the Valley of Mesilla, and all along the Río Grande, farmers invoked the blessing of San Isidro upon their fields. The sun shone warm and sweet, and the seedlings in the earth were just breaking the thin crust above; every care had to be taken to coax them to grow. Judiciously watered and carefully cultivated, the alfalfa, chile, and cotton were just up and almost out of danger from wind and freezing temperatures. The vineyards were budding, too, and these were shielded from harm—around each plant or hillock the earth was neatly patted and dampened.

Throughout the entire day, matachin dancers swirled in rhythms which courted the old gods as well as the Christian god of San Isidro. In the towns and the family placitas in those towns and everywhere along the river, there were altars in his honor where the image of San Isidro was displayed, the plowman of Spain who wanted to pray instead of turning over the earth. An angel hovered beside him, guiding the plow while Isidro folded his hands in prayer. To do him honor in the villages, a little girl—malinche—was the center of the group; she represented the laborer, the sower of seeds, and the young life of the grain. Heading the procession was the leader, the mandadero, with dark mask and a goat hair cloak. El abuelo, the grandfather, or the old one, followed bearing a rattling gourd and a whip. Four mayordomos came carrying the wooden figure of San Isidro surrounded by flowers, fruits and sprouting grain. The parish priest, the violin player, and a drummer followed, and then the dancing matachines. The faithful walked behind, swaying back and forth like branches in a light wind. A sweet, incongruous song to the Virgin Mary rose above the clack of shells on moccasined feet and the music of violin and drum. Guns fired to ward off evil spirits; there were sparks and smoke and the smell of gunpowder. El Abuelo wound in and out of the procession threatening the small Malinche. At least, slain and fallen to the ground, he was covered with yucca blades. Then the whole procession reformed and the dancers began again with El Abuelo rising ready to dance at the next altar.

By August of 1863 Union troops were no longer occupying Mesilla and martial law was discontinued. Even though residents of Mesilla had resented confiscation of their grain and foodstuffs, such a well-kept peace in the cantinas and the four fandangos held there, made them appreciate the civil order kept by the military. Now they had to depend on local courts and officials, and it made them uneasy.

The August heat rose in waves from the sands between Mesilla and Las Cruces. It was still damp where the old riverbed had been; the man in black trousers and a white shirt stumbled downhill— sweat rimming his chin. He wiped his sleeve against his head, pulled up his sagging trousers, and tried to step with energy and force. Judge Knapp had been arrested at two-thirty in the afternoon in Mesilla, and forced to walk the three miles to Las Cruces. The judge had objected to what he considered the usurpation of his civil authority by Colonel West who had named himself Judge of the District Court and had presided over it. For that defiance as well as his refusal to carry a military-issued pass, Knapp was arrested and was ordered brought to military headquarters in Las Cruces.

A mile out of Mesilla, Judge Knapp appeared exhausted in the heat of the noon sun, and Sam Gillette rode up to him offering his horse to ride. The military guard shook his head and motioned Gillette back. "He'll walk," he said, "Orders." When at last, the judge had arrived at Las Cruces, damp shirt sticking to his body, sand clinging to his shoes and trousers, he was jailed. Eventually the Judge lost his fight against military authority and he was removed from office in 1864.

Judge Knapp was not the only man to feel the wrath of Colonel West. Toward those whom he considered "vile Secessionists" he was relentless. Colonel Samuel J. Jones had taken the Oath of Allegiance after being allowed by General Carleton to go to Washington to clear up his accounts as customs officer. Jones had been accused of selling corn and lumber to the Confederates among other matters, and of acting as customs officer for the Confederacy at El Paso.

There were also charges by West against General Carleton: that he issued passports to known Rebel sympathizers including Sam Jones and that he allowed Jack Swilling, an out-and-out Rebel, to come into the territory. West also accused Carleton of not allowing Secessionist sympathizers—Frank Higgins, Charles Hoppin, Henry Grandjean, Thomas J. Bull, and Edgar Griggs—to be punished. There were some men who were not so zealous toward the Rebels but who cooperated when impressed by them: Frank DeRyther, George Putman, Henry Jenkins, Peter Deus, Joshua Sledd, and Clarke. Colonel West himself wanted to prosecute Sam Jones for his aid to the Texan invasion of New Mexico. He even hinted that Jones and Carleton belonged to the "Knights of the Golden Circle," an organization among those sympathizing with the South.

However, citizens of Mesilla petitioned the release of Jones because, as they claimed, he had rendered valuable aid to the Union under the Confederate reign. He managed the return of confiscated money and property to John Lemon and Jacob Applezoller, he saved the life of Domingo Cubero, he prevented William Steele from destroying the town of Mesilla upon his retreat from New Mexico, and he publicly denounced Colonel John Barlow. Among the many who signed the petition for the release of Samuel Jones were Father Baca, Domingo Cubero, P.R. Tully, Daniel Frietze, Nestor Varela, A. "Mauran," Cristobal Ascarate, Rafael Rueles, C. Duper, William McCleave, John Lemon, Jacob Applezoller, Pedro Aguirre, and Cesario Duran. There was even a testimonial received in regard to Jones' character from J. Cooper McKee, the Union surgeon at the fall of Fort Fillmore, who qualified his endorsement by saying that he was glad Jones had "returned to his old flat."

Although Samuel Jones was popular with the people of Mesilla, West considered his acts prejudicial to good order and discipline and unbecoming an officer and a gentleman. Before he was finally released from suspicion and arrest in 1864, he had taken the Oath of Allegiance to the government of the United States three times in three different places: in Mesilla, in Santa Fe, and at Fort Craig.

Before the termination of the Civil War in New Mexico, there were confiscation actions and convictions of treason against many citizens of the area. Charles Holcomb suffered, as did Rafael Armijo who owned property in Mesilla, Sam and Roy Bean, George Frazier, Eli Redford, and William Clarke. The property of the *Mesilla Times* was found to be in legal process with Sam Jones the executor for Robert P. Kelley's heirs, and no judgment was found against it. Anastacio Barela, gone to Texas with the Secessionists, had had the foresight to put some of his property in the name of his wife, Rafaela Garcia Barela, and no judgment was brought against him. Other properties of Anastacio Barela near the Gran Plaza were attached by Speigelberg Brothers after confiscation. The Overland Mail Buildings, the Gran Plaza dwellings of L.S. Owings and Samuel Jones were also confiscated.

October, 1863 saw Mesilla occupied with additional Federal troops, and by November, Captain J.S. Thayer commanded the post with one hundred thirty five men of the Fifth Infantry, California Volunteers and to the First Infantry, New Mexico Volunteers. Four pieces of artillery strengthened his command. Colonel Rigg was at Fort Craig with the First and Fifth US Infantry and the First Cavalry, California Volunteers. On October 16, the citizens of Doña Ana County petitioned the governor of New Mexico, Henry Connelly, for the reinstatement of martial law. Once again the border had become a refuge for every sort of criminal. Residents pleaded that the jails were not strong enough to hold criminals and there was no money to make them secure, and the process could not be served without danger to the server. Connelly refused, reasoning that Judge Kirby Benedict resided in Mesilla and could properly administer and enforce civil law.[182]

Land around Mesilla was still wet in November and December, the earth still damp from summer and fall rains. The roads on the north side of Mesilla, above the plaza were negotiable—wagon wheels found firm base in sand. But on the south side, puddles still straddled the streets; clay clung to wheels of carriages and sometimes mired them fast. Muddy boots and wet trouser cuffs were impossible to avoid; women, if they had to walk, lifted their long skirts away from the ooze and stepped gingerly and as quickly as possible. Fevers were rampant, deaths many—caused laid to the "miasma" or the "vapors." Many died of pneumonia, diphtheria, and scarlet fever, but burial books of the parish considered these deaths, principally among the aged and the newborn, as "throat trouble" or "lung sickness."

The threat of a Texan invasion, so imminent in previous months, had faded. News of their activities still came up from Chihuahua sent by Ruben Creel.[183] He reported that affairs in Mexico, those involving Benito Juárez' resistance to French military occupation of Mexico, were very bad—much worse than reported in newspapers, but that there was nothing definite happening in Chihuahua—the principal authorities of that state were fighting among themselves for power, instead of against the French intruder. Creel insisted that reports that Governor Terrazas was selling powder to the Rebels was false—a lie manufactured by Terrazas' political enemies to discredit him. The Texan threat to Union-occupied New Mexico seemed even more remote. From their sources came the news that martial law had been declared in Texas. Confederates, desperate in their final hours of struggle, were trying to confiscate wheat and impress unwilling Texans into the army. Farmers banded together in opposition; rebel Texans deserted their units, hungry, tired and angry. There was danger for men with Union sympathies caught in Rebel-held territory. But there in Texas, the Confederacy was dying.

Chapter 9 | AFTERMATH

When in February of 1864, the end of the Civil War was in sight, the promise of an early spring was upon Mesilla. Federal troops had departed for Franklin, or El Paso as it was sometimes called now.[184] Another in the long series of military occupations of Mesilla by men in uniform had ended. There was still frost in the early mornings, but by noon a quiet heat warmed the earth. As the men from California left, the countryside was again in relative peace, and life in La Mesilla became close to normal again.

The old timetable of Mexican daily life once again settled upon the land. The green of the valley of Mesilla surprised even the oldtimers in that year. The river was still in intermittent flood stage; the water in the old channel swirled and snarled in muddied frenzy as it tried to find a new path. It cast its waters to the west of Mesilla, washing out fields and ejidos, crumbling adobe houses and corrales, bringing seeds from one field to another, covering others newly planted with layers of alluvia. Branches lay across the road from Las Cruces, lank and silted, half-buried in damp sand. The ferry operated when it could, when the channel filled at the ford. Otherwise, when water stilled and flowed in the new channel to the west, wagons picked their way toward Las Cruces across the mud and debris of the old river bed. As spring greened the valley, early verdure covered the hills and the mesas up through the foothills of the Organ Mountains. From the old river channel, one could see the distant pines and the green ground covering between them when the evening sun hit the crest of the mountains.

Cycles of life—birth, marriage, and death—persevered in the Mesilla Valley, notwithstanding the occupation of armies of invasion. And now that the soldiers were gone, other considerations arose; progress of modern economy and the presence of hard currency dictated that now in 1864, instead of fanegas of crops—corn, *frijol*, etc.—coins and bills would be collected for *primicias* and diezmos[185] for the Church of San Albino. It was difficult now in the '60's to sell the usual offerings of crops for cash the church needed.

In the mid 1860's, *Los Inditos* de Las Cruces danced in front of Saint Genevieve's Church for the feast days important to their Indian and mestizo heritage. There were several large wooden crosses with piled stone bases around Saint Genevieve's church, and there were two curved stone mounds hidden in the mesquite about a block and a half north of the church. These all had significance to the Inditos, but stories varied and only those in that small, inner circle knew their real and proper function.[186] On holy days, and especially on the feast of Saint Genevieve on January third, fires burned on the mountain sometimes in the form of a cross, as they had for the novena of Guadalupe. Occasionally after 1850, the figure of the devil was burned, but Father Ortiz frowned on this practice and the devil burned no more. And in front of the church, Indian feet still beat time in the ancient steps of Tiwa dances, mixed with remembered and almost forgotten ethnic rhythms of Piro and Manso from Paso del Norte. These were the rituals of the Río Intermedio which had persisted throughout the centuries of foreign intrusion.

On the last day of May, Gervacio Luna's daughter was to be married at the Church of San Albino to a young man from Doña Ana, Gregorio Torres. It was Gervacio's place and his family's, to make the *chicharronada* for the wedding, so the pig which had been fattening for just such an occasion was readied for the kill. He was washed with lye soap, squealing and protesting until he could be heard from his corral on Callejon Guerra up into the plaza itself. Then Gervacio straddled him holding a sharp knife, and at just the right moment his throat was slit. Nothing was wasted in killing an animal—the blood was caught in a basin and would soon become pudding. The pig was skinned with a layer of fat to be cut up and fried into *chicharrones*. His paunch was washed with the same lye soap, rinsed and filled with water, a vessel to be used in the kitchen. There was an abundance of lard to be rendered from the carcass, enough to cook with for weeks to come. Some of it was saved for candles. And a portion was saved for nourishing harness, boots and saddles. It was all accomplished quickly and with gaiety, for a wedding, and a wedding eagerly hoped for as this one was, was an occasion of joy.

Holy day followed holy day in Mesilla, sacrament followed sacrament, feast followed feast as the church was the center of their small universe. On June 25, the Day of San Juan, the joyous shouts of the bathers in the river and the ditches greeted the dawn. They had been in the water an hour before the sun came up. The ritual eating of small green apples preceded the swimming, and while others might sicken with such an ingestion, none of these bathers suffered, and before they emerged from the water, long ends of hair were chopped off encouraging growth. This was the day in which the faithful, amid laughing and splashing, remembered that John the Baptist had baptized Jesús in the River Jordon.

In the early morning chill of a January day in 1865, the wooden coffin with the body of old Silvestre Nicanor Guerra was carried from the Church of San Albino after the funeral Mass to the wagon waiting to take it to the cemetery back of Callejon Guerra. The plain pine box had a few paper flowers on it, and the men who carried the coffin were relatives and close friends. They tried to walk in time to the band music, but the uneven ground made their steps falter. Some of the mourners added other small flowers to the handles of the casket, and sorrowing, watched while the body in its box was slid into the wagon, grating on the rough boards. Don Nicanor had been for many years the *mayordomo de las aguas*, the ditch

boss, in the village and its surrounding fields, and, as such, was a respected senior member of the community. It was his father, Simon Guerra and his wife Josefa Sisneros, who had in their later years been first settlers, who had come from San Lorenzo with sons and nephews to take up land with Father Ramón Ortiz. Don Nicanor was the first of many who died in this year at the close of the Civil War; his was a death of old age and complications. Others died later in the year of the mosquito-borne fevers, malaria and yellow fever following the receding waters of the Spring-flooding Río Grande. Many were the funerals during that summer and fall.

The Apaches relentlessly pursued their campaign against the people of Chihuahua and New Mexico. The Gileño Apaches were especially vindictive around Mesilla; they killed Juan Pasos in a raid and blending into the moonless dusk, silently stole from the corrales of Domingo Cubero forty head of cattle.[187] The fact that Indians still grudged the white man the parajes where his ancient water holes and his hunting grounds had been, never lessened the enmity between colonist and Indian.

Beginning around 1865, emigrants from Paso del Norte and the pueblos around it once again began an influx into Mesilla and Las Cruces. Again carts drawn by burros and mules plodded up the trail, this time on the west side of the new bed of the river on the *Camino Paseño* between thickets of mesquite and newly-opened fields. Some, tired, hungry, disillusioned at the length of the journey, stopped at Canutillo and Refugio and the new town of La Mesa. Their coming resulted from the conflict in northern Mexico between the Republican forces of Benito Juárez and the Emperor Maximilian's army sent by Napoleon of France.

Fighting in Mexico had accelerated by 1865— Benito Juárez repeatedly sought refuge from the French in Paso del Norte with officers of his government and his hungry and bedraggled men. On December 10, the Mexican President entered El Paso, Mexico, with Colonel Luis Terrazas after the French commander Agustin Billaut had taken the City of Chihuahua. Although opposed to the Juárez

Plate 21: Simón Guerra, blacksmith and judge, held court in front of his adobe blacksmith shop in Mesilla using his anvil for a desk. His ancestors migrated to Mesilla from San Lorenzo de Real, one of the pueblos south of Paso del Norte. Photograph taken in the 1970's by Mary D. Taylor.

regime, Father Ramón Ortiz begged from his pulpit in the old Guadalupe church at Paso food and clothing for them, and even though the people there were hard pressed in supporting the newcomers, the response was great. But this presence of Juárez, in the villa opposite Franklin, together with the expanding intrigues of Terrazas and his guerilla bands rankled the ordinary people. The levy of four thousand pesos upon the inhabitants of Paso for the expenses of the federal government also aroused the wrath of those taxed. These conditions did not enhance Juárez' popularity. Furthermore, the clergy in the pueblos around Paso,[188] and in the city itself, were pro-Empire because of the religious abuses of the Juárez regime, and the Indians and mestizos were of the same mind. To secure his position with local officials and with others of his associates, Juárez granted these important men lands which had for two centuries been the property of Indians indigenous to the area around Paso.

To make matters worse, the Laws of Reform, having been in force since 1858, were intensified: religious processions and dances outside the church were banned; the ringing of church bells was strictly limited. To the Indian and the mestizo, the processions associated with the feast of the Virgin of Guadalupe and the ringing of bells on this and other feast days were the most important and happiest events of their lives. And during these contentious years, additional conflicts had arisen between citizen or vecino and the Indian-mestizo regarding the stoppage of water on ditches for the building of grinding mills by the wealthier landowners, the *ricos*. For this purpose, *rebalses*, or wooden dams, were built which caused fields to be either flooded or parched. The vecino, in addition, increasingly asserted his authority in the celebration of the Feast of Guadalupe in December—the lower classes did not consider him a part of this feast at all. Controversies arose and were never settled. And so the Indian-Mestizo, to better his condition, began to look northward again, upriver along the Río Grande where his cousins and uncles had migrated in the early 50's under the guidance of Cura Ramón Ortiz. A new exodus began, and new names appeared in the parish books of La Mesilla and Las Cruces. More of the families of Samaniego, Blanco, Carrillo, Ginso, Fresques, and Acuña were written in the marriage, baptism and burial books. More relatives of Fierro came, and places of origin revealed that times were hard all over northern Mexico. Settlers came from Camargo, Balleza, and Santa Rosalia in the State of Chihuahua; from Durango; from Atotonilco del Alto in Jalisco, and from Coahuila.[189]

In April, 1865, Fort Selden was established at the southern end of the Jornada del Muerto across from the mountain of Robledo and in the vicinity of the old paraje near the ford which cut an Apache trail to the northeast. The garrison was a bastion against the incursions of the Indians, and a guard for incoming settlers and travelers on the old Camino Real.

In that same month, cash money changed hands in St. Louis, Missouri, paying for a flouring mill to be delivered to La Mesilla. Now that Fort Cummings was a sentinel on the trail to California and Fort Selden had been established, travel and commerce increased. It was an auspicious year to begin to grind wheat and corn for the forts and for commercial ventures up and down the trail. The enterprise was called "Frietze, Blake, and Company": price of the mill itself was $4,350; interest and freight increased the cost to $5,681. Pablo Chavez of Mesilla freighted the machinery from Leavenworth, and such names as Stephen Elkins and Miguel Otero also appear in the accounts of the creation of the milling enterprise. Otto Bombach, Peter Holtzhausen and Mariano Talamantes did the carpenter work. Evangelisto Cháves brought vigas from the mountains for roof beams. Virgil Mastin brought lumber from the Mimbres. For weeks, the hammer on Antonio Garcia's anvil struck sparks in the semidarkness of his blacksmith shop as he fashioned pieces of ironwork for the heavy machinery. The stores of Reynolds and Griggs and Agustín Maurin were two blocks up Calle Principal, and nails and manta, paint and bolts found their way to the site where building was going on.

Ysabel Ruis brought in heavy logs from the mountains for vigas, lintels, and supports for the machinery. Antonio Constante sold permission to cut cottonwood logs in his piece of bosque. Juan Medina brought cartloads of lime from the Picacho lime pits for the masonry or plaster of the mill walls. Daniel Frietze examined land all over Mesilla until he found a suitable expanse of unoccupied and good clay ground for making adobes. It belonged to Dona Josefa Saiz and she was glad to have the twenty dollars in return for permission to make the adobes there. Wooden molds were brought and peónes there employed to work the wet mixture with bare feet. They scooped it then into moulds so the sun could dry the clay bricks, and finally these were carried to the site of the building and laid in long rows for the walls. An enormous fireplace was erected. The resulting housing of the mill was a massive structure of adobe and lumber, iron and stone. The heavy wall around the mill and the corrales was finished in June and the boiler was filled on August 1. The mill worked from waterpower from the acequia madre, and the buildings, a block in depth, faced on Calle Principal south of Calle Parían. When the ditch ran full, and an old cottonwood leaned over the water in the evening light, there was a shimmering reflection of the smokestack and its rising smoke on the surface. The engines hummed, and men had all the work they needed in Mesilla.[190]

The Spring flood waters also provided work in caring for the acequias. Time after time the bocacequias were destroyed and heedless waters ripped up new fields. Countless times the men of La Mesilla and the other river colonies were called to ditch duty or fatigas. For each period of digging, a man was awarded a small paper certificate worth about seventy-five cents. Sometimes he could make two or three **fatigas** in a day. In this way, even if the fatiga didn't benefit him personally, he could sell it to a larger landowner, a rico, or even to someone who didn't want to or couldn't perform his work on the ditch.

Before the chill of daybreak, the mayordomos trotted on horseback through the streets of Mesilla crying *"A la tarea, señores, con palos y cabadores!"* [191] To work, men, with shovels and hoes! Goodnatured banter flew between neighbors as residents shouldered tools, and with a few tortillas and some coffee, men started for the acequia madre to begin work. In early Spring the days began cool and sweet, but the ditch bottoms were low and damp where the weeds and grass grew, and as the day warmed, so did the work. By noon sometimes, shirts were wet with sweat, and tiny *myotes*, small flies which live among the weeds, fretted eyes and ears.

Often the overgrown ditches became asylums for peónes fleeing from their masters because they tired of servitude to him and because the penciled black strokes of his debits he kept in his crude ledger outnumbered those of his wages. It was easy here in the acequia to bend over the steamy work and blend in with the other workers. Under the wide straw hats, faces were hidden; the sweat-stained shirts were similar, the chops of the hoes and the swing of the scythes concealed the refugees. Casildo Pena's son Pedro worked there for a while, hoping to get away when night came. He owed twenty-three pesos to his master, his ama, José Jacques, and could see no way ever to work it off—the debt kept increasing instead of diminishing. Anastacio Lujan labored there also; he owed one hundred six pesos.[192]

Fatigas on the ditches became, as well as occasions for backbreaking work, times of joy as well. At midday as men rested and ate, a song lifted across the fields where the households nearer the ditches could hear. Usually, it was music of romance and bravado which lifted their spirits from the monotony of the labor they performed.

The waters of the swirling Río Grande, as they receded from their old channel, as well as disclosing fertile lands, revealed fine clay deposits. Two of these were at Bosque Seco and near La Mesilla where the river used to curve around the ferry landing. One April evening, late, Agusté (in Mesilla he was called "Agustín") Maurin, a Frenchman who had immigrated from Mexico to Mesilla in

1852, stooped low over the wet ground near the old ferry in the curve of the west bank of the river at Mesilla. He took up a handful of wet earth and squeezed it through his fingers. Some of it filtered through, falling in sifts, but dark, wet chunks of pure clay lay in the palm of his hand. He looked east to the mountains and smiled to himself—right here was his gold mine, his opportunity to further his fortune.

Here, early in the 1860's, he established his "*maquina*," a kiln to manufacture brick, measuring off for himself in the absence of any official qualified to do so, a terreno of land, 525 varas by 125 varas, including the clay deposit, "*barro propio*," the material necessary to form brick and square tile. He petitioned and won preemption of this terreno from the Probate Judge of Doña Ana County. And he immediately began the construction of a proposed two-story building on the southwest corner of the plaza, described later in the *Mesilla Times* as a true Parisian-style building.

Agusté Maurin was a handsome man, quiet, successful in whatever he set about. He was a collector of fine art and European masterpieces hung on the walls of his home. He lived well, but simply, and the best of French decantered liqueurs caught the light of the sun from the window on the west side of his rooms at evening. There was a porcelain figure of the Blessed Virgin in a *nicho* in the brick wall. He usually cooked for himself, wrote in ledgers by candlelight into the night, and kept his own counsel. He accumulated property: he acquired the Velarde ranch, that of Pablo Alvillar who had owned the lot which his brick building now occupied, and he owned bosque land. He had a claim for $22,000 outstanding with the United States government for loss to himself during the Civil War; he claimed $10,000 more for timber cut by Federal troops in his bosque land during that period. His kiln now kept him busy—his bricks and floor tile were finely done and widely distributed. At the Velarde Ranch on a sunny field, bricks and tile were set out to dry in rows, then fired and stacked.

It was said that he had a woman friend, a Mexican woman who was his confidant and companion. Among his few close friends were Dr. Mariano Samaniego of El Paso del Norte and Numa Grandjean of Las Cruces. He had three brothers: Louis César, André Casimir, and Cir of Anduze, Department DuGar, France. They corresponded with each other and, since Maurin family members were merchants, words of advice crossed the Atlantic many times.

By early April, bricklayers were mortaring bricks up past the roofline of Maurin's building—up to the rectangular beginnings of the second story windows. Mesilleros looked with pride on this new addition to their plaza; to them it was a fine thing to have a building made of home-manufactured brick on the old plaza, the first such building in all New Mexico as far as they could tell, and a building with such continental flair. Unfortunately, this building also would house tragedy later in the 1860s.

At mid-morning, April 10, 1868, shutters and doors on the brick building were still unopened and there was an air of complete silence at the otherwise busy establishment. When entry was forced into Agusté Maurin's rooms, they found him in the kitchen where he had been cooking his supper. He was face down and even before they turned him over, it was evident that his skull had been smashed with the bloody axe on the floor. His throat was cut. In the corner of the room, in the hearth before the fireplace, there was a large, newly-dug cavity—large enough for an olla, an earthen jar presumably containing gold coins. At noon the bells of the Church of San Albino tolled a *doble* announcing his death.

Considerable speculation in the *Mesilla News* in later years and gossip around La Mesilla accused the *amante*, the lover of his woman friend, of the murder, he having been an employee of the dead man.[193]

Newton Rosecrans readied the body in Mesilla for burial—Maurin wore a satin vest and a black satin neckerchief to hide the slash in his throat, and a body watcher was hired for the night after the murder. Jesús María Rey made the coffin and its enclosing box for twenty dollars. Agusté Maurin was buried in Las Cruces by Father Damaso Taladrid with a few close friends as mourners. It was said that his traitorous female companion died a year later of remorse over her complicity in his death and of disappointment over not inheriting the property, and she died refusing the sacraments of the Church. The alleged murderer, a fugitive from the law in Chihuahua, fled to Guadalupe below Paso del Norte, fell drunk in an irrigated corn field and drowned. In his pocket was found a large French gold coin.

Las Cruces in 1866 was growing in size and population. Calle Alameda was lined with cottonwoods, and there were large homes alongside *hortalizas* in that garden section. The acequia madre coursed through the town showing a line of green along its banks and almost always now the sound of moving water refreshed the heat of day. The several fields of crosses still were there: East of Campo Street was one group, close by the house of "Black Chihuahua" who was still an Indian citizen of Mexico and who had one of the oldest homes in Cruces. His and Tino Zamora's houses were on the east side of Las Cruces, where it was sandy, and the L-shaped adobe homes had small patios with geraniums in tin cans resting on wooden benches against the walls. A cottonwood struggled here and there.

Another field of wooden crosses was just to the east—the weathered wood by now had lost all trace of names and leaned at will in the sand. There were said to have been crosses down by the Alameda; more on the northern mesa by the cuesta, the slope, leading down to Francisco Fletcher's home. Travelers on the trail felt that Las Cruces was properly named.

The Indians dancing before St. Genevieve's Church were joined by other Indian immigrants from the south. They began to fuse into their dress and headdresses small mirrors, feathers, shells from other Indian origins in Mexico.[194]

St. Genevieve's parish in Las Cruces had begun its own record keeping in 1859—baptisms, marriages and deaths were recorded in long brown ledgers. It was under the jurisdiction of the Bishop of New Mexico unlike Mesilla which was firmly presumed to be part of the Durango diocese. By 1866 Bishop Lamy of New Mexico had made a visita to his jurisdiction all the way down through Franklin to Socorro and the other pueblos below. In Las Cruces at St. Genevieve's he noted that Father Donato Rogieri had built a convento, bought two bells for the church, and made repairs inside and out.

Indian campaigns against the Gileños and the Apache "renegades" at Cañada Alamosa yielded children taken captive and placed in homes in Mesilla and Las Cruces. There they were baptized, reared with the rest of the children but served the family. In many instances, their children were the master's also, thus *mestizising* the population of the valley to an even greater degree. At the home of Christian Duper and Dolores Mireles in Las Cruces, María Ysabel and Felipa Parra were Apache women in their service. María Ysabel, "*yndia Apache*" at the age of twenty was judged instructed well enough in religion to be baptized at St. Genevieve's by Father Rogieri. In front of the wooden altar she stood, a dark girl in her first white dress, her face expressionless, receiving the sacrament of baptism. Christian Duper, old soldier veteran by now, was her padrino and the candle he held glowed bright in the dimly lit church.

She bent her head and knelt, and water was spilled over her long black hair, and she became a Catholic, a Christian, and should have forgotten her ancestors' gods and the Apache ways. She served the Duper family all her life until she was not able anymore, and then they cared for her until she died.

On the plaza of La Mesilla in the 1860's, on the west side, was the Barela store and residence. Rafaela Garcia de Barela lived here with her son Mariano who was a merchant as his father Anastacio was, and his father before him. They were descended from a family of traders near

Albuquerque, and here in Mesilla at the hub of the trails, Anastacio had established his business. During the southern occupation of Mesilla in 1861 and 1862, he had chosen the side of the Confederacy, and had fled to Texas with the other Southern sympathizers. But, before Anastacio left, he deeded his property worth $10,000 to his wife Rafaela so that it would not be subject to confiscation by the Federal regime. By now, María Rafaela Garcia de Barela had grown used to doing without Anastacio, and, as she had been astute in business before he left, she now became, behind the facade of her son Mariano, the head of a minor empire in the valley. She loaned money, held mortgages, foreclosed, and was the head of the Barela clan. Mariano was a young man of twenty-five in 1866 and was in love with and wanted to marry a girl whom his mother considered beneath the Barela class. Rafaela, being the matriarch, did not allow the marriage.

Mariano's younger brother Manuel was no such man to be dominated by his mother. A problem to the family from the beginning, he drank and danced and gambled the days and nights away. Where there was trouble, he was there. He married Margarita Bean at an early age—when he was nineteen and she was fourteen. Years later he was to die by hanging for a murder in Las Vegas.

Anastacio did not come home for years, and then when he did return, it was to die. His wife sued for divorce on the basis of adultery and abandonment several years after he left. In the meantime, he had established another family in Texas,[195] but when he grew old and sick, he began to long for the alamedas and the sound of water rushing in the acequias of home.

The Barela residence on the west side of the plaza was firmly settled into the old ways of Mexican living, even though many of the refinements of architecture and eastern culture now embellished the adobe structure. The Barela family had established another home on the Gran Plaza across town to the east during the days of the Confederacy, but the great fortress-like home on the plaza still hosted a multitude of residents and visitors. Behind the store in front were dark adobe rooms, walls whitewashed with yeso, deep nichos cut into them where shadows played upon figures of Nuestra Señora de Guadalupe and San José—shadows cast by candles lit in sconces of worked tin. There were adobe *bancos* along the walls, where guests were seated and floors were made hard by mixing mud with goat blood. Jerga—a straw matting—covered them, and on hot afternoons these were swept with damp brooms. Windows were covered on the outside with *rejas*, a wooden grillwork, and deep window sills held geranium plants and ferns kept soft and green by careful watering.

The cool interior of the Barela home enclosed by the thick walls of this house was the financial and political forum of the county. Doña Rafaela's power and that of her son Mariano was a recognized force that superceded all others. Mariano was the southern terminus of the Santa Fe Ring,[196] being allied with Thomas B. Catron in numerous dealings in land and finance. His power in southern New Mexico was to be a force lesser politicians were to consider substantial. In 1866 he was elected sheriff for Doña Ana County.

Along the tree-lined streets of the Mesilla plaza in the busy days after the Civil War walked men in wide-brimmed hats and jeans with strapped-on guns, men in top hats and canes, the working man with his feet in huaraches, his head shaded by a wide sombrero. Alongside women in hoopskirts and lace bonnets from the East, were Mexican women in wide skirts and rebozos.

In the evenings, men and boys gathered at *rebote* courts to play hand ball. A high adobe wall was marked off into rectangles and points were scored by the ball being bounced, then hit into these targets 'midst much laughing and shouting and good-natured ribaldry. Those who were not too weary after the day's labor in fields, in blacksmith shops, or making and building with adobe, rode horseback or muleback along the roads cooled from the heat of midday and afternoon.[197]

Gradually the old river channel dried out enough to begin thinking about a road from Mesilla to Las Cruces. In January, 1866, the Territorial Legislature authorized a commission to study the possibilities of such a road. John Lemon, Probate Judge, appointed Anastacio Sisneros, Pablo Alvarado, Anastacio García, Daniel Frietze and Thomas Massie to the commission. They were to examine the land between the two towns to find the most advantageous route and also to investigate ownership of such land and what recompense the owners would expect. On May 12 the commission reported on a recommended route: sixteen varas wide, it was to start at the plaza of Mesilla and pass the house of Samuel Jones along the old Gran Plaza of Confederate days through the lands of Mariano Barela to the plaza of Las Cruces. It was to be bordered, at least along private property, by a wall four feet high formed of puddled adobe made with sufficient straw.[198] Here on both sides of the old river channel were terrenos of land held in private ownership since 1851, so Juan Garcia, Pablo Garcia and others had to, for a consideration of pesos, yield right-of-way for the road to pass on its way to Cruces. Construction of the road was tortuous during the summer with heat and mosquitoes. But once it was finished, coaches and horsemen moved more easily from town to town.

La Mesilla began to communicate with a wider world on the east side of the old riverbed more readily; the northern part of the state occasionally took the southern part into legislative consideration. A special act of the Legislative Assembly of the Territory of New Mexico approved January 31, 1866, provided for the construction of jails and courthouses in different counties where security of the judicial process was not sufficient. Taxes were to be levied on the residents with this in mind. On June 2, Probate Judge John Lemon announced:

I, John Lemon, Probate Judge, within and for the County of Doña Ana, in virtue of the authority conferred on me and in complying with the duty of my office, have taken into consideration the existing funds of the county, and I believe that an obligation of work to finish

the courthouse which is now being built, and to build a jail within the county will be hard on the residents of the county. I issue this order and I command that each and every person who resides within the limits of the County of Doña Ana who has a yoke of oxen or horses or mules will bring to the courthouse in the Villa de La Mesilla one or more wagons of stone for use in construction of the Jail of the County.

In June of that year the hauling of stone began before sunrise on summer mornings. To a man who made his living by farming in 1866, his quota of stone brought from the Black Mesa south of Mesilla he tried to deliver on *dias de fiesta* (holidays), weekends especially Sunday evenings. The trip in wagons down to the mesa was easily and swiftly accomplished, but the trip back to Mesilla with a load of stone was heavy and slow. The horses and mules strained at the unaccustomed burden. The receipts put into their hands upon delivery assured Mesilleros that their part of this fatiga was done. There were those who wished to contribute cash instead of stone, and this was accepted. The courthouse frontage on the east side of the plaza was bought from Ernest Angerstein and Louis William Geck—this had only to be remodeled and expanded. The stone jail rose at the rear of the old solar de casa to the east and was a source of pride for residents and those who came to view it. Judge Lemon assured citizens that the completion of so stout an edifice would insure the county against all disorder and would guarantee protection of life and property.[199]

Now that life and property seemed to be assured, and the authorities of Doña Ana County more confident in the establishment of what was considered to be law and order, citizens took up the tasks of everyday life again. The spirit of the Mesilleros turned inward toward their own Mexican customs and the consolation of the Church. Births were celebrated and deaths marked. Before Benito Madrid died in 1865, Father Baca brought him the sacrament of Extreme Unction in his black carriage. A runner preceded him, with a small tinkling bell; people on the road removed their hats, and some knelt until the coach was out of sight. A national sense was nonessential—the whole of the village became a community of relatives upon whom life itself depended. With this, the Mesillero was able to brace himself for the next upheaval which, in view of the past, he considered inevitable.

Chapter 10 | THE HERMIT AND VIOLENCE IN SOUTHERN NEW MEXICO

In early December, 1866 Mesilla was sprinkled with sunlight fragmented by branches of leafless cottonwoods. The last winter trickle of the acequia madre, rimmed occasionally with giant trees, gleamed in paths of light as the sun climbed to its zenith. From the third to the twelfth of December, the novena was begun to the Virgin of Guadalupe, and for these nine nights, altars in homes glowed with candles as the old words were recited. The novena was said in the evenings, and under clear, cold night skies, Mesilleros wrapped themselves in *jorongos* and *rebozos* against the chill. The star of the east was unusually bright as the feast day grew near.

On the morning of the twelfth, the Feast of Nuestra Señora de Guadalupe, a light snow unexpectedly fell. By the time the first bell rang for Mass, a crust of white lay over the plaza and little banks of snow lay against the wall around the church. Parishioners brushed snowy feet against paths leading from the plaza, scuffing off the wet so the tiled church floor would not be damp during Mass. Then the lilting air of "*Manañitas*" lifted as an affectionate greeting to the Virgin. All the verses were sung, and the candles lit against the dimness of the early morning glistened in the little patches of snow on woolen-covered shoulders. The image of the Guadalupe was a bright lithograph on the altar, and red paper roses clung to the wooden frame. A curtain of lace was draped behind the image, and from it hung small tin bells and *milagros* in thanksgiving for favors received or those petitioned from Nuestra Señora de Guadalupe. Family groups knelt; clans clung together as they were reminded of all the reasons they had come to this village and to this adobe church on the twelfth of December.

Sunlight had begun to melt the crust of snow when Mass was finished. Parishioners leaving church embraced each other, jubilant on this traditional feast day when they could proclaim their allegiance once more to a universal figure, who was, after all, Indian and Mexican—a Virgin of their own. Already at this early hour the fiesta was being readied on the plaza. Close to the buildings *puestos*, or booths, were being erected, each with wooden panels as protection against the bulls in the coming bullfight. A rope with suspended little red flags stretched around the plaza to mark the circumference of the corrida to come.[200]

A little after two o'clock in the afternoon, with a thin line of shade falling on the plaza, the torrero Antonio Acosta, the main bullfighter, entered the ring. He wore a red shirt and slim white trousers held close against him with a sash of black silk. With a bow, and holding both banderillas, he dedicated the fight to Mariano Barela who sat with his family in chairs close to the rope barricade; and to Rafael Bermudes and William Jones who were seated there also. Musicians, most of them Mesilleros, struck up tunes familiar to corridas everywhere. The temper of the crowd quickened when Acosta made a good paso, and the roar of voices rose over the music of the band. Silver dollars threw up little dust clouds as Barela and the others tossed them into the ring in appreciation. The bulls were from Chihuahua and some were fierce, pawing the dirt and snorting to the delight of the crowd. But when the fight became more spirited, some of the more agile took refuge on rooftops and ladies and children withdrew.

Fiesta lasted on into the night with the musicians playing tunes for dancing on the packed earth of the plaza and upon board platforms. In other placitas of Mesilla, those more conscious of their Indian heritage danced the old steps and chanted sounds they had heard since infancy. To the southeast, three trails of fires glowed again upon Tortugas Mountain as those of Indian and mestizo heritage

Plate 22: San Albino Church in 1881. Built by Bonifacio Gamboa in 1856-57. Photograph by Stiles and Burke. Courtesy of Museum of New Mexico, negative number 14299.

Plate 23: San Albino Church. A new brick bell tower was added to the front of the old adobe church. Mary D. Taylor Collection.

descended in procession with *quiotes*[201] they had fashioned. Far to the south at Paso del Norte, in spite of the anticlerical stipulations of the Laws of Reform, luminarias glowed atop homes, and fires lit the mountain to the west of that villa. People in the whole length of the Mesilla Valley welcomed the coming of Nuestra Señora with devotion, celebration, music, and dance.

When the actual Vigil of Christmas approached, the ancient drama of Los Pastores, an enactment of the eternal story of the Nativity, was performed at Mesilla and Las Cruces. Sometimes the play lasted eight hours, and the characters of the Holy Family, Bartolo, Cucliarón, and the others were recited and sung in verse, sometimes in Mesilla all 2261 stanzas. The play was learned by verbal recitation— father to son, mother to daughter. Occasionally, a written copy was consulted, but only a few of these existed. Brought in essence from Spain through Mexico and up to the towns along the *frontera* "it is like some old court garment, discarded in a forgotten corner, disfigured by stains, rents, and coarse patches, but still showing the richness of the original material." [202] Some of the original props, the cloaks, the staffs, the brilliant colored beribboned costumes are still in the hands of those families who took part in La Mesilla.

In the middle of February, 1867 sand from the western mesas and the desert below began to blow across Mesilla with spring fury. The usual winds came early this year, and the streets held hills of sand between intersections. As the winds grew in intensity, the cemetery southwest of the plaza was almost completely covered. Sand over grave markers had to be brushed away by those who knew where family stones and crosses were, and even so, it was difficult to read the lettering worn by wind and sand.

Father José de Jesús Baca, Francis DeRyther, Thomas Bull, Joseph Reynolds and Rafael Bermudes as trustees for the town of La Mesilla, paid two hundred dollars for a piece of ground south from the plaza to serve as a new cemetery and a right of way leading to it.[203] The land had been cultivated and had grown corn, so the sand fill was minimal. The old cemetery was lost under a great sand dune.

While the town trustees were in harmony over this purchase, political divisions were deeply rooted in Mesilla. This division had its beginnings in the 1855 New Mexico election. José Manuel Gallegos won this election against Miguel A. Otero for delegate to Congress from the Territory of New Mexico. It had been a vicious campaign with charges of fraud by both candidates, and Father José de Jesús Baca[204] of Mesilla had been accused of tilting the voting totals towards José Manuel Gallegos and away from Miguel Otero. Guards at the polling place, a number of them in favor of Otero, had closed the polls about six o'clock near dusk, refusing to provide candles so the rest of those in line could cast their ballots. Father Baca, sensing the hostility, bought candles himself, and with the aid of one man, took the tally books and boxes down to his house and continued the voting until all had had a chance to vote. It was afterwards charged that he had stuffed the boxes with votes for Gallegos, but witnesses later testified that this was not the case.[205]

The charge of illegal aliens voting came up also: some of the settlers were accused, as they tried to cast their ballots, of never having sworn allegiance to the United States, and of never stating their citizenship preference as provided by the Decree of 1848, thus sacrificing the validity of their votes. Poll officials and other legal authorities did not acknowledge the understanding that anyone within sight of the official flag-raising on the plaza of Mesilla in 1854 became an automatic citizen, and that this entitled them to vote in this election without any oath or other formality.[206]

When Congress was called upon in 1855 to decide whether Gallegos' election as delegate was fraudulent as Otero claimed it was, the American-educated Otero's fluency in the English language while pleading his case, his eloquent accusations that Gallegos favored Mexico and that he, Otero, was the patriotic American candidate, convinced

Plate 24: Bells in the tower of San Albino Church were cast in 1886. Photograph by Mary D. Taylor in the 1970s.

that body to unseat Gallegos and seat Otero in his place. José Manuel Gallegos claimed that Bishop Jean Baptiste Lamy of Santa Fe had used his influence to defeat him and to support Miguel A. Otero, and the argument became a national and ethnic conflict between the two candidates. Gallegos had always given his spiritual allegiance to the Diocese of Durango, Mexico and refused to acknowledge Lamy's ecclesiastical jurisdiction in New Mexico; therefore, Gallegos' civil allegiance was also considered Mexican. Gallegos and the men who gave testimony regarding the voting had no great fluency in English at that time and were at the mercy of translators; the Congressional transcript shows the great misunderstandings and misinterpretations which occurred. As a result, Congress having awarded the congressional seat to Otero, Gallegos returned to New Mexico.

Elections after 1855 in southern New Mexico only accelerated bad feeling and acts of violence due to political enmities. Miguel Otero won three terms in the Congress of the United States, defeating Spruce Baird and then José Manuel Gallegos again in 1859.

Old animosities reached back to the early years of settlement and to the always-present rivalry between the Bishop of Durango and Bishop Lamy in regard to ecclesiastical jurisdiction over this section of New Mexico, which in popular opinion far outweighed any civil contest in an election. Father Baca and his congregation at the Church of San Albino still gave their allegiance defiantly to the Bishopric of Durango, which was the last bastion of Mexicanism left them.

In 1863 in the election for delegate to Congress, José Manuel Gallegos lost once more his bid for delegate to Congress to Francisco Perea. Locally, John Lemon won over Rafael Ruelas as Probate Judge of Doña Ana County. In 1865, Colonel J. Francisco Chavez defeated Colonel Francisco Perea as delegate to Congress.

It was not until August 1867—before the September election for the next delegate to Congress and for other territorial and local offices—that the first startling hint of real violence surfaced in Mesilla. The candidates for delegate to Congress in that election were Don José Francisco Cháves[207] and Charles P. Clever.[208] By now, the divisive electoral spirit born in 1855 was full-blown. It was in this election that Probate Judge John Lemon drew red lines through names and totals with the word "rejected" alongside. Whole precincts were disallowed since only one set of delegates appeared on the tally sheets.[209] The stage was set for coming troubles.

In Mesilla it was not possible to debate the issues without coming to blows. Loyalties continued to be created by personal alliances and old hatreds. In the home of Father Baca, a supposedly peaceful political meeting was to be held in August by members of both parties.

They appealed to John Lemon, Probate Judge of Doña Ana County and he answered:[210]

Señores:

Your letter arrived last night at 8:15 showing the opinion of the people of Mesilla in regard to the violence and outrage committed upon some peaceful citizens, inflicting bold destruction of life and property by Federal officials and those of the Territory.

In your communication, you say that some men in the peaceful pursuit of their official duties were outraged and violently assaulted by an official of the county and of the territory and that you are informed that federal officials of the territory and of the county were present and even participated. You direct your communication to me as Juez de Pruebas that I might afford such protection of life and property as the law guarantees to all citizens.

Nevertheless, you have not made a specific accusation against any official in particular, nor against any body of officials, nor have you made known the crime which you say has been committed, but only in general and indefinite terms. In this way you have formed a general accusation against each and all officials within the county without distinction, thus letting the world infer that the officials of the territory...are individually and collectively...a group of disorderly and dangerous men. This conjecture I consider false as your fears of being outraged are without foundation. It is not necessary to assure you that it is not urgent that some new steps be taken to assure safety of life and property. Nevertheless, señores, if the time should come that such measures be necessary, I hope that I will find you as quick to give protection as you are now to ask it. The resolutions which you give to understand to have been adopted "for a great gathering of people interested in the peace and prosperity of the county" neither have been seen nor even understood by a tenth part of the citizens of Mesilla. The resolutions have been conceived in injustice, and produced in obscurity... born and strengthened purely as a political strategy, with the purpose of bringing hatred to persons of consequence and of character...I feel very much, señores, that you believe that such procedures have been necessary and indispensable for a fortunate conclusion of your desperate cause, and I am still sorry that Señor Don Francisco Chabez has lent his favor to a project so unworthy...if you are so desirous of securing peace and harmony and you are so religiously opposed to all violence and outrage, why did you not last Sunday morning, when an unarmed man was attacked with knife and pistol in Chabez' meeting, shout peace and ask protection of the officials of the county? Was it because you thought you were then in the majority, or was it that you were not fully aware of your danger?...If some citizen, whether or not he be an official, has been guilty of an outrage to a person or property, the law clearly recognizes the course that has to be followed to repair the grievances, and it is not only the duty of every official but of every individual to protect the indefensible one from injury, and, finally, señores, permit me to say that I believe that your fears of personal outrage and violence are entirely unfounded and only a product of a disturbed imagination...I have only to say that if some member of your group wishes that I respond personally for whatever event which might occur, that will be the way it will be. I am the man most easily found in the County of Doña Ana.[211]

But at the meeting in Father Baca's home that evening, there was trouble. The two factions clashed. Manuel Barela, the black-sheep younger brother of Mariano Barela, was there. Frederick Burkner held a six-shooter against Barela's chest and threatened to kill him. Atilano and Juan Baca, Father Baca's nephews, Silvestre Maese, N. Y. Ancheta, Ygnacio Gonzáles, and Ygnacio Orrantia beat Barela. Thomas Catron was the District Attorney who drew up the indictments on August 20, 1867 against Frederick Burkner and the others who had illtreated Barela. Mariano Barela was sheriff at this time. Plainly, the lines were drawn in the political arena in southern New Mexico.[212]

United States Marshal John Pratt assigned deputies at the polling places as the September election date arrived, but José Francisco Cháves, in defeat, charged federal lawmen with interfering with the actual voting. There was much dissension, and the image of politics in southern New Mexico became defined and remained so for many years.

The later years of the 1860's were ones of increasing unrest and aligning of political factions. The political opportunities which some Mesilleros now realized that they could effect, caught their imaginations. The idea of "one man, one vote" gave some of them a sense of governmental power they had never known under Mexican rule. The candidates involved in the election claimed the voter's allegiance through personalities such as Father Baca, John Lemon, Ignacio Orrantia, or other men of importance in the village. Scarcely ever did they consider the elections in any other light than local; scarcely ever did the Mesillero consider the candidates from a national, American viewpoint.

During these days of political division, new settlers still were coming upriver from the area of Paso del Norte and from deeper in Chihuahua and central Mexico. The laws which Benito Juárez imposed on the nation, calculated to free common men from the burdens of the Church, were causing those very people to leave Mexico to search out the old customs of the Church. Around Paso del Norte and in all Chihuahua, *caciques regionales*, chieftains of separate regions, fought among themselves for supremacy in that state. Benito Juárez, as president of the Republic of Mexico even though in exile at Paso several times, overlooked this because these leaders, even though struggling among themselves, helped him put down guerilla action in other northern states to stabilize his term of presidency.[213]

As a consequence of this unrest along the frontera and in northern Chihuahua, to refugees of the late 1860's fleeing the oppression of a newly republican Mexico, the future seemed brighter in the colonies along the American side of the river in contrast to that which they had left. *La Democracia*, a Chihuahua newspaper wrote, December 14, 1868, in an article called "Los Campesinos":

> Democracy in Mexico is apparent...here in the haciendas and in the rancherias there are 100,000 workers with their families...and the adjacent pueblos of Indians. They all live as domestic servants of the owners of the finca or its mayordomo. The major part of them do not have property; agriculture for them is prohibited if it does not benefit their masters. When they have land to cultive, the most fertile ground is left to the Señores... Politically, no one reads or signs the cédulas—the administrator or his scribe casts the vote for all of them. The electoral college uses without permission their names for the selection of representatives...The collector of contributions comes; the recruiter of soldiers to march them off to war; the minister of development comes and they have to work for him by force; the police come and cast them into jail; the executioner comes and they die; for the campesino this is all part of a mysterious calamity, and he doesn't understand that by virtue of their authority, all these

opportunists appear periodically to torment him… these same legislators forget...that they derive their power [from the governed].

> The emigrants came upriver. And when times were hard, and they were oppressed and taken advantage of by American politicians or landlords, or by fellow Mexicans who were now Americans, they looked longingly back toward their mother Mexico. "La Patria" was more an ideal than a reality—more a sentiment than a fact." [214]

Mescalero and Mimbreño Apaches still threatened the inhabitants of Mesilla and the families who homesteaded and broke lands at considerable distance from the ejidos of the Mesilla grant. The Indians ran off stock, lanced those who worked newly broken fields, carried off women and children. Isolated as they were, it became impossible for them to defend themselves. On January 14, 1869, the *soto aguacil*, Sheriff Doroteo Duran, and José María Barela and Cleto Maese received an order:

> By these presents, you are ordered to name Ygnacio Gonzáles 2nd, Jacinto Alvarado, Mariano Barela, José María Alcántar, José Ran, Ylario Morales, Jesús Olivares, Rafael Lucero, Reyes Gomez, Estanislado Olivares, Luz Padilla, Teofilo Tapia, Guadalupe Morales, Roman Tapia, and Blas Duran so that from them might be named a comandante before the Justice of the Peace of the fourth precinct [so that he might] go out and assist the families who are besieged by the hostile Indians who war against us. [These men] will come armed, mounted, and with supplies of food. No excuse will be admissible. Given under my hand officially in La Mesilla and by order of the Probate Judge of Doña Ana County. Bartolo Madrid, Juez de Pruebas.[215]

The old Mesilla Guard once more rode in defense of their families and friends.

In that same year, 1869, Antonio Garcia in his *mesón* west of the Church of San Albino kept an unlicensed gaming table in his establishment and was fined for it. The same charges were leveled at José María DeCamara and Newton Rosecranz. Sheriff Mariano Barela was cited for having a *chusas* gaming wheel in his commercial house. Although Francisco Salazar kept for the least wealthy of Mesilla a pawn shop, Monte de Piedad, he was fined for not having a license. Francisco also closed his eyes to the fact that some of the articles brought him to sell were stolen goods. Eli Priest of Las Cruces, Christian Duper's son-in-law, claimed that a fusil, a musket, in Salazar's shop belonged to him and had been stolen.[216]

Vicar J. B. Salpointe of Arizona hovered in Las Cruces at this time between attempts to contact, through visits and many letters, the new Bishop of Durango, Vicente Salinas. The Bishops of Durango, José Antonio Zubiria who had died in 1868, and Bishop Salinas, his successor, had continued to hold off yielding jurisdiction over La Mesilla and towns on the American side of the river below Paso del Norte until a message from Pope Pius IX had directed this move.[217] Salpointe was determined to take jurisdiction with or without such a directive. He had brought six priests from Europe to replace certain Mexican priests now in charge of these towns and they were now inactive, waiting for assignment. The Vicar also awaited the arrival of Sisters of Loretto to begin a school and convent at Las Cruces. To the people of Mesilla, this only made stronger their allegiance to Durango and made firm their opposition to the ecclesiastic authority of the French prelates of Santa Fe.

Mesilleros went about their daily lives with the same timeless patience their ancestors had shown for decades. The moon came full and then waned to silver thinness; this was noted as were the positions of the stars, and planting and watering were done in compliance with the heavens. Yet violence was soon to visit them again. This time it would involve religion not politics.

In 1863, at Las Vegas, New Mexico, the caravan of Miguel Romero y Baca returned from Missouri. The Romero train had traveled the Santa Fe Trail for many years transferring passengers and goods and had been captained by Romero y Baca. The man who walked with staff in hand beside that train as it entered Las Vegas was unusual, and people on the plaza of that town stopped and stared. He was sixty-two years old, had a long white beard, and wore a cape partly concealing gray clothing which some considered immediately to be an old Confederate uniform. A small bell was attached to his walking staff—a light tinkle sounded as he walked beside the wagons into the plaza. Under his cowl, the old man's long white hair and beard hid whatever facial expression he might have had. Miguel Romero was quick to explain to those who questioned him: "A holy man," "a hermit," "*el solitario*," "*el hermitano*." He had refused to ride across the plains; he had walked the whole way.

As he was a stranger and knew no one, the hermit was offered hospitality by Miguel Romero at his house on the Las Vegas plaza. The hermit's curative powers, his herbal remedies, his devotion, his suffering from self-imposed privation quickly drew attention. Streams of the faithful sought his presence, each one with some particular favor to ask or some illness to cure.[218] The solitude he had come to find in this far northern part of New Mexico was quickly interrupted. And so he withdrew to a cave on Tecolote Peak, El Cerro Tecolote to the north of Las Vegas. But even here the faithful came; men built him a cabin for shelter near a spring close by. The Hermit lived on a type of corn mush he made, trading for corn meal small religious emblems he had carved. When he came down on his infrequent visits to town, inhabitants of Las Vegas could hear the small bell sound as he moved his walking staff. He was offered hospitality everywhere, and when he did accept it, he slept on the floor of his host's home. When he went back to Tecolote Peak, he told those with whom he had stayed that if ever they failed to see a fire glowing before his cave, they were to come because the "trouble" had found him. In a few years, he grew restless again, gathered his few belongings, and walked away from Las Vegas.

When he walked into La Mesilla in 1866 alongside the wagon train of Don Ramón Gonzáles coming from Kansas City through northern New

Mexico on the Santa Fe Trail, citizens greeted him with surprise, but they offered him the same hospitality as had been afforded him at Las Vegas. Strangers often entered the plaza of Mesilla, strangers of all sorts, dressed in every type or combination of clothing. But this man was an exception. Never had they seen an old one such as he; never had they looked into eyes so wise. Every sort of hospitality was again offered. He stayed a while with the Barela family, and then with the family of Antonio Garcia. But soon he tired of people and town, and the Organ Mountains to the East beckoned him; he had heard of a cave at the entrance of Soledad Canyon. For a year he stayed there, and then his wanderings took him to the Cerro Hueco below El Paso. From here he walked to Paso del Norte and took residence in the Cerro de Zapello a few miles to the south of that villa and west of the *médanos*, the sand hills, of Samalayuca.

By this time, something of his background became known—he had revealed a sparse outline of his troubles and travels in Europe and the New World. He had lived as a hermit seven years in the mountains of Italy, then becoming part of the religious community of Sant' Antonio Abate, an order having Portugal as its origin.[219]

At Cerro del Zapello he found a cave to give him protection and there he lived for a time. He came down only to find water and provisions. He was befriended by Father Severo Borrajo at Paso del Norte, by Mrs. Escobar, by Doña Lola Uranga and by Father Ramón Ortiz' sister Doña Refugio Samaniego.

In March 1869, or perhaps 1868,[220] he returned to Mesilla, to his cave in the Organ Mountains. He told Doña Rafaelita Barela there that three men from Paso del Norte had appeared at his cave at Zapello one night with intentions of killing him. Fray Juan María had come out, lantern in hand and held it up to light the three rough faces. "Here I am, sirs. I know why you have come." At these grave words, the three turned and disappeared into the darkness. Before he left the Paso area, he gave Señora Escobar the journal he had kept.

It was written on fragile paper with charcoal he had manufactured. He also wrote with *almagre*, a reddish sharpened rock. His "*memorias*" did not survive for long, the words flaking off as the journal was handled.[221]

From La Cueva, he came down only occasionally, renewing his friendship with Father Baca, fashioning rosaries from dried flower paste to give to friends in exchange for his scant supplies.

Teresita Fountain was eight years old in 1869; she had already made her First Communion and on Sundays she was allowed to wear the starched white dress and veil handmade for that event. There were small ruffles from the hem halfway up the skirt, and the bodice had real Alençon lace at the collar. El Solitario had made her father Antonio Garcia a rosary, and Teresita, especially on Sundays, liked to stand at the big west window and run the rosary through her fingers because it gave off the odor of roses. Her mother, Soledad Bermudes, had told the little girl to say the rosary slowly—Ave María by Ave María. Teresita usually said two decades slowly and then close to her face, ran the rest of the flower beads through the palms of her hands. That way she could inhale the fragrance and imagine a whole garden of roses outside the window.

Fray Juan María, when he came down from his cave to visit Mesilla, used to say the rosary in the big room at the home of Mariano and Rafaelita Barela. Father Baca had urged his parishioners to attend the rosaries the hermit recited and to listen to his preaching.

Most of the parishioners of Mesilla crowded the old house, and around the kneeling figures there was no room to step. There was in good weather sometimes an overflow past the doorway. Before the Hermit left to return to La Cueva, Teresita's mother Soledad Bermudes always sent with him a small earthen *casuela* filled with *biscochos*.

Mesilleros occasionally visited him at his cave bringing sick friends or relatives. Antonio Garcia once took such a one to see El Solitario. They both had to bend down to enter the Hermit's cave

Plate 25: The "Hermit." Undated Photograph. The Mary D. Taylor Collection.

entrance, and Antonio had to support his friend because he was weak from the long ride and the climb to the cave. As they entered the cave and stood upright, they could see the dim figure of the Hermit sitting motionless behind his fire. There wasn't very much in the shelter—a straw pallet with the Hermit's cloak folded over it, a slender torch fixed in a miner's spike into the wall of the cavern. He had only two clay pots, casuelas, over the coals. One was to cook the cornmeal he made a mush from; the other held water already boiling. He always seemed to know what was needed before the need presented itself. There were some roots and herbs tied together and suspended from a second spike in the cavern wall. As Antonio Garcia stood with his friend silently before the Hermit and his fire, Fray Juan María regarded the sick man quietly. He finally rose, selected some of the dried herbs, and dropped them into the already boiling water. Antonio eased his friend down to sit by the fire and crouched beside him still saying nothing.

Antonio Garcia had ridden a spirited horse, leading the horse his friend rode. Garcia's horse was now hobbled below the cave and he fretted, whinnying and rearing restrained by the hobbles. With still no words among these three men, the Hermit's gaze never left the sick man. Rising finally, Fray Giovanni brought a gourd with some of the hot, brewed tea to the man who was ill. Antonio helped him hold it to his mouth until he had swallowed all of it. The Hermit returned to his place behind the fire and spoke, looking at his friend Antonio. "Loose your horse from his restraints. He will remain where he is." Antonio rose and went out to free his horse as the Hermit had bidden. The sick man for the first time raised his head and looked at the Hermit. He rose without help, smiled and made the Sign of the Cross. El Solitario's gaze never left the man, and he rose also. When Antonio returned, he saw his friend standing and smiling; he also blessed himself, inclined his head toward the old man. Antonio Garcia and his friend, now walking erect beside him, went down to their horses. Antonio's horse was quiet and remained so as Antonio mounted. Both men rode out of the canyon towards Mesilla.

In April, 1869 the Hermit descended from his cave and walked to Mesilla towards the house of Antonio Garcia. The family saw him coming and heard the small bell tinkling on his staff. Teresita ran towards him and when she reached him, he smiled and put his hand on her head.

There was in Garcia's home that day a man of dubious reputation who had come to ask Antonio to lend him some money. As the cloaked figure approached the house with Teresita, that man approached the Hermit and held out his hand, asking for his blessing. The Hermit stopped, and the wrinkled face became grave; he did not extend his hand. Instead, those amazing eyes seemed to penetrate the man. "Return the horse you rode here to its rightful owner. You are a thief. When you have made restitution, I will give you my hand and my blessing."

On that April afternoon, after he had eaten his usual simple meal, he motioned Antonio Garcia to come close. Teresita and her mother Soledad stood at a distance. Fray Giovanni María d'Angostino in a low voice said to his friend: "I am pursued even here. There are those who wish to kill me. I will return to La Cueva, and there will be a fire in front of the cave every Friday evening. When there is no fire, come and find me. They will have killed me." When Antonio's face expressed alarm and he started to speak, the Hermit raised his hand and blessed him. The Hermit then made the Sign of the Cross on Teresita's forehead and on Soledad's. He turned and went back the way he had come. The Garcia family knew that this was his way; they said nothing and made no effort to call him back.

Antonio Garcia and others—Mariano Barela, Father José de Jesús Baca, and those of the Bermudes family—watched every Friday night for the Hermit's fire in the Organ Mountains. When the tiny, faraway glow appeared, they were reassured of the Hermit's safety. Sometimes on Friday, clouds hung down in storm; lightening flashed, thunder rolled in early April rain. The Holy One's friends came together waiting for the clouds to lift so they could see the glow of the distant fire.

Plate 26: "Grandma" Teresa Fountain was the author's source for much information regarding persons and events in La Mesilla. Photograph taken in the 1950s by Mary D. Taylor.

On one night, that of April 16, there was no fire visible. And the night was clear with full moon and bright stars. Since Garcia was the Hermit's good friend, it was he who set out at dawn on horseback to see what was wrong. He rode steadily over the sands of the foothills approaching the mouth of the canyon which led to La Cueva. He tethered his horse when the ascent to the cave became too steep and made the rest of the climb on foot. As he approached the cave, in the ever-present silence of the mountain, Antonio's throat tightened and grew dry in apprehensive premonition.

Stooping to enter the cave, Antonio straightened and looked around. The Hermit was not there; his books and his pallet, and some small articles lay neatly in their places. But his gray outer clothing and his cape lay folded neatly in a corner. Antonio Garcia felt sure by now that something had happened to the Hermit; he searched near the cave but found nothing. He descended from the cave and rode back to Mesilla. On his way, he met two sheepherders taking their sheep toward the mountains. To Antonio's questions about the Hermit's whereabouts, they shook their heads. At the promise of five dollars in gold if they found him or his body, they agreed to come to Mesilla if they should find the Hermit.

On Sunday morning just after sunrise, one of the sheepherders came into Mesilla and told Antonio Garcia that they had found the body of the Hermit. He had been dead for several days by this time, but the shepherd declared that the body was in perfect condition, and that the coyotes and vultures had not gone near it. Mariano Barela, Antonio Garcia and a few other men began the trip to the Organ Mountains. When the sheepherder led them to where the body laid it was some distance from the cave and he lay face down. Since he had on only his underclothing, it seemed that the intruders had come at night while he slept on his pallet. As his friends turned him over, they saw that his fingers were still around his crucifix. The position of the body indicated that he had knelt and then was dealt a heavy blow to the back of his head, and he had been lanced twice through the upper back.

At the Barela home, his friends gently laid the Hermit on a bed to prepare his body for burial. When they removed his underwear, they found an iron ring with spikes around his thin waist so deeply imbedded into the flesh that they were not able to remove it. They clothed him once more in his gray coat and trousers and wrapped him in his cloak. Then his friends carried him in a wooden coffin to the Church of San Albino where he lay in state. Candles were kept lit throughout the night, and during these hours parishioners knelt and prayed the Rosary. It was the custom that the decades be recited aloud all night at a *velorio*; the adobe church was crowded all night, and the glow of many candles shone through the arched windows and lighted the open doorway where those who loved this man found a place to kneel. Father José de Jesús Baca knelt near the open coffin sometimes leading the rosary; others led the recitation during the long hours of the night and early morning.

Father Baca said the funeral Mass the next morning; then the pine coffin was carried to the cemetery; men alternated in bearing the box on their shoulders. The inscription on the wooden cross which was to be replaced with a carved stone read:

"Don Juan María de Justiniano Hermitano del viejo y nuevo mundo. El muriô el dia 17 de Abril de 1869 a los 69 arias de edad y los 49 haviendo profesado una vida rara en este siglo XIX."

"Don Juan María Justiniano Hermit of the old and the new world. He died April 17, 1869, at the age of 69 years, having professed for 49 years a rare life in this XIX century."

His death and funeral are recorded in the *Libro de Entierros* at San Albino's for May 2, 1869:

Juan Ma. Agustiano, adulto de nacion Ytaliana. Solitario de los desiertos, no rescibio Sacramentos par haber muerta asesinado en la sierra y para que conste firme.

Juan Ma. Agustiano, adult from the nation of Italy. Hermit of the deserts, he did not receive the Last Sacraments because he was murdered on the mountain and I testify to all this.

Father Baca signed this entry.

It was later speculated that Apaches had murdered him. But this seemed unlikely to residents of La Mesilla for several reasons. The fact that he had repeatedly indicated to friends in Paso del Norte and in Mesilla that he would be murdered by men who had followed him—perhaps this had been the reason he left Italy, traveling through South America, Central America, to New Orleans, up to the beginning of the Santa Fe Trail and had followed the Romero y Baca wagon train to New Mexico. It was said that after his death in the Organ Mountains, a few Italian gold coins changed hands locally. Some thought his assassin could have been apprehended easily, but that no authority made a move to apprehend him. There were many such rumors. A charge was brought against Father Manuel Cháves of St. Genevieve's Church in Las Cruces for complicity in the murder of the Hermit. He was kept in jail one night and then released. Angered and resentful, the people of Mesilla and Las Cruces accused those in power, citing even the French prelates' influence in the detention of Father Cháves. There were some who claimed it was politically motivated to discredit the Catholic Church and the "native" clergy. A Las Cruces correspondent wrote that the charge was made from malicious motives with the object of removing him from his position of parish priest. "In the deplorable state of public morality in the melancholy times in which we live, it wouldn't be out of the question that the evidence in this case hadn't been calculated with dollars and cents, so it would be known before-hand what it would cost in the humiliation of this congregation." [222]

Nothing in the next two years could match the excitement over the death of El Solitario, Giovanni María Agostino. The mound of earth over his grave was kept smooth and damp by constant and loving care of those whom he had befriended and those who loved him. In the spring and summer fresh flowers were spread over the mound of earth and paper flowers were fastened to the arms of the wooden cross. Albert Fountain later carved the same inscription on a flat sandstone which replaced the cross. And even then the Hermit's friends brought flowers to spread over the stone. An iron fence was erected around the plot, and the place became a shrine throughout the territory. [223]

By midsummer, the acequia madre ran full as the rains greened the land from desert to western hills and eastern mesas. Mesilla was still and hot; the early mornings and late evenings were cool oases in a time of intense heat. It was then that Mesilleros filled ollas with water to drink; then wrapped the clay jugs in wet burlap to stay cool, and hung them in shade away from the midday sun. Bathing water was drawn from the ditches, also, and some mothers, when the water was not running so swiftly, brought children and washed them with amole, the soap plant, in the cool water. In the evenings and early mornings, bathers splashed in the waters of the acequia—in the heat of summer, Mesilleros could not resist the freshness of the water.

In July, 1969, the Mayordomo de Aguas of Mesilla, Santo Tomás, and Bosque Seco asked Daniel Frietze, Probate Judge, to notify the inhabitants of the precincts involved that they must help with fatigas on the acequia. It was necessary for the water to flow unobstructed by weeds and unnecessary earth so that all the fields could be watered at proper times. The *Jueces de Paz* were ordered to assemble the people, or peónes they had hired to replace them, with tools to hack the growth away. The cycles of seasons and life evolved with the old ways of seed, water, crops and harvest; of birth, life, marriage, and death. The *Río Intermedio*, Middle River, for an interim, was at peace as though life for the people there might at last be one of peace and prosperity. Unfortunately that was not to be.

Chapter 11 | THE RIOT OF 1871

Chuzas was always the game that attracted more people at a fiesta than any other. It was around this roulette-type wheel for which little colored balls could be bought in order to play, that *señoras* and señoritas, properly chaperoned, traded family news and gossip as they tried their luck. On the feast day of the Virgin of Guadalupe, all up and down the Río Intermedio, there were always chuzas tables decorated with colored paper and images of the Virgin. In Paso del Norte and in Las Cruces, in Mesilla and Doña Ana, on the *Dia de Feria*, the day of fiesta and fair, all work stopped for the celebration. There were musicians and dancers and cockfights, bullfights, and the smell of good food cooking. Since the twelfth of November, luminarias glowed in the mountains around El Paso del Norte, and in December they lighted the small, peaked hilltop behind Tortugas across the old riverbed from Mesilla. With these, the Indians of the valley lighted the way for the Virgin and heralded with matachin dances the approaching Fiesta de Guadalupe.[225]

By 1869 Father Ramón Ortiz, *cura parroco*, was gone from El Paso to the mountainous area of the Tarahumara Indians, and Father Real y Vásquez had replaced him in the old Mission of Guadalupe at Paso del Norte. This curacy was still the old Paso del Norte curacy and Mesilla was still considered an integral part of the Mexican diocese. San Albino de Mesilla parish also served small settlements nearby including Picacho, La Mesa, Chamberino and all the ranchos between those places. Father José de Jesús Baca cared for all these.

In the Mesilla Valley Indian depredations continued; mail riders were shot and robbed, wagon trains were ambushed. The Pass of San Agustín was several times the scene of Indian attack. The Indian question was further tortured by political maneuvering of growing proportion in 1870. There were some who wanted to deal with the Indians as peaceably as possible, drawing them in to areas of civilization and farming. There were others who rejected the idea of reservations and advocated the theory that "any good Indian was a dead Indian." Lt. Charles E. Drew, beloved of the Indians and able to talk with them and have them come in to the agency of Cañada Alamosa, was severely criticized by Republican John Rynerson. Rynerson held the Cañada Alamosa Indians accountable for most of the depredations in southern New Mexico. He claimed that Drew was babying the Indians, was being hoodwinked by them and that he operated through an alcoholic haze most of the time.[226]

Three times a week the mail rode into Mesilla—the mail rider threw down his mail pouches from behind his saddle and stepped into the station for a meal and refreshment before going on. Covered with dust from the trail, he looked forward to the fine food and wine of the valley of Mesilla. After the populous northern part of the trail, towns for the rider were farther apart: Sabinal, Lemitar, Socorro, Ft. Craig, Paraje, Alemán, Leasburg, Ft. Selden and finally Mesilla. It was up to him to make the fastest time possible, and slapping the reins on the horse's neck, he rode hard to get past the dangerous Jornada del Muerto to Mesilla. The next stop forty miles away was the station called alternately by now El Paso and Franklin.[227] Another route that traveled through perilous Apache country once a week was from Mesilla through Fort Cummings, Mimbres, Piños Altos, and on to Arizona and Los Angeles. Fort Stanton sent the mail through the high country through Tularosa down to Franklin. Mail riders had to be daring men, men of endurance, afraid of nothing, good horsemen. Many a mail was bushwhacked by the Indians, the rider left for dead and the mail stolen or scattered in the wind.

The colony grants were in peril by 1870, making life even more difficult for the settlers. Newcomer Anglos were moving in on the terrenos and ejidos, squatting and claiming the land they considered vacant in the Mesilla and Refugio grants.[228] On November 16 and 17, 1870, on the old plaza at La Unión, sometimes called El Pueblo del Refugio, Juan Simon Enriques stood up in public meeting and asked that a committee be appointed to divide officially and finally the lands of the Merced of Refugio. Juan Simon's hair was pepper and salt by now—he had been one of the first settlers—and a light breeze that autumn day brought a shock of it across his forehead. He held his hat tightly in two hands in front of him, and those hands showed the cracks and calluses of hard work and weather. He said that every day they were seeing their rights being violated, and this was through their own negligence. And that negligence was in not recording the deeds properly when Ramón Ortiz had given them to the colonists in 1852. There was a murmur of agreement and approval of Juan Simon's words. As a result of those words came the appointment of José María Garcia as commissioner to protect the Merced, and to apportion the vacant lands to proper residents of the grant. A register was to be made with each property owner entered. They would register the hortalizas; straighten up the streets and the *callejones*. The president of that association was to be Juan Sisneros; Juan de Dios Garcia and Leon Alvarez were to be secretaries. Immediately they all took heart, and upon the conclusion of the meeting, there were abrazos, slaps on the back, handshakes—just as though it all were settled—just as though there would be no more trouble now that they had all agreed on this action.[229]

On Sunday, April 13, the same sort of meeting was held in La Mesilla. Locust blooms were fragrant in the night winds, but during the day, and especially this one, stronger winds coated them with fine dust. Citizens met in the courthouse at the corner of Parián and Guadalupe streets to consider ways to counteract the same type of landgrabbing which had gone on at Refugio. The Honorable

Pablo Melendres, Juez de Pruebas, Probate Judge, of Doña Ana County was elected president of the assembled landholders, and John Lemon and Daniel Frietze were elected vice-presidents. A commission to study the situation was named: J.D. Bail, N.V. Bennett, Cristóbal Ascarate, Thomas J. Bull and Ygnacio Orrantia. After the Surveyor General of the Territory failed to come and after several delays, the commission levied a tax for expenses in proportion to the land and solares each settler possessed in order to complete the task themselves. It began to appear hopeful that the Mesillero could retain land granted to him and triumph over the claim jumpers.

In the Spanish section of *The Borderer* for March 15, 1871, *El Fronterizo*, words were directed at Hispanic landholders. Sympathy for early settlers was evident; advice was given in regard to registering land grants. The writer declared it necessary without delay to put the proper and pertinent documents in the hands of competent lawyers to assure titles—this was to protect those persons born and reared here and those who had made their homes in Doña Ana, Mesilla, and Refugio. There was no doubt as to the legality of these grants, he said; nevertheless, the government required all titles that they might be properly confirmed. The paper further stated that the federal government knew nothing about the claims; that not even two people in Washington had ever heard of them. This year there would be a surveyor on these lands, but newcomers, seeing the terrenos and ejidos with no visible inhabitants, and believing them to belong to the government or, in fact, knowing that they had legitimate owners, occupied them. There was no law to prevent this. Each colonist must register his land.

The long fingers of politicians in Santa Fe were not idle in the fight over lands and they were familiar with the Mesilla Valley. Thomas B. Catron and Stephen B. Elkins were graduated from the University of Missouri in the same class. Catron came to New Mexico in 1867 after serving in the Confederate army during the Civil War. Shortly after, he became District Attorney for the Third

Judicial District, moving from Santa Fe to Mesilla to serve. In 1872, Stephen B. Elkins obtained from President Grant an appointment for Catron as United States District Attorney.

Stephen B. Elkins served the Union in the Civil War; after discharge, he was admitted to the bar in 1864 and moved to Mesilla. He served in the Territorial Legislature of New Mexico from 1864-1865 and as Attorney General for New Mexico from 1868-1869. He was United States District Attorney from 1870-1872 and became Territorial Delegate to Congress in 1873. Catron and Elkins formed a law partnership in Santa Fe, taking a prominent part in New Mexico politics during those years.[230]

They were expert land title lawyers. They helped adjudicate land grant problems in northern New Mexico and, by means of claiming a certain fraction of land in the grant as a fee for their services, were to become the richest landholders in the territory. And they had friends in southern New Mexico, fellow politicians who used the same methods and reaped the same rewards. There were other issues linked with land that involved the Santa Fe Ring of which Catron and Elkins were members; while professing to befriend the Hispanic population, they were dedicated in reality to acquiring their lands and to keeping many of them in bondage by favoring the extension of peonage. Suspicion rested heavily also on some of their Hispanic compatriots who allied themselves—crossing party lines, moving openly, moving covertly—with Anglo speculators. By 1870 Mariano Barela of Mesilla was deeply involved with the Catron and Elkins ring.[231]

The Anglo-American population of the Territory of New Mexico who were largely of the Democratic party, especially after 1869, took an anti-statehood stand in the battle over whether New Mexico was to become a state or not. All the governors of the territory up until 1871 had been appointed by the President of the United States; all were Anglo-Americans; all were dedicated to the principle of separation of church and state. However, if the governorship of New Mexico as a state were left up to the vote of the people of the territory, the ruling class would surely lose to a Hispanic vote for a Hispanic governor. And this would certainly change the status quo of the separation of church and state.

In this anxious year of the forming and cementing of party lines, 1870, the forces of this intrigue were working in the land grants of La Mesilla, Refugio, and even Doña Ana, causing the colonists anxiety, and the meetings which were held in La Unión and Mesilla were results of this feeling. The inhabitants of the river villages became even more suspicious and reluctant to commit themselves politically.

Below Santo Tomás where there were still lands to be settled outside the Miguel Sánchez y Baca Grant, a new town was being established. Settlers had cultivated fields there years before—those from Mesilla, Santo Tomás, and the Baca grant. Young apple and peach trees were planted in the old tradition of the grant; borders were turned in good loam soil; new plants set out with cuttings from the older vineyards and carefully tended. Cattle were contained in new log corrals; herders, using evenly plaited rawhide, made new ropes the size of a man's smallest finger. They frayed and fastened these ropes at *lazo's* end, and spliced in a loop with great care to carry the rope's play as it dropped over a running calf's head. All these things were done in attentive detail as it had been done in the first colony towns. Citizens applied for a *sito del pueblo* in 1871 for a town to be called La Mesa.

The chill of early spring still lay over Mesilla early in March, 1871. It was too early for the winds to start, and fog rose from the still undrained bogs of the great flooding of the late '60's. The old river bottom, grown over with *tules* and bosque, held the fog longer than other, higher areas, and moisture clung to harness and leather and made shadows of human figures. In ten minutes' time, when the sun broke through, all traces of mist had disappeared.

On the plaza of La Mesilla, cockfight pits still remained, and the owners and their cocks began to drift toward the center of town on weekends in early March. The fiesta of San Albino, traditionally held the first week of that month, was over and remnants of spent fireworks had been swept up, but the cocks and their owners still took bets on fights all day and into the night. Acequias were being cleaned for water to come from the river to the fields—the Mesillero either made his own fatiga or paid a peón to do his ditch cleaning for him. Calle Principal was gradually being cleared of sand dunes which restricted pedestrians, horses, and wagons. The few prisoners from the jail had begun once again with shovels loading wagons and hauling off sand.

As that morning drew on, Mesilleros were on the plaza, and because it was Sunday, the bells of the Church of San Albino rang for later Mass. The church was being renovated and whitewashed— there were still some heaps of white lime outside in the atrium, waiting to be ground and mixed with hot water and wheat paste. No one leaned against the church walls today lest some of the whitening come off on dark clothes. In a few days, the mixture would dry, and the white coat would be almost permanent. Conversations that day were political—of alliances and feuds, of friends turned enemies, of fear and misunderstanding. Political division was already deeply rooted in Mesilla, but political discussions were carried on mainly in English, and this tongue most of the Hispanic inhabitants of Mesilla did not fully understand. Even in Spanish, the talk was high-sounding, full of words and phraseology which humble people did not recognize. The working class man, the ordinary laborer, the *jornalero*, was content to tend his garden and work for wages. If he had a small plot of land, this became his realm. He tended the fruit trees lovingly, his hands cupping the soil around the roots of trees and grape vines, and around the plantings of chile and corn and squash. As long as his tiny garden was in order, his life was, also. But now it seemed that persons outside his little world expected him to pledge loyalty to some candidate for a cause he did not understand, and unless someone he trusted told him what to do in his own language, he felt lost. In Mesilla, most

of his loyalty was toward his patron and toward his friends, and he failed to understand the principles of the struggle going on. He did feel the necessity for a loyalty to something outside Mesilla. The heat of argument he felt; his heart pounded wildly with cheers and hurrahs at political rallies. He struggled to understand these intricacies and render loyalty, but to precisely what, besides his allegiance to the Church of San Albino and in turn to the Bishop of Durango, he never really knew.

In Las Cruces, much of the same atmosphere prevailed. The political parties were firming up, and the inhabitants in that town and in Mesilla took sides from political allegiances and from loyalties born of relationships through blood or marriage. But stronger than these feelings was a strong undercurrent of fierce loyalty to Durango and to the ancient mother Mexico. They feared the pretensions on their parish of the French prelates, Bishop Jean Baptiste Lamy in New Mexico until 1869 when the Vicariate of Arizona was created in New Mexico, and then they feared those of Jean Baptiste Salpointe, Vicar Apostolic of Arizona. News had come upriver of Salpointe's encroachment on Durango's jurisdiction in the parishes by Paso del Norte, news that he was pressing to take over the parishes on the American side of the river by El Paso and to annex to Arizona the Mesilla jurisdiction also. This preoccupation weighed heavily especially upon Mexican residents of Mesilla.[233] There was also the sad knowledge brought by refugees from an El Paso beleaguered by the struggle between Benito Juárez and Maximilian, that their beloved cura Ramón Ortiz had fled into the Sierra of the Tarahumara to escape retaliation for his imperial sympathies.

Lesinsky's store on the corner opposite St. Genevieve's Church in Las Cruces, boasted a coat of new slate-colored plaster, in contrast to others white or unplastered. The store was large and long, stocked with merchandise unequalled in the immediate area. For customers' pleasure, there were cigars, a barrel of wine, and a barrel of whiskey. Lesinsky, a Jewish merchant, also had an interest in the flour mill in Las Cruces and was a partner of Ernest Angerstein in a mercantile establishment in El Paso, Mexico. Close by the store were the offices of *The Borderer*, the Democratic paper, the only newspaper in the southern part of the state. Since Lesinsky professed to be a Democrat, the establishment quickly became the center for Democratic rallies, political decisions, and just plain talk.

The Borderer was anti-statehood in its editorials. It advocated annexation to Arizona as preferable to becoming the State of New Mexico. It also pronounced against public records kept in the Spanish language, English being preferred. And its editor, N. U. Bennett, advocated the reenactment of the peón law allowing peonage, recommending that the peón have the privilege of leaving, or trying to leave, within thirty days to escape being indentured.

In Santa Fe, *El Nuevo Mexicano*, a Republican paper, had advocated the year before that New Mexico should not be made a state until the law passed by the United States Congress abolishing peonage in 1867 was enforced in New Mexico. In 1871, the days of servitude of peónes were not ended as many claimed.[235] Many of them were older now, twenty years older than when they had first come with the beginning of the colonies. Many were grandfathers, with sons and grandsons who were peónes also in all practicality. They worked for wages, bought supplies from their master or from his store, and kept worn, small handmade books which recorded with strokes of pencils the degree of their indebtedness. They labored long hours for small wages, and the rows of marks of indebtedness many times were longer than the rows marking their working days. They had small garden plots, too, with frijol, chile, corn, and squash, but they did not own even these small gardens. The ground was part of the master's land, and the peón was expected to hand over choice fruits from his labors. The grandfather, his sons, and their sons carefully tended the land, and in the late summer and fall gathered the harvest. Strings of drying chile hung on ropes stretched from crooked poles, and the smell of it was enough to delight master and laborer alike. These men were expected to render their votes as well as their labor. Dutifully, most followed their masters.

From Mexico came increasing knowledge that the bright light which President Benito Juárez had shed was dimming. Once hailed as the savior of Mexico, now he barely held together vestiges of the promised democracy. On January 1, 1871, Juárez' wife died in Mexico City and two of his children had died in exile in Washington, D.C.; he himself was dead by 1872. Then began the *Porfiriato*—the long rule of Porfirio Diaz—which prolonged and intensified the undemocratic system of *hacendados* and peonage in Mexico.

During the last part of April, 1871, political unrest in Las Cruces and Mesilla began to crystallize. In Las Cruces, a Republican mass meeting was held and Manuel Nevares was elected president. Francisco Baldonado was there, as was Perfecto Armijo; George Maxwell and Benjamin Davis came from the precinct of Organ, and there were others, prominent men from all the precincts. It was a feverish meeting, where insults of "Copperhead Secesh" and "traitors" were hurled at the Democrats.[236]

On May 3, the Democrats organized in Mesilla. They called themselves the "Democratic Club of Doña Ana County," and they announced themselves the first of such organizations in the territory. The courthouse was full of men and cigar smoke. Since three o'clock, carriages, horsemen, and buggies arrived from Doña Ana and Las Cruces, accompanied by a wagon on which Thomas Bull's brass band played patriotic airs and the familiar tunes of Mexico. A carnival atmosphere prevailed; ladies in carriages twirled their parasols in time to the music and there were snatches of song as the procession moved along toward Mesilla. A time or two an exuberant horseman fired gunshots into the air. On arrival at Mesilla, it was apparent that the courthouse could not hold them all so they overflowed into the plaza—about six hundred persons filled the square cheering for the Democratic cause. From the courthouse tumbled benches, tables, chairs which were pulled under big shade trees for freshness on that May afternoon. Thomas J. Bull called the meeting to order, as well as he could for all the cheering and enthusiasm echoing up from the plaza. There was not much business or resolution accomplished that day, but with the noise, the flow of whiskey, and high-sounding words, the Democrats frenzied themselves into a state of anticipatory victory.[237]

In that May of 1871, the west side of Mesilla along the road which led to California, in the district called "California', petals from peach and apricot trees suffused orchards with pink; in the late afternoon, rays of sun slanted golden against adobe walls. It was here that the stage bound for Soldier's Farewell and Cooke's Spring—both stops on the stage line west—rattled on towards California. The driver cracked his whip above the horses' heads with energy, much to the delight of small boys playing in the fields. It was a brave showing, and the fact that Apaches were hidden along that long and dangerous road seemed remote in that agreeable time of evening in Mesilla. John Davis had just bought the old Orrantia property from Colonel Joseph Francis Bennett for one thousand dollars cash. And from the corrals of the station where the stage had loaded boxes and mail, there rose a slim column of smoke trailing from the blacksmith shop of J.M. Reed, wagonmaker. It was peaceful and busy in Mesilla in May; there was little sign of the trouble to come.

In the same issue of *The Borderer* in which José María DeCamara of Chamberino congratulated the Democrats on their coming victory, the Democratic paper printed a song made up for the Republican candidate José Francisco Cháves:[238]

I am a Republican; these are the qualities that recommend me: Don't you remember? A Republican should be a Negro. I am of good blood, the son of a fraile my grandfather; my compadre Pedro can help me with the penetentes where he lives.

There was more, and it was not any prettier. It seemed that at this point, there would be no

holds barred in the struggle for votes in the coming election. The verses referred to Cháves' background and to his appointment while in Congress of a Negro to West Point. The allusions to "frailes" and to the "penetentes" were garbled attempts to malign Cháves' followers.

In Mesilla in the months preceding the election, it became increasingly apparent that there were ethnic innuendos, spoken and unspoken, and written in the ribald rhymes which the paper had published. Residents of the Mesilla Valley were dismayed and confused by the issues and by the candidates themselves. The previous careers of these contenders for a congressional seat in the House of Representatives of the United States did nothing to dispel these feelings.

Both candidates were Hispanic: José Manuel Gallegos, the ex-priest, unfrocked by Bishop Lamy in 1852, was born in *Abiquiú*;[239] Colonel José Francisco Cháves, was born an aristocrat in Los Padillas. In truth, both Cháves and Gallegos were remarkable and admirable men, but in very different ways. José Francisco Cháves had led an exemplary life, a heroic one, and his career in both politics and the military seemed impeccable. A man of patrician background, a native of Valencia south of Albuquerque, Cháves drew the vote of those residents of the Mesilla Valley whose roots had so recently been in Mexico or who had early married into Mexican families and were firmly entrenched in the Mexican life of Mesilla.[240] Father Baca campaigned against José Manuel Gallegos who had, whether by his own fault or by a series of unfortunate allegiances, incurred serious animosities in New Mexico. Father Baca was outspoken in his criticism of Gallegos, of the French prelates of New Mexico and Arizona, and he was a champion of the Bishop of Durango. Gallegos was, however, the Democratic choice for candidate, and Father José de Jesús Baca of Mesilla was his determined Republican opponent. Dedication to Cháves was due in Mesilla and Las Cruces to loyalty to local candidates such as John Lemon and to the exhortations of Father Baca.

As growing animosities along the river valley became intensified, ordinary duties continued to take up much of the time of the Mesillero. The streets of Mesilla were still being cleaned of sand. Several streets had such large sand hills blocking them that wagons could not pass. Pedestrians found it difficult to walk—on the streets north of the church, black skirts and trousers always had fringes of fine dust along the hems. Clearing the sand away was a slow process for when one end of a street was cleaned it seemed the spring winds blew sand from the other end. It really did seem, as the paper said, that it would be easier to move the town. When the process of loading sand into wagons was going on, inhabitants drew their shutters closed and barred the windows. There was dust on everything; little ruffles of fine sand clung to the outside pediments over doors and windows. By evening tiny buttresses of sand had built themselves into the sides of doorways.

That same May, the new governor of New Mexico was reported en route to Santa Fé. Governor William A. Pile, another appointee to whom the Democrats applied the term "Radical Republican." He was never to attract either censure or approbation, except for the fact that he allowed the remaining archives of Santa Fe to be used by nearby merchants as wrapping paper for soap and candles.

Late in May, a more serious meeting was held by Democrats at the courthouse in Mesilla, and the ticket they nominated included Pablo Melendres as candidate for probate judge. Two years previously, he had run as a Republican against Daniel Frietze, Democrat, for this position and won. Now, of course, he was considered a traitor to his party and a turncoat. Mariano Barela was to be the candidate for sheriff; he had been defeated twice by Fabian Gonzáles, Republican, in other years. The campaign was warming up—old friendships were wavering; men began to clean their rifles, and to fill leather pouches with paper cartridges. Wooden pedals worked whetstones from which knives threw out small sparks, blades taking a fine edge.

Even though political plans and meetings occupied Mesilleros and residents of Doña Ana and Las Cruces, because for the most part it was a new thing and out of the ordinary, business in the mercantile establishments went on as usual. Frederick Burkner's store on the east side of the plaza of Mesilla as well as the Reynolds and Griggs mercantile directly opposite, sold dry goods, shirts and shoes, shawls and dresses, sugar, coffee, tea, and assorted groceries. There were provisions for miners: boots, drugs and medicines.

On a June morning, when Mass was beginning, the aroma of Burkner's coffee grinding assailed the senses of as yet unbreakfasted parishioners. It was the feast of Corpus Christi, the day when altars were erected and decorated with wheat, grapes, and flowers in Mesilla and Las Cruces. In Las Cruces a procession walked from St. Genevieve's. Surrounded by mayordomos of the parish in the center of the procession, Father Boneard carried the ciborium containing the Blessed Sacrament. He held it high so the people lining the streets could see it clearly, and rays of sunlight glinted from it. White satin and lace had been brought out from between folds of blue paper, polished brass and silver candlesticks gleamed against their altars. First as always the musicians came playing, and the parishioners sang the old hymns in Spanish as they walked. The summer morning was cool, and the music was heard softly up and down the streets. Then they played the music of the community: marches, waltzes, polkas. Little boys of the Visitation Academy carried banners, and the girls and young ladies in white followed. Dolores Duper had arranged a magnificent altar across from the Montezuma Hotel—this was the procession's first stop.[241]

A similar procession was held in Mesilla, and the seven customary altars were set up in the plaza and down Calle Principal. At four o'clock in the afternoon there was Benediction of the Blessed Sacrament in the newly whitewashed church of San Albino; parishioners sang a cappella the old remembered songs, the music they had brought from the pueblos below El Paso. A fine incense haze hung over the altar; candles lit the adobe church. This was the beginning of real summer, a summer that seemed peaceful in prospect after so devout a beginning. The political agony to follow was remote on the traditional day of devotion.

Toward the last of June, Republican delegates from southern New Mexico began to arrive in La Mesilla for a convention. Every house had extra relatives; the two hotels were full. Don Blas Duran represented the local Duran family; Cesario Duran and Reducindo Duran came from Tularosa. Perfecto Armijo arrived, having taken this time from his business in Tularosa and Las Cruces. There were seventy-five delegates in the old courthouse, and although it was customary to close doors and windows against the heat of mid-morning, they were thrown open to allow people to breathe more comfortably. By noon the delegates were in shirtsleeves, and whenever a breeze stirred leaves outside in the plaza, there was welcome relief. Blas Duran became temporary chairman; Cesario Duran became president. Jacinto Armijo, Fabian Gonzáles, Rafael Bermudes, José Miguel Trujillo, Atilano Baca, and Marcelino Gallegos held lesser offices. At convention's end, nominations for county officers were: John Lemon, probate judge; Atilano Baca, Father Baca's nephew, probate clerk; Perfecto Armijo, sheriff; Marcelino Gallegos, treasurer. The fact that J. Francisco Cháves and J. Manuel Gallegos vied for delegate to Congress was overshadowed by the candidacy for local offices.

On June 29, 1871, as the district court was readying itself to function, a Tularosan appeared as juror. He had sold the last of his corn in order to come when called, and he had been sworn in open court. When the jurors were called, his name was not among those on the list—it was a political move—he belonged to the wrong party. The man was entitled to, but never received, eleven days' service pay and one hundred forty miles travel costs—he had been counting on this, using his corn money against that which he would earn at court.

Down in La Unión, León Alvarez, Republican, told Democrats Juan de Dios Garcia, Juan José Belarde, and Agustín Duran that *El Fronterizo*, the Spanish section of *The Borderer*, was not going to be published any more. This was untrue, of course, but the story made them cancel their subscriptions. The campaign was gaining momentum.

Mesilla was not oblivious to the ever-present Apache. News came that early in the summer, troops from Ft. Bayard under Captain Kelly, Eighth Cavalry, had pursued the Apaches who had stolen animals from Cienega. With him were twenty soldiers, seven citizens and a guide intent on overtaking the thieves and recovering the stock. The trail led up into the shadowy Gila country, south into the Burro Mountains, to the Tucson road, then into the Chiricahua Mountains. It was still snowing in the Sierra Madre when the troops finally found the Apaches. Fifteen Indians were killed, Bigfoot among them—the head man whose foot measurement was thirteen inches. In the Sierra Madre where their wikiups were, the soldiers found jerkied meat, mescal, salt, sugar, calico, and domestics—evidence that these Indians had been given rations at an agency. There were also indications of raids upon villages and wagon trains: a doll's dress, unfinished; a priest's cassock; and a blanket with the Mexican flag and ensign in the center; Mexican coins, military papers. There was even a very small bag with black curly hair inside. The troops took everything they wanted: scalps, carved leather saddle bags, beads, baskets. Captain Kelly ordered everything else burned, and the Eighth Cavalry detachment started on the long journey back to camp.[242]

The Indian wars were to last a long time. In another savage battle, Salvador, Apache chief of the Cañada Alamosa colony and reputed son of Mangus Colorado, was killed in a fight with Kelly's troops west of Silver City. The *Santa Fe New Mexican* published a double-edged, sarcastic editorial about Agent Orlando F. Piper's handling of the colony during these Indian crimes—which were apparently committed by Indians from the agency—and about these encounters in particular. Attempts were made to settle the Apaches on reservations, but civilian and military demagoguery frustrated such plans. Dan L. Thrapp said it best: "Few ever seriously considered acceding to their simple request to remain where they were, in their traditional homeland where they had been raised, and whose mountains, valleys, deserts and canyons they knew and loved." [243]

The Apaches never really gave up; only Loco, the headman of the Mimbres tribe had indicated his willingness to settle down at the agency at Cañada Alamosa. Other headmen waited to see what would happen to Loco before they compromised their people. And even then, on an occasional outing without permission to leave the agency, the warriors would come back quietly, some with bloody scars, weary, silent testimony to illegal raids. Gomez, the old fox who was supposed to have died, surfaced again and raided wherever he pleased. The Indians were back to their old tricks of raiding in Mexico, then running back to the southwestern United States for cover; then back to Mexico again when depredations in New Mexico and Arizona forced them to flee.

There were those who still wanted to treat the Indians with kindness and lead them into the white man's civilization, only with gentleness. These were the residents who understood the Indian hesitance over abandoning his own heritage to come into the agency to adapt to the white man's way of life. And then there were those who advocated force, annihilation, punishment. They rejected efforts of Lt. Charles E. Drew, agent for the Mogollon, Mimbres, and Gila Apaches, and Vincent Colyer of the Federal Indian Commission to establish the Apaches on reservations. The fact that the Indian had been there when the white man came, that the hunting grounds of the Apaches were now the pastures of the white man's cattle had been almost entirely overlooked or rejected.

Even though the Apache presented an everlasting threat, the year 1871 found citizens of southern New Mexico more interested in politics than in anything else. After the polarization of the Civil War, men were beginning to resolve themselves definitely into being either Republican or Democrat. In Las Cruces, Lesinsky, for all his free whiskey and cigars, appeared to be losing business. His mercantile establishment had become Democratic Headquarters, and in the early part of July, when one hundred degrees had been measured in the shade, men stood about in their free time on shady street corners. Every discussion, every argument, and the acceleration of the campaign made men sweat and fan themselves with their hats. Excitement was the sweltering generator of anger and dangerous thoughts. In Mesilla, they sought places under locust trees or any patch of shade they could find. Standing still and exerting no energy made for a little coolness. Moving about and thrashing arms in gestures made it become necessary to loosen collars and remove coats. Generally in other summers, the accepted policy was to stay in out of the heat to rest during the hottest part of the day, from noon until three or three-thirty in the afternoon. But early in July Democrats had held a political rally in Picacho,[244] and on the way to their respective homes, had stopped in at Lesinsky's for one last drink. The band was with them, and anywhere there was music, a crowd gathered, no matter what the time. Republicans began to gather that afternoon as well as Democrats: there was camaraderie and the whiskey flowed freely. Then the heat began to intensify the effects of the whiskey; the crowd became quarrel-some. Each side began to cheer for its own party "...la libertad y el partido republicano," and "viva" many times. The cheering became a roar, and a Democrat hit a Republican over the head with the butt of his pistol after a particularly slurring remark. Immediately, those who lived close by started home for weapons. Those who had come in wagons, and had left rifles in them, began to back away toward those wagons. A silence settled over the crowd broken only by muttering and the moving of feet. A woman cried out and then leaders who were sober or, at least, more sober than the rest, moved among the crowd with calming tones, and cajoling and joking in English and in Spanish, brought some order to the group. Sullenly the Democrats got back into carriages and wagons, mounted horses and slowly rode on. Republicans tried to resume normal conversations, and then they, too, dispersed.

A burst of patriotic enthusiasm greeted the Fourth of July, 1871, in Mesilla and in Las Cruces. On both plazas, flags were raised and the Grand Army of the Republic with its blue-uniformed veterans of the Civil War was proudly prominent at each celebration. A hiatus in political arguments made the birthday of the nation a celebration. Cannonades were fired for each state in the Union. There were fireworks made by local Mexican artisans, the Declaration of Independence was read in English and Spanish, and in Las Cruces, close to *The Borderer* office, Mrs. Christian Duper set out an elegant meal. There were toasts to the longevity of the Union in both towns.

Soon after the Fourth of July, Rafael Bermudes, one of the most prominent men of Mesilla, a Republican, made it known that if any more disturbances occurred between the parties of the county, the Republicans would go into Las Cruces and burn down Lesinsky's store. He reminded Democrats that their candidate for sheriff, Mariano Barela, was already under several indictments of assault with a deadly weapon.

There were marches and counter-marches almost every Sunday—processions, speeches, waving of flags. Rallies were held in Doña Ana, Picacho, Mesilla, Santo Tomás, La Mesa, Chamberino, and La Unión. Men wore arms and carefully loaded their pistols. Long coat tails were folded precisely so as to give the hand ready access to the gun belt. Sometimes a knife handle protruded from the right boot. To the "vivas," both sides began answering with shouts of "Death!" to the Radicals or Democrats. Most of the words were said bilingually, but even if they were shouted in one language, most residents caught the drift through the tone of voice.

In the election year of 1871, there were a few men who were more prominent than the rest. Pablo Melendres attracted the attention of the press and of the voting public because he had changed parties.[245] He was tall and fair, good-looking with a well-kept beard. He was a fine speaker and was one of the first colonizers of Doña Ana. Such a man was interesting and an easy subject for conversation. Where he had been a Republican before, he was now a Democrat. Probably it had all stemmed from the violence of the 1867 election—there never had been an entirely peaceful election in Mesilla under the Mexican government or now during American territorial days. There were murders in 1867, changing of voting tallies—it was reported that even John Lemon had drawn a line in red ink through a total, changing it to less than the crossed-out sum and defeating Perfecto Armijo. Lemon had run as an Independent in that election, supporting Charles P. Clever. As a result, Melendres felt he had been betrayed, and that John Lemon was the Judas. Now in 1871, he revealed to *The Borderer* even more intended treachery at the hands of the Republicans. In his letter to the paper, he claimed that Ygnacio Orrantia, Clerk of the Probate Court, had come to Melendres at his home in Doña Ana about noon on the thirteenth of July. Here he laid out a plan claiming it would make Melendres one of the greatest political leaders of New Mexico. Speaking in a subdued voice in the closein dimness of the great old house, Orrantia offered to Melendres the position that Rynerson held at the customs house—maybe one hundred twenty-five dollars in gold or silver. If this offer were agreed to, Orrantia and Melendres would go into Mesilla that evening, meeting with Rynerson, Father José de Jesús Baca, and maybe even John Lemon. All Melendres had to do was to rejoin Republican ranks and keep it quiet until just a few days before election. If he were asked why he had changed parties, he could say he'd always been a Republican; he had just joined the Democrats' ranks to insure the ruin of the Democratic party. Ygnacio Orrantia, according to Pablo Melendres, ended his request by saying that the Republicans would win the election even if they had to do it with guns, bullets, clubs, rocks, or blows. He added also that he wanted secret control of the office of Probate Judge until just six days after the election; this way he could have jurisdiction over the ballot boxes.

Plate 27: Thomas Bull Band playing in a Mesilla street in the 1880s. López family photographs, RG 84-159c, Rio Grande Historical Collections, New Mexico State Library, Las Cruces, New Mexico.

Pablo Melendres refused the alleged offer, wrote a letter to the paper reporting what had transpired, and no one seemed to doubt his word. The Republicans viewed this revelation and its effect with great agitation.

In these hot summer months, the Democratic paper also reported a "love-test" in the Republican camp. John Lemon had, at a campaign gathering, confessed that he had thrown out enough votes to defeat Perfecto Armijo in 1867. Now that they were on the same ticket, he publicly asked pardon from Armijo. The paper jeered at the abrazos, embraces all around, and taunted the Republicans with this humiliating development.

An advocate of the Republican cause, Father José de Jesús Baca told his parishioners that if Mesilleros voted for a Democratic ticket including as representative the ex-priest José Manuel Gallegos, they would see the Texans come again and they would lose their property and their religion. This, to many residents, was the ultimate in maledictions. The Texans had been the nemesis of Mesilla and New Mexico many times, and, if Father Baca said this, surely it would come to pass. He was also obliquely referring to the threatened takeover of Mesilla by the Vicariate of Arizona: the French prelate of that vicariate was, from time to time, visiting the parishes on the middle river from Las Cruces to Ysleta in Texas, sending threatening or cajoling messages to their pastors or the Bishop of Durango regarding Arizona's jurisdiction. The Republican vote of many of the Mexican residents of Mesilla and the surrounding towns within Father Baca's curacy was solidified. Fear set in on the plaza of Mesilla especially; plans were made and weapons readied. Neighbor became suspicious of neighbor; family members drew together in clans. On the street, eye contact was hard to come by.

July found processions still marching up and down through the river valley towns of Doña Ana, La Mesilla, La Mesa, Santo Tomás, Chamberino, and Amoles. Rallies were held in each of these towns by both parties. As excitement mounted for the September election, anger, defiance,

and fear enveloped the communities. The two principal newspapers, the Democratic *Borderer* of Las Cruces and the Republican *Weekly New Mexican*, of course, gave conflicting accounts of the successes and of the numbers attending these meetings. Unimportant incidents were magnified into confrontations; words were misinterpreted. It was a time to be a careful reader. There were some niceties of these processions; not all were showers of insults and threats. On one occasion, the Democratic ladies showered their favorite marchers with bouquets of flowers wrapped around with slips of papers inscribed with poetry. And there were frantic efforts on both parties' sides to garner votes. Speeches were made before great numbers of people; candidates spoke before a few idle persons on street corners. On every block of every town gathered knots of concerned voters, most of them quiet and thoughtful. In Richard Coleman's blacksmith shop in Mesilla, the sound of his hammer on the anvil was louder than any other sound. Passersby could see the fire rising up in his shop, the waves of heat, and the sparks. A few kept up the din of slogan shouting, but for the most part, toward the middle of August, residents of the valley became apprehensive and quiet.

On August 5, 1871, Pedro Telles from La Unión wrote to John Lemon asking clarification of a point which had been troubling him and some of his neighbors: the articles of the Treaty of Guadalupe Hidalgo stated certain rights of a Mexican citizen after he had resided in United States territory for more than two years. Did he, or did he not, on such grounds, have the right to vote in the coming election? Pedro Telles and his neighbors could remember other elections in which their votes had been challenged because of their former Mexican citizenship.

The Feast of San Lorenzo fell on the tenth of August. The first bells rang at eight o'clock in the morning for High Mass, and men with big hats and dark suits and women in black rebozos hurried along Calles Parián and Principal. Some carried bouquets of late roses and green leaves wrapped in moist cloths to keep them fresh until they were put before the statue of San Lorenzo in the Church of San Albino. Some of the older people and some of the younger ones had come to Mesilla years ago from the pueblo of San Lorenzo below Paso del Norte, and this was a day of special devotion for them. The rejoicing of the bells was a welcome relief to the air of tension that had lately lingered over Mesilla. A woman, white lace shawl over her head, hobbled along on her cane, a bright pink cascade of Miguelito held tightly in her hand. Years ago she had brought the seeds from Camargo in Chihuahua, and today she had brought the flowers for the Feast of San Lorenzo.

The calm of the feast day was soon over. The newspapers kept bringing up the fact that John Lemon, candidate for Probate Judge, had never taken up arms for his country as had some of the veterans of the California Column. They repeated again and again the fact that he had had several government contracts; in fact, one of them involved the building and maintaining of Ft. Selden since 1865. The paper claimed that in one political demonstration, Lemon had waved the flag in the face of a Democratic Union veteran and shouted "Hurrah for the Union!" This didn't sit well with Democrats. After all, he had never born arms. They had forgotten or never knew of his imprisonment by Confederates during the Civil War and of his close brush with death at the hanging episode in Doña Ana. Besides this, Democrats claimed that John Rynerson, when Protestant Bishop Randall descended from the stage dressed in black with a white Roman collar, had said that he was a new Catholic priest whom the Democrats had brought here to work for them politically in Mesilla and Las Cruces. Rynerson retorted that this news was published in the English portion of the paper, but not on the pages in Spanish.[246]

The early September election was approaching. Ylario Moreno, son of the Democratic candidate for the territorial legislature, on the way to a *baile*, was shot at, but not hurt. Manuel Barela, always a contentious young man and brother of Mariano Barela, Democratic candidate for sheriff, camped one August night on the outskirts of town with a party of cattle drivers. Someone out in the darkness away from the campfire, called out to him. He answered but did not rise. There was a volley; the shots were wide, nicking the harness on one of the wagons but hitting no one.

In the latter part of August in one of the last meetings in the campaign, a hopeful crowd gathered at Doña Ana to await José Manuel Gallegos. Doña Ana was almost completely Democratic, and an enthusiastic reception was planned for their candidate. Pablo Melendres was there waiting, as was California Column veteran John Barncastle and his wife. Otto Bombach, carpenter from Prussia, Herman Greenwald and Peter Ott sought out the shade of a portal to wait. At the edge of the crowd, some of the troops from Fort Selden's cavalry had come up to sample the excitement. Older residents of the town, colonists for more than twenty-five years, were subdued, apprehensive, for although the town was Democrat in sentiment, there was deep fore-boding for relatives in other areas along the river where allegiance was divided. When Gallegos arrived, there was a night meeting, more speeches, some drinking. Anticipation of a final procession downriver, planned days before, woke a sleepy-eyed Doña Ana the next day. Again there were wagons and carriages and ladies with parasols. The band played, and thunderheads gathered in the northeast. There was not the slightest trace of breeze. Six miles they traveled to Cruces where citizens from that town and Mesilla met them and joined the caravan. Thomas Bull's band tuned up again, seated on a large, flat wagon bed. The air was still, but above them the clouds rolled in a separate current of air. José Manuel Gallegos' buggy was near the front of the procession, and at intervals he mounted a fine bay mare. He was a good sight on horseback—in his sixties, he still sat easily and erect in the saddle. When the procession finally arrived at Chamberino, the old Chamberino down in the valley, the Church of San Luis Rey was glowing with light. The twenty-fifth of August is the Feast of San Luis Rey de Francia, and the celebration was underway. There was a full moon and a feast of food lay on tables in the placita. Republicans with the Gamboa band were already playing patriotic tunes interspersed with Mexican polkas and paso doble. When the Democratic band arrived, each amicably took turns at playing. Over in front of José DeCamara's home, a small platform had been built and here Gallegos made a rousing speech. His old training as an orator had not forsaken him. There was a grand ball until daylight with both bands and local musicians playing.

At dawn on the twenty-sixth, the return trip upriver was getting underway with thoughts of tomorrow's rally at Mesilla. The snorts and whinnies of horses cut through dust curling up from moving hooves; there were sounds of leather slapped against rumps of horses—harness snapped into place. The ladies waited in Mrs. Horace Stephenson's parlor, fanning themselves, and at last the word was given that all was ready. The twenty-seventh of August was to be another such celebration and rally, and it was a cheering thought that all had gone so well in Chamberino on the Feast of San Luis Rey.

Dawn in La Mesilla on August 27, 1871, was soft and cool. The oppressive heat of yesterday was tempered; there were a few people on the plaza to savor the fresh morning. August clouds on the southeastern horizon again promised rain. As the sun rose higher, Mesilla began to bustle with preparations for the expected political rallies. This day had been selected as appropriate for demonstrations of party solidarity by both Republicans and Democrats, and as Mesilla had not known such specific loyalties before, there was anticipation of excitement on both sides. Both bands tuned up early—the Gamboa band in the plaza and Thomas Bull's band down by Lemon's mill. The notes of a trumpet practicing lingered faintly and echoed from street to street. And there was the usual activity in town; bells for Mass rang early today. Down by the corrales where horses and wagons were kept on Calle Principal two young men put the finishing coat on the greasing of wagon axles with crushed fruit of tuna cactus for the long freight haul down the Camino Paseño on the west side of the river near the mesas.

As the day grew warmer, concerns which ordinarily occupied Mesilleros were forgotten: the constant threat of Apaches, the daily routine of survival. Even though secretly prepared for the possibility of violence, the Mexican residents quickly attached fiesta atmosphere to the political meetings; they put aside their daily tasks to devote this day to the excitement in store. Even the windows and doors, which ordinarily would be drawn against the heat of late summer by noon, were left open—no one wanted to miss anything.

The plaza began to fill with people early; the hard-packed earth had been dampened to withstand the scuffing of many feet. They came from Las Cruces, Doña Ana, La Mesa, La Unión, Chamberino, and all the small populations in between. There were groups of men who talked of politics and strategy; there were others who knew little of politics, and who only followed Father Baca's views. And there were those who were advocates of Gallegos and his Democratic supporters. Many were little concerned with anything but the excitement; almost all were still confused as to the issues.

José Manuel Gallegos, Democrat, suggested a joint discussion, a debate—leaving out personalities and reviewing only the issues. The Republicans wanted to air the political history of the candidates together with their private and social lives. And since the parties could not agree, it was decided that the Democrats would rally on the plaza in front of the Reynolds and Griggs store, and the Republicans would hold their meeting down Calle Principal from the plaza in front of the mill.[247] Gallegos would have his forum, and Father Baca and John Lemon theirs.

Before the hour set for the rallies, Horace Stephenson—being apprehensive of the outcome in the face of preceding threats of violence—rode in from La Mesa with one hundred armed men. In a little while, after talking at length to members of both parties, he and his horsemen returned in the direction from which they had come.

The scheduled meeting was at least half an hour late in getting started. By now, the heat was intense; there was not a movement of air anywhere except for an occasional light breeze high up in the trees around the plaza. The separate meetings began and Democrats and Republicans, each bearing banners, marched through the streets of Mesilla. That afternoon most men had been drinking, and as the heat increased, alcohol took its toll. The processions began to chant "Viva;" then other less complimentary words took the place of the "Vivas." Epithets were traded. There was a slight and abortive confrontation as the processions passed each other—I.N. Kelly, a printer who had been on the staff of *The Borderer* told John Lemon that the interruptions in the Democratic rally by the Republicans were unnecessary—many said later that this was friendly exchange. The processions formed, broke up, and reformed as the afternoon grew later. Ill will was mounting.

In front of the Church of San Albino, Teresita Garcia was swinging on the gate in the center of the adobe wall around the churchyard. She pushed back and forth with her foot, and each time she swung outward, she had a clear view of the plaza. She watched the processions and wondered. The air was electrified with tension, and even small Teresa began to be afraid. She had come to hear her grandfather Antonio Garcia play in the Republican band, and the music made a good beat to swing back and forth on the gate. The Honorable José Manuel Gallegos, Captain Sena y Baca,[248] and William T. Jones had just finished addressing the Democrats in the plaza, and the ladies had retired to the home of Mariano Barela on the west side and were seated in the long, cool sala sipping lemonade. Teresita noticed that while the speeches were being made, a man interrupted twice and was shouted down by the crowd. She recognized him as Ygnacio Orrantia, a friend of her grandfather's. Most of the Republicans had gone to the home of Thomas Bull, and then there was a period of quiet. Teresita almost gave up swinging on the gate because everything seemed to be over. Then she saw groups of men reforming into lines, and both parties marched out of sight—Teresa could

still hear the music. By now, it was nearing five o'clock and still Teresa swayed back and forth on the gate. As the lines of men came back toward the plaza, approaching the area in front of the church, she stopped pushing her foot and peered through the closed gate. The lines began to counter-march around the plaza, each band trying to outdo the other in decibels of music. Suddenly she heard loud words—Teresa knew they were angry words. Through the swirling crowd she lost sight of her grandfather and his horn. She left the gate and the churchyard and began to run home. As she ran, she heard what she knew to be a shot, and she began to cry because she was afraid.

When the leaders of the Democratic and Republican processions met in their countermarch around the plaza, there was a second's awful silence, and then louder and angrier words which then became shouts. Someone fired a shot into the air—they said later it was Apolonio Barela. Someone thrust the American flag into the face of I.N. Kelly, the printer, reportedly a former Secessionist, who was at the forefront of the Democrats. Then more shots. It was said that upon being insulted by Kelly, John Lemon declared that he'd just as soon shoot him as anybody else. And then Kelly struck Lemon in the head with a heavy wooden club, either a pick handle or a wagon spoke. There were many more shots—the printer fell to the ground with five or six bullet wounds. Felicito Arroyas y Luera fired at Kelly first, and then fell dead himself of a bullet wound. The building belonging to Mariano Barela took several bullets, and the ladies inside began to scream. Little Teresita Garcia was nearly home by this time, crying out for help from her grandfather. The procession lines broke; the marchers and onlookers alike began to run for escape routes through the narrow streets leading from the plaza—several were trampled. There were some who crawled on all fours trying to avoid the bullets. Men scrambled to the housetops, and the buildings of Mariano Barela and Frederick Burkner on opposite sides of the plaza became party bastions in the fighting. Pedro Garcia, in one of the last actions on the plaza, had held a gun on Mariano Barela against the doors of the latter's

Plate 28: Men gathered in a Mesilla Street in 1880. López family photographs, RG 84-159b, Rio Grande Historical Collections, New Mexico State Library, Las Cruces, New Mexico.

Plate 29: Boys playing in a Mesilla Street in the early 1880s. Doña Ana Historical Society Photograph Collection, MS 0153002. Rio Grande Historical Collections, New Mexico State Library, Las Cruces, New Mexico.

home; Garcia in turn, had been shot in the back, whether mortally or not, no one knew.

Earlier in the day on August 27, General Devin from Fort Selden had passed through the towns around Mesilla and Mesilla itself and had declared the situation peaceful and that a military presence was not necessary—he was now on his way back to Selden. A courier was sent to overtake him.

In Las Cruces, news quickly spread of the riot in Mesilla; a man just come from there rode jubilantly through town brandishing the knife he had sunk into Kelly's body. The dreadful scene on the plaza was now abandoned. Men still fired sporadically from rooftops at any movement below. Several of the wounded had been spirited home; it was said that nine men died. Some still lay on the plaza; others disappeared as it grew dark. Only a few dared go to help the wounded: Dr. Black had been shot through the hand as he attended a man lying there; Dr. U.H. Woodworth did his best to help, and W. Heintzelman and the Reverend Francisco Bouvard from St. Genevieve's parish in Las Cruces had tried to stop the killing, but now retired also.

Troops from Ft. Selden arrived about ten o'clock that evening, halting in front of Colonel Jones' residence on the Gran Plaza. Cavalrymen galloped into the plaza, order was quickly restored and the firing stopped. Residents of La Mesilla began to come out of their homes and carry away the wounded and dead.

John Lemon lay in his home on Calle Principal, head bandaged, still alive and conscious. From his deathbed he dictated a will to John Bail—a short will because had had not much strength left, and not much time. Because a verbal will was declared as binding as a written document, the brief statement was not hard to remember. John D. Bail, Oscar H. Woodworth, Jacob Appelzoller, and Jules J. Jeannerett were at hand as witnesses:

> I give all my property to my wife: Everything I possess I wish her to have: Everything belongs to her: She will have my debts: I give all to her,

and I wish her to be my Executor.

John Lemon died at ten o'clock that night.[249]

In every town along the river it was traditional that there be a group of mourners who wept and prayed at every velorio or wake. A velorio could not be considered successful unless there were those who professionally mourned—the greater the grief expressed, the more honorable the wake and funeral. Lazaro was one of these—he was crippled, having lost the toes on his right foot from frostbite one night when he fell asleep outside in the cold of a winter snow. This ancient man who mourned at all the deaths in Mesilla and Las Cruces sensed the tragedy, having been in Mesilla all day and late afternoon. A little after ten o'clock he heard the cries of sadness. Following the sounds of sorrow, he inched his way, supported by his staff, through the doorway of the house and through the relatives and friends of John Lemon and fell to his knees. He began to recite the Rosary, and tears ran down his lined face. He swayed back and forth still supported by his rough stick, and repeatedly struck his heart with a calloused hand. Luciana Pope de Lemon's lips moved silently with the words Lazaro recited.

From his camp with the detachment of the Eighth Cavalry near Colonel Jones' house, General Devin on August 28, issued the order that Captain William Kelly and thirty-five of Troop C would remain in the vicinity of Las Cruces and Mesilla: Fifteen troopers at Las Cruces and Lt. Goodwin and Kelly with twenty at Mesilla. These officers were to visit the detachment at Las Cruces once a day to discourage more violence.[250]

At ten o'clock on August 28, 1871, John Lemon's funeral was held at the Church of San Albino with Father José de Jesús Baca officiating. Lemon and his two daughters were the only burials ever made under the church walls.[251] In spite of the fear that still gripped the town a large number of persons attended the funeral Mass. The day was hot again; the sun overhead was bright against the threatening clouds in the east. Lemon's widow, Luciana, was dressed in black, *todo luto*, with a black veil over her face. Her son, John, Jr., wore a black armband and carried a black hat in his hand; Candelaria, Juliana, and Catarina followed their mother and brother behind the casket into the church. For John Lemon, the bells tolled long and melancholy; there were no words among the mourners. Violence had stunned the town to silence—even Father Baca's brief eulogy seemed to shatter the quiet that engulfed Mesilla.

Fabián Cortes and Felicito Lueras were buried from the church that day, too. The stillness and the hush even when words were necessary, the absence of people on the streets of Mesilla, the presence of the troops from Fort Selden—all this brought a remembered fear of violence and disaster.

These were not all the dead. More died in the fighting on August 27, 1871: Sotelo López and Francisco Rodriguez were two—there were said to be others, but no one ever knew for sure. No record was found of their burials. Neither was the number of wounded ascertained. Relatives carried them away; some of them crawled into the darkness and disappeared. Juan Barela, Juan de Dios Saenz, Francisco López, Leandro Miranda, Jesús Cubero, Hilario Moreno, José Quesada, Cesario Flores, Manuel Neváres, Jesús Calles, José María Padilla, and Jesús López were all reportedly wounded. Daniel Frietze narrowly escaped with four bullet holes in his coat. Mesilla was once more invaded by fear. The streets were deserted for many days.

Newspapers and mail riders reported that there were many Mexicans on the road to Mesilla from Paso del Norte and Guadalupe below on their way to help in what they considered a battle between the two groups. There were more angry words exchanged, and the coming election was anticipated with apprehension. There were still political speeches being made by candidates in Mesilla and Las Cruces. Major Kelly held his detachments ready.

Shortly after the political riot in Mesilla, an advertisement, a token of the ethnic consciousness of the times and an effort to thwart the Republican influence on Mexican residents, appeared in *The Borderer* on September 20, 1871: "Wanted: A good boy who can read and write English and Spanish, to make a devil of. As the Radicals pitch into us occasionally, we need some of their own weapons. Hence the want."

To ward off the entrance of evil into households in Mesilla, crosses of salt were retraced over doorways. During the last days of August and the first days of September, the rains came and the weather cooled a little. But even so, doors were opened cautiously—a crack to see who called before opening. After dark, no light showed at a window; no door was left unbarred.

The election was set for the fourth day of September, and before the election and even before the riot in Mesilla, several citizens and officials had asked that they be allowed to vote in other precincts: Fabian Gonzáles, Republican candidate for sheriff; Felipe Guerra, Juan Guerra, Pablo Garcia; Perfecto and Pablo Cháves; Fletcher Jackson. When election day came, the people of Mesilla banded together in groups to vote, fearing to go singly to the polls. Entire family groups of men went together, sometimes with knives or pistols hidden, fearful of attack. And there were guards posted to insure the safety of the ballot box. The dismal mist of September rain, welcomed in other years, was now accompanied by rushes of wind and it swirled around the men at the polls. Some were in mourning, wearing black armbands—there was no joyous, bustling activity in Mesilla now. Anxiety and intimidation kept many residents at home—some were already secretly packing belongings to depart from Mesilla.

Toward the middle of September, Judge Johnson of the second judicial district was in Mesilla to investigate the riot. The town had been, for the most part, without a judge for four years, and now through hindsight, the extent of disorder in the southern part of the state was realized.[252]

A grand jury for the county was called: among the members were Ygnacio Orrantia, Frederick Burkner, Cesario Durán, Manuel Banegas, J. Edgar Griggs, Thomas Bull, and Ramón Nevares. Juan José and Evangelisto Cháves from Picacho were excused. A Territorial grand jury was also called in the face of the disaster. Neither of the juries ever functioned. Judge Johnson handed down indictments: "The Territory vs. Felicito Lueras" for drawing deadly weapons—when the judge discovered the Lueras had been killed in the riot, the charge was dismissed. Vicente Dominguez was indicted for murder. James Hutchinson, John Lemon and Michael Cronin were indicted for assault with intent to kill—Lemon's indictment was dismissed also when the court became aware of the details. Mariano Barela, Felis Armenta, Juan Bernal, Francisco Baca, Santiago Ackenback, Rafael Bermudes, Silvestre Maese, Juan López and Julian Torres from Tortugas were all indicted, but nothing ever came of the indictments. The grand jury was to convene in November; Judge Johnson came in October, reportedly "cleaned up his docket" in November, and left for Grant County.[253]

A little over a year later on the twenty second of December 1872, William Logan Rynerson married Luciana Lemon de Pope in the parish house a few streets away from John Lemon's tombstone in the wall of the Church of San Albino. The ceremony which Father Agusté Morin, the new French priest, performed was short; the occasion was not joyous. Many of the residents of Mesilla and Las Cruces wondered at the union—a little more than a year had passed since John Lemon's death, and Rynerson had been his friend and fellow Republican. Bishop Salpointe had given them a dispensation to marry because of the difference in religion and because it was Advent, the week before Christmas. Thomas Bull, Francisca Bull, Joseph Reynolds, Mariano Barela, James Edgar Griggs, and Eugenia Ascarate Griggs were witnesses.[254] William Rynerson, Luciana Pope de Rynerson and the Lemon children went to live in Las Cruces after the new year. It was said by many that their home was not a happy one.

Chapter 12 | MIGRATION

As political rivalries built in Mesilla for the 1871 election, the channels and fine lines of political reasoning were not clear to many of the colonists and their descendants. But their loyalties and affections were strong and fierce, and most rendered fealty to their candidates along with a loyalty to their former mother Mexico. The colonist now was an American and had technically all the rights and privileges of voting and citizenship, but through the years of invading armies and confusing flags in the back of his mind were the dual banners of Nuestra Señora de Guadalupe and of the Eagle and the Serpent, the tricolor of Mexico. In the months of July and August, a movement spread to find new lands within Mexico because, as had happened before, when ever the people along the river had become confused, frightened and threatened, they looked south to Mexico and what they had considered in the past as home. There had been exodus before, and now another was planned by Republican party members who surely must have felt that they would lose the election.

It was said afterwards that Ignacio Ascarate had told them that the land around Ascención in Chihuahua was good land, and that Mariano Samaniego of Paso del Norte had procured for them from Benito Juárez permission to colonize there. The document the prospective emigrants drew up was headed "Comición Central de la Emigracion de Acención," the Central Commission for Emigration to Ascención:

Los Caballeros Marcelino Gallegos, Favián Gonzáles and Vicente Mestas are named for a preparatory meeting to be held on the ninth of the current month and year. The Commission is for the Fifth Precinct of La Mesilla in order to write down the names of all and each one of the Republicans who desire to emigrate. This registration will declare the family members and what each family possesses, notifying them at the moment they sign that on the nineteenth of the same month at nine o'clock in the morning, there will be a meeting of all the emigrants in the house of Don Rafael Bermudes in La Mesilla to set the time of emigration and to let all those interested know the details of what has been done and the steps taken.

It will be your duty to return on the day cited to the Central Commission named below with blank form attached to this so it can be signed by the persons [to be] in your charge.

Blas Duran, Ygno. Orrantia, Central Commission.

Apolonio Barelal A. Ancheta, Secretary.

After the riot Republicans in Mesilla made ready to immigrate to Mexico to Ascención in northern Chihuahua. Colonel Emilio Langberg, military commander of the line of colonies established twenty years before to act as a buffer on the Mexican side of the boundary between the United States and Mexico after the war between those two nations, had suggested this location as a good one in 1850 for such a colony.

It was near the Ojo de Ascención where Langberg reported wood, water and forage plentiful. Juan Ascarate from the Ascarate family near Janos recommended it highly as a refuge for the defeated Republicans who felt that Mesilla could no longer be their home. One hundred and twenty families were to have emigrated by 1872, and Democratic residents of the territory felt secure enough to taunt the Republicans:

Se van, se van
Se van los republicanos
A Ascención
Porque los democratas

Ganaron la elección.

The Republicans are going
To Ascención
Because the Democrats
Won the election.

Some of the *ancianos* remember other words, too, words describing the fracas in Las Cruces where behind the cottonwood trees there were political machinations in Lesinsky's store along with the selling of sugar and bacon. These words were, of course, a Republican reply to the Democratic taunt.

And so the defeated Republicans sought refuge in Mexico again as other Mesilleros had in former crises. The first archbishop of Durango, Don José Vicente Salinas y Infanzón, had finally conceded in 1872 the ecclesiastical jurisdiction of the territory of the Mesilla to the new Vicar Apostolic of Arizona, the Right Reverend Jean Baptiste Salpointe. But Mexican residents of the Río Grande del Norte, in view of their latest misfortunes, were unwilling and unable, as had been the case in earlier disputes, to forsake their loyalty to Durango and accept the authority of the new French vicar of Arizona. As they were encouraged in this loyalty by Father José de Jesús Baca and discouraged by the tragedy of the riot in Mesilla, they turned toward Mexico. Here would be the haven they were seeking.

When the first wagon train left Mesilla in the fall of 1871, hope for a better, a more tranquil life rode with it. Some of the women wept; their dark rebozos served to wrap against the chill and to wipe away their tears. The smaller children in the wagons cradled close to the women; the older boys walked alongside the wagons with the men. Whips cracked above the heads of oxen and mules; others herded cattle along the trail. The movement out of town was heralded with the taunt of the Democratic song again, but none of the departing Republicans turned a head to notice and none looked back. Slowly the covered wagon train left Mesilla along the road to Janos, a long, pale caterpillar undulating, swaying toward its destination.[255]

They were disheartened at the first glimpse of the Ojo de Federico and Ascención—the land was intermittent desert and bosque and had been alternately washed by floods from heavy rains and then left dry, arid and cracked in the sun. There was much to do to improve the earth, and as soon as work began, the emigrants took heart, the effort making them feel as though they would succeed.

The town was begun as Mesilla had been, with chozas and jacales—huts of mud, logs, and branches. Families settled there in clans again; extended families formed placitas, brothers and brothers-in-law came from Mesilla to help. A town was established, houses built, streets laid out, a church begun. The Apaches attacked them relentlessly from the nearby recesses of the Sierra de Carcay, but Mesilleros knew how to defend themselves. Remnants of the old Mesilla Guard and their sons, now grown, mobilized as they had before against the Indians hostile to new colonists. Land was broken, and fields were watered from the Ojo de Federico; once again capricious waters alternately blessed them and cursed them.[256]

During some of this year, 1872, Bishop Jean Baptiste Salpointe was in residence in Las Cruces pressing for the full power of administration in Mesilla. On January 6, 1872, Father José de Jesús Baca wrote to Cura Don Antonio Severo Borrajo that, according to priests from Las Cruces, Salpointe had been called back to episcopal headquarters because the Papal order had been received for the taking over of Mesilla and its jurisdiction. None of the Mexican priests had heard that the Bishop of Durango had received any Papal order, and for this reason refused to yield to Arizona.

By the end of the year, December 13, 1872, Father Baca wrote to Bishop of Durango José Vicente Salinas:

I suppose by word of Sor. Cura del Paso del Norte that Your Excellency knows the decision of the Vicario Apostolico of Arizona to take possession of these churches which belong to the jurisdiction of Your Excellency and which are within the boundaries of the United States...

But as that resolution has been already placed in execution, I find it my duty to notify Your Excellency...After the Vicario Apostolico notified us of the aforesaid decision, the Sor. Cura of San Elizario, the Sor. Cura of El Paso, and I met to see if we could avoid a scandalous conflict so injurious to the faithful. The step which seemed most judicious to us was to obtain an interview with the Vicario Apostolico [Salpointe was at Las Cruces] and to beseech him that he suspend his resolution until this question could be determined by the proper order [word from Salinas that he had received the Papal order]...Unfortunately he did not, and the act has been consummated. The first day of the present month after I had celebrated Mass and the other functions of the day, the Vicar appeared at the door of the church which already had been closed and immediately commanded that I turn over the keys. I refused...as I had not had any order from my prelate to turn over the jurisdiction, I had no order to turn over the church. Then I asked the intervention of the civil authorities, but they, even though they were in my favor, could not take any part in the affair...After this, the vicar withdrew from this pueblo leaving a priest to administer it in a private home ordering him to take charge of the rest of the churches which are within the comprehension of this filigrecia...This, Your Excellency, is the situation in which the priests who administer these churches find themselves, especially I who find myself [residing] next to the one who has involved all of us in this unfortunate affair. I have to see with sadness the terrible division among the faithful, some of whom are on one side and some on the other. I must, at the same time suffer the most grievous insults made to my person as much by the same French priests as by their followers who always have been enemies of the church. I believe my life in danger...My remaining in this administration can only heighten the difficulties because of my feelings against the French clergy which quickly spread to the faithful...I beg Your Excellency to...let me go

to administer a new town that has formed in a place called Ascensión within the boundaries of Mexico and six leagues from the presidio at Janos. The inhabitants who have populated this town were all residents of these same places which I administer. They have emigrated to their native country seeking the protection they lack here...they have only been there a year...I will [get a church built as quickly as possible]. [257]

On July 9, 1872, these new colonists at Ascención sent a petition to the Bishop of Durango stating that they had returned to their native Mexico and asking that they might receive Cura José de Jesús Baca, still in Mesilla, as their resident priest. He was old and tired, but he said if they wanted him and if Bishop Salinas gave his permission, he would go to them.[258] He served there until his death in 1885.

Some of the Ascención colonists—finding life too hard, constantly menaced by Indians, and seeing their crops fail in the fickle, capricious waters from the spring and river—returned to Mesilla and settled into life again. Teresa Garcia[259] was one of these. Fabián Gonzáles, Remijio Saenz, Apolonio Varela, Atilano Baca, Juan Holguin, members of the Duran family, the Mestas, and Rafael Ancheta formed the nucleus of those who remained in the new colony.

For those who remained in Ascención, the independent spirit of the Mesillero never died. Political divisions rose again; leaders developed devoted followers; government influence, this time Mexican, was again introduced to the colonists. Little by little, some of them took the long road north returning to the valley of Mesilla—in Ascención there were more rivalries and embattled positions in which deaths occurred. The colony grew with arrivals from Janos and Corralitos; the Mesilla population there diminished as hopes grew cold, and from time to time the old settlers from Mesilla and their sons came home again.

Others also had moved away from Mesilla in earlier times of trouble and heartache. The Civil

War and the flooding river gave motivation to some to look toward the Sacramento Mountains to the East. They found a road to where the green, fertile banks of the Tularosa River beckoned. There it was quiet and they could open fields in peace.

Some of the family of Duran went there: Reducindo, his son Victor; Cesario, his son Pablo; Francisco Baca, his wife Paula Saucedo; José María Villaseñor; Nieves and Antonio Duran; Domingo and Nicolas Duran. Juan Mirabal had gone there, he who had ridden with the Mesilla Guard, and Remigio Saens went, José María Pino and José Barela too.[260] Some of these older men saw the land, set stakes and had gone back to Mesilla for the others to come.

Among the settlers who came later to the Tularosa in family groups or clans from the valley of Mesilla was Atilano Gallegos—he had an ox train and did freighting and would ultimately come into mortal conflict with the Texans. José Delfin came, Maximo Padilla, Claudio Lechuga, Perfecto Telles, José María Bernal—all farmers. The Bruzuelas looked forward to opening fields along the Río Tularosa; the family of Lucas Escajeda and some of the Guerra clan came.

They should have been reluctant to cross the San Agustín Pass—Apache attacks there had been frequent and disastrous. A few years before, merchant Perfecto Armijo and a military escort had been ambushed there. Indians suspected of belonging to the Cañada Alamosa Agency had killed a corporal, wounded a private, and had killed two horses.[261] Mesilla travelers were always wary, sending scouts ahead, watching rims of canyons as they passed, eyes searching among scrub oak and pine on hill profiles. The thought that heartened them was that the old warrior, Captain William McCleave commanded Ft. Stanton up on the Bonito River,[262] and having survived the Civil War and endured the presence of the California troops in Mesilla, Mesilleros knew McCleave, by his reputation and experience as a match for the Apache. Knowing that the Tularosa would be within that soldier's jurisdiction, they dared once

again to think of opening fields in untilled, new ground.

Settlers from the Valley of Mesilla[263] marked off a townsite, a *hortaliza* for houses and orchards; they dug acequias from the Tularosa river to the fields of wheat and to the garden plots. They also brought their Catholic faith with them; the church of San Francisco de Paula was a small jacal at first, but it served them until a larger adobe one took form. They brought their customs, their cures; *matachines* danced on feast days as they had always done along the Río Grande.

In April and in May each year, a fiesta is still celebrated honoring at once the defenders of Round Mountain, on April 17, 1868, when Apaches attacked the settlers, and honoring San Francisco de Paula to whom they promised the dedication of the church if they were successful in battle. Along the Río Grande, remembering the ceremonies of their Indian forebears, it was the occasion of a candlelit procession up Round Mountain and there were bursts of gunpowder lit as cannonades under heavy anvils, and matachines danced before the Church.[265]

They dug in, as they had at Mesilla in the early years and in all the colonies along the Río Grande. They called them chozas,[266] homes that were half holes in the ground—the top halves with jacal-like structures, thatched. Each of the forty-nine blocks had its little choza, its garden and water brought to it by the acequia and smaller ditches dug from that.

The scatterings of trouble began before 1871 between Anglo-Texans, some ex-soldiers, and the Mexican settlers. It began just as it had in the pueblos below Paso del Norte after the War with Mexico, and as it had at a later date in the Mesilla Valley with an earlier invasion of Anglo-Texans. By now, the settlements around the Tularosa were ethnically much like those of Mesilla, Las Cruces, Refugio, and Doña Ana in the 1850's. There were a few Indians, remnants of the Manso and Piro, and mestizos; there were immigrants from northern New Mexico, from Jarales, and from Belen. Anglo-Texans and other Anglo mixtures had come here from Missouri, Kentucky and New York. The old concept was at work: any land lived upon or held by "Mexicans" was seen as vacant; to most Anglos, they were not real citizens and had no right to own land.

Along the Río Tularosa, in the summer of 1870, wheat fields[267] shone golden yellow; they curved and waved in winds from the foothills of the Sacramentos. Up higher in the canyon where the river cut its channel, newer immigrants—Anglos and even some of those who had come from the Mesilla Valley,[268] dug ditches to water their new fields. This, of course, diminished and almost cut off the flow of water to the fields below and to the hortalizas, the blocks of the townsite.

One morning late in that summer, 1870, Antonio Jaramillo struck the bank of the acequia a furious blow with his spade. The trickle of water in the ditch had not even come up to the gate where it could be let into the fields. Clods of dry dirt rolled down into the stream and the water separated, running sparsely in two thin trickles. Within one half hour, Jaramillo, some of the Duran family, Teodocio Carrillo and other farmers along the acequia were striding up the ditch toward the blockage of the water. A quarter of an hour later, they were at the first of the dams; Father Pedro Lassaigne had joined those bent on destroying the dams. This time Antonio Jaramillo struck a blow which made a difference—the wall of the dam crumbled and the water ran freely downriver again. A shout of victory went up. At the second dam at the mouth of the Cañon de Tularosa, the men found owners of the higher fields in company with José Cháves, Constable. They had established fields on the upper river and their labor had helped build the dams. Now they stood in the mud of the released ditch water, both sides threatening each other, waving guns about.[269]

Ultimately, the dams were repaired, and charges were filed. Such phrases as "malicious mischief," "chancery," "assault with intent to kill," "resisting an officer" appeared in court dockets for 1871.

On May 18, 1871, L.G. Murphy, Probate Judge for Lincoln County, published a proclamation:

Inasmuch as sworn declarations have been made by citizen residents within the disputed boundaries of this County and that of Doña Ana and who have taken up homes in conformity with the land laws of the United States within those disputed boundaries that armed persons in defiance of the law have interfered by force with the rights of said citizens notwithstanding that all the affairs in dispute have been submitted to the decision of the next term of District Court which will be held for the County of Doña Ana. And inasmuch as said declarations state that their lives as well as their property are in imminent danger with such unlawful people, that they have no hope for help from any other place. Now, for that reason, I, L. G. Murphy, Probate Judge in and for the County of Lincoln, issue this my proclamation, calling upon such armed persons to desist in their illegal actions while the affair is pending in District Court, and I state to such persons thus occupied that they will be held in strict account for their actions as disturbers of the public peace, and, accordingly, punished.

In testimony of which I have placed my signature and the county seal today, May 1 1871.

Lyon Philliporski, secretary for Judge Murphy.[270]

Thus the settlers from the Mesilla Valley and others who were, for the most part, interested only in survival of their families and their fields and crops, became embroiled in a small war which was at once political, ethnic, and which had at stake the most precious commodity in all this little world of green river banks and rocky valleys: water.

By that same month of May in 1871, the year of political upheaval all the length of the Río Grande, the year of the defining and cementing of party lines, matters climaxed. Pablo Melendres, Probate Judge of Doña Ana County,[271] who would ultimately be responsible for the written and legal distribution of land to the settlers, wrote an answer to a plea for help from Reducindo Duran, remembering that in January, 1869, Lincoln County had been separated from Doña Ana County and that the Tularosa townsite was positioned exactly on the dividing line between those two counties: he said that he had received Duran's communication of May 11 which told of events in Tularosa which concerned the bad treatment of Duran and others who had killed three or four persons. Melendres stated that neither the authorities who were after Reducindo Duran and his allies nor any other authority at Tularosa had any power over them. The authority to prosecute this crime, he said, rests with officials of Doña Ana County. The Judge encouraged Duran to get someone like Perfecto Armijo to act as Justice of the Peace—his name alone would calm things down; that the *alcalde de las aguas* (ditch boss) would be respected and his orders obeyed. Pablo Melendres further castigates Father Lassaigne, for he said that Lassaigne had said Melendres was a Mexican and had no authority at all; he invited the priest to infringe upon the law and see how quickly he'd be brought before Melendres to be judged. In farewell, the Judge enclosed for Duran a list of the Democratic candidates in the coming election and asked for his vote.[272] The settlers from Mesilla who had come to the Río Tularosa with high hopes of molding new lives free from persecution and highhanded political manipulation, were old hands at solving difficult situations by themselves. They had fought this same fight over water again and again through the years, and while they were not resigned to it they were accustomed to self-reliance. They had fought oppression, famine, disease and Apaches by themselves; there were clans bound together by blood ties and those of compadrazgo. The sanctuary they had sought had become a battleground.

Cesario Duran[273] and a few others went back to northern Chihuahua as did other families. Other settlers continued to fight. By 1873, a new eruption of violence disturbed that year's shaky peace.

Troops from Ft. Stanton were called in[274] to restore order as a result of a new and determined effort of the Mexican settlers in the lower lands to free the water from the Cañon de Tularosa for their crops. Spring was giving way to summer, and the water in normal times would have been cascading down the canyon in abundance. But again, newer fields lately opened drew little water from the acequias. The wheat, the corn, the chile, the orchards lay in the delta plain below waterless in the sun, and, among the early settlers, tension grew. On the 24th of May, an armed band of thirty-five men came up the canyon from the drying fields, grim and silent, determined to destroy the upper dam and release the water for their own use. Felipe Bernal and José Marques led them, and they marched ahead of the others, hats pulled down firmly, rifles cradled in their arms. The guns were cocked, fingers light on the triggers. The others came behind them, some already veterans of the same battle two years ago. These were rough, dark-faced farmers, bitter before this new battle which must be fought. The first dam they reached was that of Andrew Wilson who was a sometime-freighter and had a Mexican wife. With the tools some of them carried, they broke his first dam, and then the others below it. Then they returned to town after telling Wilson and his friends that they would never have another drop of water for irrigation.

On the twenty-seventh, a Tuesday, they came again, the same men, and broke the same dams which had by that time been repaired. This time they camped, took up fortified positions, and threatened to shoot if any man lifted a hand to mend a dam. Tuesday and Wednesday they stayed there watching, and on Thursday, a few of the new settlers, came out to repair one of the dams. There was an exchange of fire, and the Mexican farmers retreated to Tularosa.

At Ft. Stanton, news had come of the trouble. Lt. Wilkinson and a detachment of five men rode to bring a letter to the alcalde of Tularosa. But the soldiers were fired upon; the fire was returned and one of the settlers was killed. The lieutenant forthwith returned to the lumber mill where families not directly involved were fleeing for safety. Frightened messengers were dispatched, messages sent to no avail. The Mexican settlers divided their group—half below the mill and the other half circling around behind the mill. A hail of rifle fire decimated their lines. They ran.

Reinforcements came from Ft. Stanton with a mountain howitzer, and the next day the soldiers rode with the gun rattling along the stony road toward town. The citizens of Tularosa made a defiant gesture at blocking the road; they were poorly armed but determined. The captain sent a messenger to ask Father Lassaigne, parish priest of St. Francis de Paula Church, and some other prominent citizens why so many armed men guarded the road where it crossed the ditch into town. They declined to give a direct answer: Father Lassaigne, José María Marques, Julius Boiseller and William Ostic.[275] A curious confrontation arose between military allied with some of the townspeople and others of the hortaliza. Brother against brother, Anglo against Mexican, and Father Lassaigne with his hoe again across his shoulders where many of the men held rifles. The military finally entered the town of Tularosa, and occupied it.

Father Lassaigne argued his own case in court and, with the assistance of Perfecto Armijo, succeeded in quashing the indictment. His brows were still a straight black line above his eyes and there was no one who dared to oppose him or meet head on that direct black gaze.[276]

In the case handed down from the bench of Warren Bristol, Judge of the Third Judicial District, the question of the use of the waters of the Tularosa River was settled finally on July 5, 1874.[277] The argument between the two factions, including the division of the Duran family, over the common ownership of the acequia which brought water to the fields and gardens was dismissed from court. But it would come up again in a future incident; the whole of Tularosa hoped that this would not be the case. Cesario Duran and his neighbors could use the water for household and kitchen purposes and watering stock. They could use the water, and they might increase the flow by opening springs and

other means; the first, the original settlers, those who dug the acequia in the first place had a right to the water which superseded all others. Judge Bristol found both sides at fault, each had to pay his own court costs and a sharp rap of the gavel on his desk ended the case. The judge had made it clear that these settlers were to agree on the distribution of acequia water, and, most important of all, that those who would deprive the original settlers of first right to water by damming or by other artificial means, would be subject to injunction.

This was a fine-sounding opinion and it had the ring of decency to it, and many respected it. But ways were found around it. In time, many of the early settlers lost their lands because the lack of water caused crop failure, and because many who paid their taxes were not marked as paid. Wily newcomers took advantage of ignorance and fear to begin large holdings by these means. Men from the California Column were among these: Andrew Wilson, Wesley Fields, John Waters, Robert Dickson, George Nesmith, and others.[279]

Troubles, then, did not end for the men who had come from Mesilla to Tularosa with such high hopes, but many survived and became ancestors of those who live there today. Others became disheartened and either returned to the Mesilla Valley or went to Ascención, to Casas Grandes, or to Janos in the State of Chihuahua, Mexico. The endless cycle of migration and immigration began again as it did in the Duran family. From Northern Chihuahua it had swept through the Paso del Norte area, up through the Mesilla Valley, to the Tularosa, and now back again to Chihuahua.

As residents of Mesilla and other towns of the middle Río Grande slipped away into other areas which seemed healthier politically, populations of the Mimbres area and San Vicente (Silver City) were augmented. And the green box canyons, El Valle de Santa Barbara and El Ancon de San Diego, beckoned settlers with easy and controllable access to water. Here was the old paraje of San Diego, the deep grass of the rolling hills down to the river which once watered Onate's expedition before beginning the long Jornada del Muerto. The backwaters of the river extending up to old Ft. Thorn had since dried out with the river moving to the west; arroyos ran only in fierce storms now—hence there were pastures knee-high in good grass ready for the taking. The towns of Loma Parda, Las Perchas, and Las Palomas lay to the north.[280] The middle river was filling with settlers, discontented in other areas, disenfranchised, debtors—good strong men whose eyes knew no horizons and whose strong hands and backs were already accustomed to breaking new lands, digging ditches, and planting fields. Many of them were the same settlers and their sons who had first colonized Mesilla and the other river colonies.

EPILOGUE

The Mesilla story does not end with the town's founding and the historical sequence of events which follow. That part of the story has been eloquently and accurately told in the preceding chapters of this book. Still, the process of what Mesilla has become and is becoming needs to be told. This brief epilogue begins with Mesilla's traditional phase from the coming of the railroad in 1881 to the present time.

Mesilla was the Doña Ana County seat from 1854 to 1881; in 1881 the county seat was moved to Las Cruces. With the coming of the railroad, Las Cruces then emerged as the growing commercial center in the Mesilla Valley. Mesilla had its local markets and continued to have direct communication on the Camino Real to Chihuahua in the south and to Santa Fe in the north. There was a connection with towns like Janos and Ascension in Mexico. And the local population had to be served; so the business establishments in and around the plaza of Mesilla were still vital to the local economy. There were political voices yet to be heard and Mesilla continued to have this voice.

Cultural elements were strong and the Church of San Albino continued to play its important spiritual role in the lives of the Mesilleros. The war with Mexico, the Civil war and the San Antonio Mail and the Butterfield Stage brought people of various backgrounds, languages and cultures to the town; these brought a valued diversity to Mesilla. Diversity was reflected in various business elements as well as cross cultural ties through marriage within the local population.

In time, as roads improved and as wagons and carriages were replaced by automobiles, greater opportunities for the purchase of diverse goods became more available in Las Cruces. This affected the local economy and business slowed and many establishments eventually closed. In time the Gamboa, Fountain, and Frietze and Alidib stores were the only businesses left. Their survival depended only on local trade and the ability of the locals to receive credit there.

The only advantage to the flow of traffic to Las Cruces is that plaza buildings were left relatively intact creating a representative architectural array of building styles which formed an historical image of the past. In time this would lead to various local, state and national historical designations.

As Las Cruces grew, citizens of Mesilla became alarmed that town would be swallowed up by Las Cruces and thus lose its identity. This resulted in a citizen petition to incorporate the town. Once incorporated, the Board of Trustees effected the transition from a county unit to a viable Town of Mesilla in 1959. To protect the ambience of the town, its cultural identity, its architectural flavor and the town's historical significance, ordinances were adopted, after great public debate, to carry out the intent of the original petition to incorporate the town.

Today the Mesilla plaza is a state monument, a national historic site, and a national landmark. Also, buildings surrounding the plaza which fulfill state and national criteria have received state and national historical site designations as well as national landmark designations. The Town of Mesilla was surveyed in order to determine if the core area could be designated as a state and national historic district. The district was so designated in 1980 and 1982.

Mesilla today finds itself at two extremes—sometimes a bustling site and sometimes a sleeping village as it once was. Two fiestas reflect the town's historical dimension and its ties with Mexico—*el diez y seis de Septiembre* and *el cinco de Mayo* celebrations. The plaza's *kiosko* or bandstand is utilized as a site for photography, a mariachi group, a wedding ceremony, a political event or as a site for child play. There is a reflection in the village of its historic past, its renewed vitality and the ever-present concerns that its people remain the true cultural element in the town.

One sees in Mesilla's architectural details the passage of time—the early period with buildings of worn curved rooflines, the more stately territorial with classical pediments and brick copings, the modified pueblo-territorial types, the Mesilla vernacular and the ever-present, towering above all, Romanesque/Mission Revival Church of San Albino. These buildings, and the people who work and carry on their daily lives within them, create the really important niche in the historic town.

J.Paul Taylor y Romero

NOTES

1. The Source

1. H.E. Bolton, *Coronado, Knight of the Pueblos and Plains*, (Albuquerque, University of New Mexico Press, 1964).

2. El Paso del Norte, the Pass of the North, is present day Juárez.

3. This location is approximately thirty miles downriver from the present-day San Lorenzo.

4. Fray Angélico Chávez, *My Penitente Land*, (Albuquerque, University of New Mexico Press, 1974), p. 154. The writer's inspiration here is Fray Angelico's description of Indian wonder as they witnessed Cortes' welcome of the twelve friars at Veracruz in 1524. Oñate's action may have been similar as well as that of other conquistadors under like circumstances.

5. Thomas H. Naylor and Charles W. Polzer, *The Presidio and Militia on the Northern Frontier of New Spain*, (Tucson, University of Arizona Press, 1986).

6. Census Records, Archivos de la Catedral de Ciudad Juárez (ACCJ); Archivos del Ayuntamiento de Ciudad Juárez (AACJ). The AACJ microfilms were examined before refilming took place. All AACJ citations refer to the old microfilm series unless otherwise noted.

7. A genízaro was a predominantly non-pueblo Indian living in more or less Spanish style, having been rescued from captivity among hostile Indians. He had forgotten his native tongue and spoke Spanish, sometimes brokenly. In northern New Mexico he had been settled into such communities as Belén and Abiqúiu, but by no means were these the limit of his habitat. They were settled in these places because they were excellent colonists and even, better fighters; they were stout defense against hostile tribes. In the region around Paso del Norte, genízaros lived, not in communities of their own kind, but integrated with the mestizo populations there. In fact, within Mexico itself, genízaros came to be considered mestizos; Fr. Ernest Burrus, S.J., Telephone interview, April, 1987. Steven M. Horvath, *The Sociological and Political Origins of the Genízaros of the Plaza de Nuestra Señora de los Dolores de Belén*, New Mexico 1740-1812. Ph.D. Dissertation, Brown University, 1979; Adrian Hermino Bustamante, *Los Hispanos: Ethnicity and Social Change. in New Mexico*. Ph.D. Dissertation, University of New Mexico, 1982; Fray Angélico Chávez, "Genízaros," *Handbook of North American Indians, Vol. 9, Southwest* (Washington: Smithsonian Institution, 1979).

8. Mrs. Edward A. Ayer, Translator, *The Memorial of Fray Alonso de Benavides, 1630*, annotated by Fredrick Webb Hodge and Charles Fletcher Lummis, (Albuquerque, Horn and Wallace, 1965); Father Gerald Decorme, S.J, *Las Misiones del Valle del Paso*, Manuscript, Microfilm, University of Texas at El Paso; Vina Walz, *History of the El Paso Area 1680-1692*, Ph.D. Dissertation, University of New Mexico, 1951.

9. Cleofas Calleros, Microfilm, Reel 4, El Paso Public Library; C.L. Sonnichsen Papers, University of Texas at El Paso.

10. The influence of Nuestra Señora de Guadalupe on the Mexican people, and particularly on the inhabitants of the Middle Río Grande del Norte, the *Río Intermedio*, cannot be measured. The miraculous quality of Juan Diego's experience is immaterial in this text. But the fact that Her image and the force of the faith She inspires is a primary factor in the ethnic awareness along the river cannot be denied. Her apparition in the sixteenth century on the hill of Tepeyac near the City of Mexico remains forever Indian, to be zealously guarded and treasured in the richest and humblest of homes as part of an indigenous, national heritage.

11. Herbert W. Yeo, *The Archaeology of Doña Ana County*, Manuscript, Branigan Library, Las Cruces, NM. The Jornada del Muerto (Journey of a Dead Man) is a waterless, ninety-mile stretch of the trail from Tonuco Mountain (San Diego) to the river near Fray Cristóbal. This jornada shortened the long journey to the north by not following the Río Grande. These ruts over the Camino Real follow a dry and elevated path which has few arroyos and which offered less exposure to Indian ambush.

12. Maude McFie, *A History of the Mesilla Valley*, M.A. Thesis, New Mexico College of Agriculture and Mechanic Arts, 1903; José María Ponce de León, *Reseñas Historicas del Estado de Chihuahua, 2ed., Tomo I.* (Chihuahua, Mex., Imprenta del Gobierno, 1910).

13. AACJ, Reel 2.

14. AACJ, Reel 3, 1827.

15. In 1836, Texas declared its independence from Mexico, and from 1840-43 tried to claim New Mexico under provisions of the Treaty of Velasco.

16. Aureliano Armendariz, Compilation, Federal Music Project in New Mexico, Works Progress Administration, ca. 1937, Mary Alexander Collection, Gadsden Museum.

17. Maude McFie, *A History of the Mesilla Valley.*

18. Records and documents in history refer to the village and parish in these several ways: Nuestra Señora de Candelaria, Nuestra Señora de Candelaria de Doña Ana, Santa María de Candelaria, and Doña Ana. The concept itself can be traced to the ceremony of the presentation of Jesus at the temple by Mary - the "Doña Ana" referring to the mother of Mary, Saint Ann. Today the parish is known as Our Lady of Purification which refers to the same biblical incident, Mary going to the temple after forty days for the Jewish purification ceremony after the birth of Jesus. The feast of Nuestra Señora de Candelaria falls on February 2.

19. Licencias, Archivos Historícos del Arzobispado de Durango (AHAD); Cleofas Calleros, ibid. In 1845, Bishop José Antonio Zubiria gave permission for an altar portatil, a portable altar, to be used at Doña Ana and for a public oratorio to be established there. An altar portatil is an altar that is transferable from place to place, a portable altar. An oratorio is a room, usually within a home, used for Catholic devotion and for Mass to be said whenever possible.

2. From Break of Day

20. The Metropolitan is the great Cathedral in Mexico City constructed by Spanish conquerors with stones of an Aztec temple there which they had destroyed.

Guadalupe Hidalgo is now within the City of Mexico itself. Here also is the Basilica of Nuestra Señora de Guadalupe, the hill where Her apparitions to the Indian Juan Diego occurred in 1531. It is now about two miles from the center of the city.

21. Guadalupe Hidalgo is now within the City of Mexico itself. Here also is the Basilica of Nuestra Señora de Guadalupe, the hill where Her apparitions to the Indian Juan Diego occurred in 1531. It is now about two miles from the center of the city.

22. The fact that Polk proclaimed the treaty in force on July 4, 1848, helps to explain the fact that there still exists in the Mesilla Valley the belief that the American flag was raised on the Mesilla plaza on that date. Perhaps someone did raise the flag in another ceremony, but written record eludes us on this point.

23. Carl I. Wheat, *Mapping the Transmississippi West, 1540-1861*, (Parsippany, NJ, Maurizio Martino Publisher, 1995).

24. AACJ, Reel 61, March, 1849; AACJ, Reel 15, Vol. 1848, January 12, 1849.

25. AACJ, Reel 15, Vol. 4; AACJ, Reel 61, February 17, 1847, December 4, 1845 and March 16, 1847; "Nuevas Colonias en el puesto de Guadalupe, March 16, 1847", amplified that the puesto's inhabitants were on the right side of the Río Grande. It was recognized as a colony in 1849 when people came from the North who did not want to remain in territory taken by the United States and who did not want to lose their Mexican citizenship. These *emigrados verdaderos* soon clashed with the colonists already in Guadalupe and those who came from other pueblos menaced by the American troops.

26. Fountain-Fall Testimony, Center for Southwest Research, University of New Mexico.

27. Archive of the Archdiocese of Santa Fe (AASF); Archivos Históricos del Arzobispado de Durango (AHAD); Hubert Howe Bancroft, *History of the North Mexican States and Texas, Vol. II*, (San Francisco, A.L. Bancroft and Co., 1884-89). Documents concerning Ramón Ortiz' life, his *limpieza de sangre* for the seminary in Durango, brought to light facts contrary to previous accounts concerning his life.

28. A visitador in the Mexican Catholic Church was not a visitor as the word might seem to indicate. In this case, for example, Juan Rafael Rascón was a *visitador* to New Mexico and the area to the north. The visitador was an ecclesiastical inspector. It was his duty as he traveled within the Diocese of Durango, to inspect the condition of churches, chapels, priests and all the accouterments thereof. His scribe kept a journal and wrote in it what the visitador said in regard to all these entities. He inspected and made suggestions of how better to keep the books; he read all wills as it was customary among the well-to-do to leave the church amounts of money or livestock or crops which could be turned into cash for the Church. This activity might seem avid or greedy, but such donations helped keep the Diocese alive.

29. That Guadalupe Miranda was Ramón Ortiz' teacher in Juan Rafael Rascón's home is ironic. During Ortiz' curacy at Paso del Norte in later years, Guadalupe Miranda was an enemy of the young priest. Miranda stayed close to Manuel Armijo and to Antonio López de Santa Ana in all political and military affairs.

30. "Libro de Sepulturas," San Antonio de Cuencamé, Cuencamé, Durango; Charles H. Lange and Carroll L. Riley, *The Southwest Journals of Adolph F. Bandelier, Vol. 1*, (Albuquerque, University of New Mexico Press, 1966).

31. AHAD. Letters from these and other priests reflect the events which formed these opinions.

32. AHAD, 1836-1837.

33. Vicente Riva Palacio, *Mexico a través de los Siglos, Vol. 2*, (México, D.F., G.S. López, 1940).

34. Fidelia Miller Pucket, "Ramón Ortiz: Priest and Patriot," *New Mexico Historical Review*, October, 1950, p. 262.

35. ibid.

36. Hugh Stephenson came to the area of Paso del Norte about the year 1824; he married Juana Ascarate of the land wealthy Ascarate family of Janos and El Paso. James and Samuel Magoffin were wealthy traders and merchants along the Santa Fe-Chihuahua Trail. James was a secret agent and was credited with the capitulation of Manuel Armijo to the

United States forces near Santa Fe, New Mexico in 1846. James Magoffin's inlaws were of the Valdes and Verimendi families of San Antonio, Texas. The family Verimendi were advocates of Texas independence, making them suspect in the eyes of official Mexico.

37. The standard grant a settler received, a terreno de labor, land to plant, was 360 *varas* by 960 *varas* [sometimes this varied due to the curve in the river or other topographical variances] This, at least, was the way it was in the Valley of Mesilla. Ramón Ortiz knew planting time was hard upon them, so he made the farming land grants first so the settlers, just having completed the ditch from the acequia madre to the fields, could put in seed in time for future harvest.

38. *El Faro*, Chihuahua, Mex., November 24, 1849.

39. National Archives, Record Group 98, Records of the U.S. Army Commands, Department of New Mexico, Letters Received, #133.

40. AACJ, Reel 15, Vol. 1848.

41. AACJ, Reel 61.

42. AACJ, Reel 35 [new filming].

43. ibid.

44. An "empresario either native or foreign…those who introduce as colonists a certain number of families. These empresarios were to receive as premiums or rewards for their services a certain amount of land…The premium or reward could not exceed nine haciendas and six labores (equal to about forty-seven square leagues). Of this, at the end of twenty years, he was obliged to have alienated two-thirds by sale, donation, or other manner." This was the rule described in the article of the Regulations of 1828. (These regulations made formally in Mexico came to New Mexico but were carried out in a somewhat diluted and customized manner - more than 2000 miles was a very long way to carry out a regulation to the letter.) Letter from James M. Lewis, Lawyer "In the Matter of the Arroyo of San Lorenzo Grant," Thomas Catron Papers, PC 29/301, Box 6, No. 37, Center for Southwest Research, University of New Mexico. A caballería is equal officially to 1104 varas by 552 varas. An hacienda of land has 5000 varas by 25,000 varas. In archives of different localities and regions, the terminology of the amounts of land given to empresarios varied. Thomas C. Barnes and Thomas H. Naylor, *Northern New Spain: A Research Guide*, (Tucson, University of Arizona Press, 1981).

45. AACJ, Reel 60, Vol. 1847.

46. AHAD, Letter from Ramón Ortiz at Paso del Norte to Bishop José Antonio Zubiría at Durango, December 23, 1849.

47. AACJ, Reel 16, Vol. 1849.

48. ibid.

49. Las Cruces was the second settlement founded on the land granted to the Doña Ana Bend colony.

50. When land grants were issued in 1851 and 1852 La Merced de La Mesilla and Nuestra Señora del Refugio - the Mesilla grant included two tracts: Mesilla and Picacho. Included within the Mesilla grant was the Santo Tomás de Iturbide area which would be separated from the Mesilla grant in 1853.

51. AACJ, Reel 61, 1849; AACJ, Reel 15, Vols. 1848 and 1849.

52. During the election for delegates to Congress in 1859, there were accusations and counter-accusations at the polls in Doña Ana, New Mexico, of ballet-box stuffing while, for an instant, the person who was officially monitoring the voting stepped outside briefly. This affair became a real dispute and many testimonies were taken from some of the oldest voters. They were required to relate their lives' stories, particularly in reference to whether they had been present when the flag was raised on the Mesilla plaza in 1854. The common belief was that if an individual was

within sight and/or sound of the raising of that flag, he/she automatically became a citizen. The ballot box argument had blossomed into a general review of the citizenship - American or Mexican - of some of the voters and of the people in charge of the security of the single ballot box.

3. Ramón Ortiz and Colonization

53. Lt. Sacket commanded the American occupation forces at Doña Ana.
54. AACJ, Reel 16.
55. ibid.
56. ibid.
57. ibid.
58. ibid.
59. ibid.
60. ibid.
61. When a suerte of land is mentioned, it means that a colonist was to draw from a hat a number which would correspond to a certain tract of land which would then be his. Correctly used this term differentiates from other terms because suerte means drawn by luck, while the use of the terms solar de casa and terreno de labor indicate lands assigned to the colonist.
62. Katherine D. Stoes Papers, Río Grande Historical Collections, New Mexico State University.
63. ACCJ.
64. *Compadrazgo* is the Spanish word applied to relationships developed by godmothers, *madrinas*, and godfathers, *padrinos*, at Baptism—all these were addressed as compadres and comadres. The fealty of this compadrazgo was as binding as ties of blood relation and sometimes was considered an even closer kinship which could be developed even further by marriage. Records of such family groups can be found in the Libro de Baustismos, Libro de Casamientos, and Libro de Entierros in the archives of the Church of San Albino, Mesilla, New Mexico.
65. Books B & E, County Clerk's Office, Doña Ana Courthouse, Las Cruces, New Mexico.
66. Grandma Fountain (her father was Pedro Garcia) related these and other tales from the early years of the colony.
67. National Archives, Military records for L.W. Geck, Washington, DC.
68. Fountain-Fall Testimony.

4. El Tratado de Mesilla

69. Colonel Sumner's sulkiness was due to a rivalry with Governor Calhoun for the reins of governmental power, and to the colonel's contention that a civil government would never succeed in New Mexico.
70. Fort Fillmore was established in September 1851 to protect Mesilla Valley residents from Apache attacks, but it also provided a U.S. military presence in the territory taken over from Mexico.

5. The Mesilla Guard

71. An earlier version of this chapter, coauthored with Nona Barrick, was published in 1976 by Texas Western Press as *The Mesilla Guard 1851-1861*.
72. AACJ, Reel 17, Rafael Ruelas, July, 1851.
73. The name Hermenegildo is of Spanish origin. It appears in this manuscript as Esmeregildo, Meregildo, or Merejildo where it is quoted directly. Otherwise, Meregildo will be used as it is in the census, baptismal, marriage, and death records.
74. Relationships are established here from the Libro de Bautismos, from the Libro de Casamientos, and from the Libro de Entierros, records of San Albino parish in Mesilla. From these and the census taken here in 1850, it becomes evident that Meregildo Guerra, the leader of the Mesilla Guard, Desiderio Guerra, Simón Guerra, Rafael Guerra, Juan Guerra, and Mateo Guerra, all pioneered in settling

that colony. The younger members, Hermenegildo and his brothers, Apolonio and Alecario, together with Juan Ortega, Cosme Ríos, Rafael Bermudes, and Silvestre Maese (or Me or Mes), all intermarried with the families of Mirabal, Durán, Cubero, Valencia, Provencio, Lucero, and Saenz. Simón Guerra's sons-in-law were Juan Mirabal, Jesús Cubero, and Jestis Belarde. The members of the Guardia Móvil who had no direct blood ties sometimes became associated with a fealty almost as binding as a blood relationship. They actually became kindred through being chosen as godfathers for infants of the Guard members. These were the comadres and compadres, the padrinos and madrinas of the 1850's.
75. According to Mariano Velásquez' *A New Pronouncing Dictionary of the Spanish and English Languages*, (New York, Appleton and Company, 1900), a ranchería is a collection of huts or shelters; then again the meaning can include a corral for horses; it can mean, in addition, the corral, the shelters, and some fields of corn which are planted and left untended in the Apache nomadic existence, only to offer a harvest when he returns.
76. Personal interview with Catalina Butler, descendant of Rafael Provencio.
77. Personal interview with Francisco Butler (who knows many good things about Mesilla), Mesilla, New Mexico.
78. Conditions exacted by the Commissioner Don Ramón Ortiz as he apportioned lands to the colonists.
79. Personal interview with Eve Ball, Ruidoso, New Mexico.
80. AACJ, Reel 62, Vol. 1852.
81. ibid.
82. AACJ, Reel 17. The Río Grande in 1853 left Mesilla on the east side of the river as Las Cruces was.
83. District Court Records, Doña Ana County, State Records Center and Archives, Santa Fe, New Mexico.
84. AACJ, Reel 17.
85. ibid.
86. Dan L. Thrapp, *Victorio and the Mimbres Apaches*, (Norman, University of Oklahoma Press, 1974).
87. Albert Schroeder Collection, State Records Center and Archives, Santa Fe, New Mexico.
88. Michael Steck Papers 1839-1882, Center for Southwest Research, Indian Affairs Collections, University of New Mexico.
89. ibid.
90. AACJ, Reel 18.
91. Rex W. Strickland, *El Paso in 1854*, with a 30 page handwritten newsletter by Frederic Augustus Percy entitled "El Sabio Sembrador", (El Paso, Texas, Western Press, 1969).
92. *Santa Fe Weekly Gazette*, February 19, 1854, State Records Center and Archives, Santa Fe, New Mexico.
93. *Santa Fe Weekly Gazette*, November 19, 1853, microfilm files, New Mexico State University.
94. The certification actually reads "in the undisputed territory," which is an error. Records of the Third Judicial District Court, Doña Ana County, New Mexico, State Records Center and Archives, Santa Fe, New Mexico.
95. ibid.
96. Records of the New Mexico Superintendency of Indian Affairs, United States Department of Indian Affairs Bureau, April 4, 1852-January 8, 1856, Microfilm Reel 25, E 173-717, New Mexico State University.
97. Michael Steck Papers.
98. Thrapp, Victorio.
99. Eve Ball Interview.
100. John C. Reid, *Reid's Tramp, or a journal of the incidents of ten months travel through Texas, New Mexico, Arizona, Sonora, and California*, (Austin, Steck Co., 1935).
101. Probate Journal A, Doña Ana County Clerk's Office, Las Cruces, New Mexico.

102. Balanquito is sometimes referred to as Belanquito or Palanquito.
103. Michael Steck Papers.
104. Ibid. Lt. Col. Dixon Miles to Dr. Michael Steck, Fort Fillmore, October 29, 1855. Here he addressed Dr. Steck as "U. S. Indian Agent, Cruzes, Doña Ana a [sic] Ft. Thorne."
105. The punctuation and spelling is Colonel Miles'. The translator is not known.
106. Michael Steck Papers.
107. Michael Steck Papers, Letter from Dr. Steck to "Sir," January 3, 1857.
108. Fort Fillmore Post Returns, War Department Record Group Number 94, National Archives, Washington, D.C.
109. Michael Steck Papers.
110. ibid.
111. ibid.
112. Records of the Adjutant General's Office 1780-1917, Letter Received, Record Group Number 94, National Archives, Washington, DC.
113. Michael Steck Papers.
114. Record Group Number 60, National Archives, Washington, DC.
115. Records of the Adjutant General's Office 1780-1917, Special Orders Number 44, Department of New Mexico, 1858, Record Group Number 94, National Archives, Washington, DC.
116. Office of the District clerk, United States Federal Courthouse, Santa Fe, New Mexico.
117. Aurora Hunt, *Kirby Benedict* (Glendale, CA, Arthur H. Clark Co., 1961).
118. Executive Records Book, 1851-1 855, May 17, 1857, State Records Center and Archives, Santa Fe, New Mexico.

6. Calle del Correo

119. Dr. Bessie Edsall, Personal letter, October 17, 1961.
120. "Pioneer Postman Brought Mail Horseback Into Infested Apache Land," The El Paso Times, April 29, 1956, El Paso, Texas.
121. ibid.
122. Personal interview and tour of premises at Mesilla, courtesy of Stith family, 1965.
123. *Mesilla Times*, July 13, 1861, Mesilla, New Mexico.
124. *Mesilla Times*, Oct. 18, 1860, Mesilla, New Mexico.
125. Confusion regarding street names came when the east line of buildings on the plaza was not there.
126. Doña Ana County Courthouse, Deed Book 3, p. 184.
127. *Mesilla Times*, June 30, 1861, Mesilla, New Mexico.
128. Capt. William Banning and George Hugh Banning, Six Horses, (New York, Century Co., 1928).
129. Diary of Phocion R. Way, "Overland By 'Jackass Mail,'" *Arizona and the West*, Spring, 1960.
130. Diary of Phocion R. Way, Summer, 1960.
131. William Tallach, "Tallach Story," *Press Argus*, v. 100, Van Buren, Ark. Centennial Edition, Section D, p. 3.
132. Diary of Phocion R. Way, Summer, 1960.
133. *Texas Almanac*, 1859, p. 139.
134. A 'stage' in the original meaning meant a stretch of about ten miles of road—between relays of animals. In between these ten or twelve mile stages were the swing stations which were little adobe huts, which housed the men who tended the stock. Such a station existed to the west of Mesilla as remembered by Angel Lucero, with whom the authors had a personal interview. His father was Vicente Lucero, one of the original colonists of La Mesilla. Mr. Lucero remembered the ruins of corrals situated just as the land rises to the mesas to the west. His father told him that those ruins were the remnants of the corrals where the horses were kept for the stage line that came out of Mesilla.
135. Captain William Banning and George Hugh Banning, Six Horses

136. Haydee Noya, Cataloguer, Dept of Manuscripts, Huntington Library, San Marino, Calif. Letter. Mrs. Noya quotes from letters of Isaiah Woods from files of the Library.
137. Pacific Wagon Roads, Microfilm, Rio Grande Historical Collections, New Mexico State University.
138. Diary of Phocion R. Way. Summer, 1960.
139. H. D. Burrows, "A two-Thousand Mile Stage Ride," paper read at Pasadena, Calif. meeting on Feb. 4, 1896.
140. Pacific Wagon Roads.

7. La Entrada

141. "Baylor's Babes" these young soldiers had earned that name because, as can be seen in the muster rolls, they were very young and they volunteered early in the Southern cause.
142. "Spy" in the days of Civil War meant "scout" instead of the meaning given it now.
143. These details have their basis in issues of the *Mesilla Times* and later accounts in Arizona newspapers and others.

8. The California Column

144. The California Column of the Union Army was composed of over two thousand men who had volunteered to march east across the desert to expel Confederate forces from New Mexico. They were under the command of Colonel, soon to be General, James H. Carleton. Six companies of cavalry, fifteen companies of infantry and one company of artillery made up the column.
145. The War of Rebellion Records (ORA), Series 1, Vol. 9; ORA, Series I Vol. 15 GO#20; *Santa Fe Gazette*, July 9, 1864; *Daily Alta California*.
146. *San Francisco Evening Bulletin*, San Francisco, Dec. 6, 1862.
147. ibid.
148. ORA.
149. Aureliano Armendariz, Compilation.
150. ibid.
151. Translated by Joseph P. Sanchez, Jerry Gurule, and David Hernandez, Spanish Colonial Research Center, National Park Service.
152. Teresa Garcia was the daughter of Antonio Garcia, and would one day be the daughter-in-law of Colonel Fountain.
153. Aureliano Armendariz, Compilation.
154. Mesilla parish books; Las Cruces parish books.
155. From the original Sanchez y Baca grant; presently San Miguel.
156. Records of the Adjutant General's Office 1780-1917, Record Group Number 94, National Archives, Washington, DC.
157. ORA, Series 1, Vol. 15, p. 596.
158. Dr. Benjamin Sacks, Personal Correspondence, Sept. 30, 1963.
159. Records of the Adjutant General's Office 1780-1917, Record Group Number 94, National Archives, Washington, DC.
160. *Mesilla Valley Independent*, Las Cruces, NM, Oct. 6, 1877.
161. Katherine D. Stoes, "Mutiny in Old Mesilla," *New Mexico Magazine*, Feb. 1950; Records of the Adjutant General's Office 1780-1917, Compiled Military Service Records, Civil War, California and New Mexico Volunteers, Record Group Number 94, National Archives, Washington, DC.
162. ibid.
163. Records of the Adjutant General's Office 1780-1917, 504-ACP-1874, Record Group Number 94, National Archives, Washington, DC.; Darlis A. Miller, *The California Column in New Mexico*, (Albuquerque, University of New Mexico Press, 1982); ORA; Dr. Benjamin Sacks, Personal Correspondence, 1968.

164. ORA, Vol. 9, Series 1, p. 576; Katherine D. Stoes Papers

165. *Santa Fe Weekly Gazette*, Santa Fe, NM, Dec. 27, 1862; Herbert Hart, *Old Forts of the Southwest*,(Seattle, Superior Pub. Co., 1964).

166. The chozas on the rivers here are half jacal, half cave dug into a hill.

167. Carleton and West had differences, but the General defended West's actions. Carleton said he ordered him to take corn. He also says people left because of the Texan threat. General Carleton claimed there were differences among citizens adjusted by the military commission on the general's orders, not West's. At this point, West asked to abandon Mesilla for Hart's Mill - a better vantage point, he thought, to stop the Texan advance.

168. ORA Series 1, Vol. 15, p. 596 et passim.

169. ibid.

170. ORA,Series 1, Vol. 15, pp. 606-636.

171. ORA, Series 1, Vol. 15, pp 681-683, Fergusson to West at Mesilla, Feb. 13, 1863.

172. Leonardo Siqueiros claimed that at Paso del Norte he traded care for sick and dying Texans for the guns. Fergusson went to see the pieces: three twelve-pound mountain howitzers, two six-pound field pieces. In turn, governor Luis Terrazas of Chihuahua claimed to have taken them from Siqueiros because such weapons were not supposed to be in the hands of private individuals. Actually, Terrazas was afraid of revolution in his own ranks. Capt. Fergusson recommended that the United States make a gift of these guns to Terrazas as a gesture of good will, as the governor was in possession of them anyway.

173. Records of the Adjutant General's Office 1780-1917, G.O. No. 1, Hdqtrs. Dist. AZ, Mesilla, Record Group Number 94, National Archives, Washington, DC.

174. ORA, Series 1, Vol. 15, P. 634; ibid., Vol. 9, p. 567.

175. ORA, Series 1, Vol. 26, p. 491.

176. Co. G, First Inf. CA Vols, Capt. Henry Greene, Cmndg.

177. From the collection of Mrs. Elizabeth Armendariz, now the property of Mary Alexander, her niece, Gadsden Museum, Mesilla. Albert Jennings Fountain became one of the most influential and well-known men in 19th century New Mexico and figured very prominently in the history of Mesilla. His rise to power came about after the period of history that this book deals with so it is not elaborated upon here.

178. Homestead Act 1864

179. J.Hall's abstract to land by the present settlement of San Pablo.

180. Personal interviews with the Mestas family; 1870 and 1880 U.S. census records; entries in the Parish books of the Church of San Albino.

181. *Santa Fe Weekly Gazette*, Dec. 27, 1863.

182. Executive Records Book, Secretary of State's Office, Santa Fe, New Mexico.

183. Ruben Creel had come to Chihuahua from Kentucky with Colonel Doniphan in 1847 and had remained and gone into business. ORA, Vol. 26, p. 920.

9. Aftermath

184. Fort Fillmore was abandoned shortly after Union forces returned to the Mesilla Valley. Troops now were stationed at Fort Bliss near El Paso.

185. Primicias are first fruits, the cream of the harvest; diezmos are collected after the tenth month and correspond to tithes.

186. Katherine D. Stoes Papers.

187. AACJ, Reel 17.

188. Doña Ana County Records, New Mexico State Archives and Records Center, Santa Fe, NM; also notes from the Gilbert Espinoza Collection, in the possession of his daughter Maggie MacDonald.

189. Francisco R. Almada, Gobernadores del estado de Chihuahua, (México, Impr. De la H. Cámara de Diputados, 1950); Thomas F. Cotner, editor, Carlos Castañeda, co-editor, *Essays in Mexican History; The Charles Wilson Hackett Memorial Edition*, (Austin, University of Texas, 1958).; AACJ reels 21 and 24; AHAD, letters from Cura Interino Real y Vasquez of Paso to Bishop Salinas of Durango.

190. John Lemon, The John Lemon Family Papers, Rio Grande Historical Collections, New Mexico State University.

191. From interviews with older residents of Mesilla.

192. Katherine D. Stoes Papers; Justice of the Peace Complaints, 1863-1878, Records of Doña Ana County, Records of State Archives and Records Center; AACJ, Reel 46 (new filming), Part 2.

193. Sources for the details of the murder of Agusté Maurin: Doña Ana County Courthouse, District Clerk's Office; *Mesilla Southwestern Old Times*, October 10, 1972; Katherine D. Stoes Papers. The *Mesilla News* had promised to reveal in a later issue other details of the murder, but then excused itself by saying that a request of importance had been made to withhold these particulars.

Inventory of Maurin's belongings for estate purposes in the Doña Ana County Clerk's Office reveal that two large oil paintings were hanging on the wall in one of his rooms—they were valued at $150.00. There were eight other large paintings in oil hanging there, also. The two previously mentioned were evidently singled out for special mention.

In George Griggs' History of the Mesilla Valley, p. 116, appears a letter from Nathan Boyd, Orejon Ranch, Mexico, August 15, 1914, in which Mr. Boyd acknowledges the loan to the National Gallery of Art in Washington of two paintings: a portrait of Beatrice Cenci by Giovanni Mazzolino and "a copy" of Titian's portrait of his daughter. He says that he found them in the home of Don Demetrio Chávez, "a Mexican then living in an old-time adobe house nearby the plaza of the town of Mesilla [his store and house were just across the street south from the brick building]. "On first entering Don Demetrio's house I noticed two pictures on the wall of the anteroom: the room was badly lighted, and at first I did not recognize what they were, but on having the heavy wooden shutters to the window in the room opened I saw that the pictures were very old and remarkably perfect and beautiful paintings, - very old copies, as I supposed, of two famous portraits, Titian's portrait of his daughter, Lavinia, whose face is enshrined in many of his pictures, and Guido Reni's portrait of Beatrice Cenci, which as you know is said to be one of the twelve greatest portraits of all time. Don Demetrio finally consented to sell the two paintings, and I sent them to London to be relined, remounted and restored." Unfortunately, he knew nothing of their early history. He said they had been in his possession many years, that he had acquired them in part satisfaction of a debt, that the old Mexican from whom he obtained them had died long ago, and that he did not know how or by whom they had been brought to Mexico.

Furthermore, of the portrait of Beatrice that I found here in southern New Mexico, in 1893, was painted by Mazzolini, and [as] competent judges have decided that it was painted by him then it is more than probable that it is the one - the long-lost original, that Guido copied."

Also AACJ, Reel 62, Vol. III.

194. Katherine D. Stoes Papers; Francisco R. Almada, *Diccionario de Geographia Y Biographia, Chihuahuenses*, (Chihuahua, México, Ediciones Universidad de Chihuahua, 1968); baptismal, marriage, and death records in the parish books of Saint Genevieve's, Las Cruces, New Mexico, and those of San Albino Church in La Mesilla, New Mexico;

AACJ, Reel 24.
195. Personal interview and visit by family from Texas.
196. The Santa Fe Ring was a network of lawyers, politicians and businessmen involved for mutual gain in acquiring and selling land granted to Hispanics under Spanish and Mexican law. They also dealt in ranching, mining and railroad interests.
197. Many interviews with old residents of the valley; Katherine D. Stoes Papers; records at the County and District Clerk's office, Doña Ana County Courthouse, Las Cruces, New Mexico.
198. Specifications for road in record in the County Clerk's Office, Doña Ana Courthouse, Las Cruces, NM.
199. "Aviso Publico," Territory of New Mexico, County of Doña Ana, Office of the Probate Court, Mesilla, New Mexico. Doña Ana County Records, New Mexico State Records Center and Archives, Santa Fe, New Mexico; Doña Ana County Clerk's Office, Deed Records, Book 3, p. 37.

10. The Hermit And Violence In Southern New Mexico

200. Personal interview with Mrs. Teresita "Grandma" Fountain.
201. Quiotes were, and are still, staffs fashioned from the yucca plant and decorated with "desert spoons," the spoon-shaped leaves of ivory consistency which must be dug from the underground growth of the yucca plant. These delicate blades of the yucca are used today to fashion quiotes, and are also used in La Mesilla, together with juniper branches, as traditional palms on Palm Sunday, Domingo de Ramos. Literally, according to the *Diccionario de Mejicanismos*, a quiote is a stalk growing from the center of a plant.
202. Onna Barret Mills Butts, *The History of Los Pastores of Las Cruces, New Mexico*, Thesis (M.A.), University of Southern California, 1936.
203. Archives of the Diocese of Las Cruces.
204. Father José de Jesús Baca had come to Mesilla in 1854, a refugee from the jurisdiction of Bishop Jean Baptiste Lamy of Santa Fe with whom he had difficulties in his curacy at Tomé.
205. 34th Congress, 1st session, House of Representatives, Misc. Doc. No. 15, Serial 866: "New Mexico Contested Election. Papers and Testimony in the Case of Miguel A. Otero, contesting the seat of José M. Gallegos, delegate from the Territory of New Mexico."
206. Fountain-Fall Testimony.
207. José Francisco Cháves and Mariano S. Otero were grandsons of Don Antonio José Cháves, governor of New Mexico 1828-1836. Francisco Perea and Pedro Perea, important in New Mexico history, were also grandsons. Ralph E. Twitchell, *The Leading Facts of New Mexico History*, Vol. 2, p.25, footnote 24. Almost all the candidates in these elections were related and descended from the same few early pioneer families in New Mexico.
208. Charles P. Clever was born in Prussia, emigrated to the United States and settled in Santa Fe in 1850. He engaged in various activities including holding office as United States Marshal in 1857; he was one of the owners of the *Santa Fe Weekly Gazette*; he was a lawyer; he served with Gen. Canby at the Battle of Valverde; he was Adjutant General of New Mexico 1861-1865, in 1867 and in 1868. He became Attorney General of New Mexico 1862-1867, delegate to the Fortieth Congress 1867-1869.
209. Poll and Tally Books, Doña Ana County, State Records Center and Archives, Santa Fe, New Mexico.
210. Names of those who addressed this letter of protest to John Lemon as Probate Judge with indications of their party affiliation: Francisco Salazar (D), Frederico Buckner (R), Fabian Gonzáles (R), Ignacio Gonzáles (D), Domingo Albillar (R), Juan Ortega (D).
211. John Lemon Papers. John Lemon's letter is translated from the Spanish, and because of this, liberties were taken in syntax to make it more coherent in English. The *Santa Fe Gazette*, Aug. 31, 1867, also reported the disturbance. Lemon backed Clever; William Rynerson was the leader of the Chávez forces aided by Mariano Barela, Ygnacio Orrantia and N.Y. Ancheta. The *Gazette*, a strongly Democratic paper, reported a very corrupt election in which it accused John Lemon of throwing out the precincts which were strongly for Chávez.
212. Larry D. Ball, *United States Marshals of New Mexico and Arizona Territories*, 1846-1912, (Albuquerque, University of New Mexico Press, 1978), p. 93.
213. Francisco Almada, *Resumen de historia del Estado de Chihuahua*, (Chihuahua, 1986. Ediciones del Gobierno del estado de Chihuahua).
214. Lansing Bloom, "New Mexico under Mexican Administration, Parts III and IV," *Old Santa Fe*, Vol. I, 1914.
215. Doña Ana County Records, State Records Center And Archives, Santa Fe, NM.
216. District Court Records, Doña Ana County, State Records Center and Archives, Santa Fe, NM.
217. Mesilla was not officially turned over by the Bishop of Durango to the Vicariate of Arizona until 1872.
218. Information from J. Paul Taylor, great-grandson of Miguel Romero y Baca.
219. Sources for information are the following on the man known as Giovanni María Agostino (in his baptismal entry at the Parroquia de S. Vittore M., Sizzano, Diocesi di Novara, December 25, 1802, his name is Latinized as Joannes Marie whose parents were Giuseppe Deagostini and Francesca Comera. His mother died in 1819 at the age of forty; his father died in 1833 at about sixty years of age.): Letters from Dr. Giuseppe Cuneo from the Archives of the Archdiocese of Santa Fe, State Records Center and Archives, Santa Fe, New Mexico; a short biography of the Hermit written by Albert J. Fountain from the collection of Mary Alexander, Gadsden Museum Collection; and personal interviews with Teresita Fountain.
220. The indefinite date of the Hermit's whereabouts in 1868 and 1869 is due to the lack of actual documentation during years of the Hermit's wandering in the Valley of the Río Grande. There are several accounts as noted, but none with precise dates.
221. Romulo Escobar, "Memorias del Paso del Norte, La Cueva del Hermitano," *Boletín de Estudios Chihuahenses*, Vol. 2, Ciudad Chihuaha.
222. *Santa Fe New Mexican*, May 18, 1869.
223. Information as to the stone marking the Hermit's grave is from a personal interview with Elizabeth Fountain Armendariz. At present in the cemetery at Mesilla, a cement marker has replaced the crumbled stone, and the iron fence has disappeared.
224. Doña Ana County Records, New Mexico State Records Center and Archives, Santa Fe, New Mexico.

11. The Riot of 1871

225. Romulo Escobar, "Las Chuzas ," from the series "Memorias de Paso del Norte," *Boletín de Ia Sociedad Chihuahuense de Estudios Historicos*, Chapter XXX.
226. Multiple issues of the *Santa Fe Weekly New Mexican* during the fall and winter months of 1869 and 1870.
227. *Santa Fe Weekly New Mexican*, Nov. 16, 1869. The old Franklin was becoming known as El Paso, and in 1872, after Benito Juárez died, the old El Paso del Norte was officially "Juárez."
228. Moreover, deeds to land granted in the colony were sometimes never recorded in the courthouse until a transaction of some kind took place: buying, selling, mortgaging. If none of these actions were ever taken in regard to the property, the colonist merely kept his original deed in a trunk or in a drawer. Occasionally he misplaced or

lost it entirely, so there was no record of his grant. Since the grant was made under Mexican administration, a copy of the instrument was supposed to be filed in Mexican archives. Unfortunately, these copies were either destroyed, lost or unavailable.

229. Acquisition 7/3. Refugio Colony Grant Lands Abstract, 1864-1909, MS 113, C.L. Sonnichsen Special Collections, University of Texas at El Paso Library.

230. Maurice G. Fulton, *History of The Lincoln County War*, edited by Robert N. Mullin, (Tucson, University of Arizona Press, 1968); "Frank Warner Angel's Notes on the New Mexico Territory, 1878," edited by Lee Scott Theisen, *Arizona and the West*.

231. Doña Ana County Clerk's Office; Larry D. Ball, United States Marshals,. p. 93.

232. *El Fronterizo, The Borderer*, Mar. 16, 1871; Katherine D. Stoes Papers.

233. Multiple references from AHAD including a letter from José Antonio Real y Vasquez to Durango regarding the fact that Lamy is coming to Las Cruces in February, 1869; Pbro. Antonio Severo Borrajo to José Vicente Salinas, Bishop of Durango, Sept. 9, 1871 indicating that Vicar Salpointe possibly was, had been, or would be in Las Cruces pressing for annexation from that point. The fact that Salpointe was, indeed, in Las Cruces is indicated by several letters from priests at that time: Antonio José Borrajo to José Vicente Salinas, Sept. 9, 1871; Borrajo to Salinas, Jan. 6, 1 872; letters from Salpointe at Las Cruces Feb. 6, 1872; Mar. 9, 1872.

234. *The Borderer*, March 23, 1871.

235. Fountain-Fall Testimony.

236. *The Borderer*, April 27, 1871. This newspaper was a Democratic sheet-coverage for the Democrats was positive, for the Republicans, negative. California Column veterans who were Democrats: Lawrence La Point, Bernard McCall Seneca Ames, Joseph Francis Bennett and his brother L. V. Bennett, Dr. Oscar Woodworth. Some of the earlier army veterans were also Democrats: George Achenbach of Doña Ana, and Conrad Aubel of Organ were two. Many big landholders and merchants were Democrats: Pierre Duval and the Ascarate family members; the Guerra family who were wagon train men, business men, and landholders—Blas, Alecario, Mateo, Jesús, and Desiderio. There were many more.

237. ibid ., May 4, 1871.

238. ibid, May 18, 1871.

239. José Manuel Gallegos was the older of the two candidates, and his ecclesiastical and political careers were blemished by his frank opposition to Bishop Jean Lamy, by his alleged immoral conduct while a priest, and by his failure in previous political campaigns.

240. Tally sheets for 1871 election returns; also census of 1870 for Doña Ana, Las Cruces, and Mesilla. State Archives and Records Center, Santa Fe, New Mexico.

241. Various June issues of *The Borderer*, Las Cruces, New Mexico.

242. *Santa Fe Weekly New Mexican*, May 2, 1871, Santa Fe, New Mexico.

243. Dan L. Thrapp, Victorio. p.99.

244. Santa Fe New Mexican, July 7, 1871.

245. Pablo Melendres, born in Valle de San Bartolomé, Chihuahua, came from El Paso del Norte to Doña Ana with the first colonists, and held the office of Juez de Paz under Mexican rule. Under the government of the United States during the invasion of 1846 he became Prefect and held office during and after that conflict under trying circumstances. He was a man whom other men respected, Mexican and American alike.

246, *The Borderer*, August 16, 1871.

247. ibid, August 30, 1871.

248. Other candidates in the election of 1871, in addition to the two principal candidates for delegate to Congress, were: for district attorney, Joseph F. Bennett and John S. Crouch; for representative to the New Mexico legislature, Manuel Nevares, Eugenio Moreno, Apolonio Barela, and Jacinto Armijo; for probate judge, Pablo Melendres and William L. Rynerson; for sheriff, Mariano Barela and Perfecto Armijo; for secretary of the probate judge, Daniel Frietze and Atilano Baca; for county treasurer, Matias Flores and Marcelino Gallegos; for justice of the peace, Robert Taylor and Longino Torres; for deputy sheriff, José Cordova and Anastacio Serna. Tally Sheets, 1871, State Archives and Records Center, Santa Fe, New Mexico.

249. Will of John Lemon, in possession of his great grandson, Fred Lemon of Doña Ana, New Mexico.

250. Sources for description of the riot in Mesilla on August 27, 1871: Ralph E. Twitchell, *The Leading Facts of New Mexico History*, Vol.3, (Cedar Rapids, Iowa, Torch Press, 1911-17) p. 193, fn 61a; *The Daily New Mexican*, Santa Fe, July 18, 1871, Sept. 1, 1872, and Sept. 4,1871; *Santa Fe Weekly New Mexican*, Oct.17, Nov. 21, 1871 et al.; *Santa Fe Post*, Aug. 27, 1871, letter to editor; Aug. 28, 1871; *Weekly Arizona Miner*, Sept. 30, 1871; *The Borderer*, Aug. 30, 1871, Sept. 6, 1871; Records of the Territorial District Court, Third Judicial District, Territory of New Mexico, November term, 1871, State Archives and Records Center, Santa Fe, New Mexico. AHAD, copy of legal matter in El Paso County: Jean Baptiste Salpointe of the Diocese of Arizona, United States, of the Roman Catholic Church, Petitioner v. José Antonio Borrajo, Defendant. Document includes a copy of the Papal Bull "Given in Rome in the Palace of San Pedro, under the Ring of the Fisherman the 22nd day of December, 1871" which gave Salpointe jurisdiction over Mesilla, but the Bishop of Durango was not directly notified of this until much later.

251. Libro de Entierros, San Albino parish book.

252. The Borderer, Sept. 20, 1871.

253. *Santa Fe Weekly New Mexican*, Sept. 19, 1871; Nov. 21, 1871.

254. Libro de Casamientos, Numero 3, de Diciembre, 1872.

12. Migration

255. The parish records of the Church of San Albino, records of purchases from the Lemon store and mill after the riot (from the Rio Grande Historical Collection, NMSU), and records in the Doña Ana County courthouse reveal that some settlers had gone ahead to Ojo de Federico and Ascensión, that some had gone and returned to Mesilla, and that there were some who did not go there until 1873.

256. Profesor Jesós Ramirez Caloca, "Ascensión," *Boletín de Ia Sociedad Chihuahuense de Estudios Historicos*, Tomo V, p. 245-249. Professor Caloca, in his article, states that Ygnacio Orrantia told him these facts and described to him the terrain when Orrantia was an old man.

257. AHAD, Cartas , 1872, José de Jesús Baca to José Vicente Salinas, Dec. 13, 1872.

258. AHAD, Cartas y Oficios, 1872.

259. Teresa Garcia, daughter of Antonio Garcia and Soledad Bermudes, married A. J. Fountain, Jr.

260. 1870 and 1880 United States Censuses; Tularosa Basin Historical Society, *Otero County Pioneer Family Histories*, Vol. 1, (Alamogordo, New Mexico, Tularosa Basin Historical Society, 1981); C.L. Sonnichsen, Tularosa, *Last of the Frontier West*, (New York, Devin-Adair Co., 1960); Personal interviews with Mr. Herman Weisner; Books E, 10,15,16, 13, County Clerk's Office, Doña Ana County, Las Cruces, New Mexico; Map of Tularosa townsite, 1885; Parish Records, St. Genevieve's church, Las Cruces, New Mexico.

261. *The Borderer, El Fronterizo*.

262. *Santa Fe Weekly Gazette*, Dec. 27, 1862, Christopher Carson, Company 1, New Mexico Volunteers, Capt. B.C. Cutler, Asst. Adj. Gen., Department of N.M. Commanding,. Microfilm, Rio Grande Historical Collections, New Mexico State University.

263. "Mesilla" used here denotes the whole length of the Mesilla Valley from which most of the early settlers of Tularosa came: Refugio, Santo Tomás, La Mesilla, Picacho, Doña Ana, and Las Cruces.

264. The whole townsite was called the hortaliza and it was watered by the first water to cascade from the Canyon of the Río Tularosa. This Spanish word is usually reserved for individual gardens, but here it includes the whole area as one large garden. Tularosa Basin Historical Society, Otero County Pioneer Family Histories , p. 159.

265. ibid.

266. ibid.

267. *Santa Fe Weekly Gazette*.

268. John Lemon Papers, "Pablo Melendres Letter."

269. For sparse details of this encounter, refer to: Doña Ana County Docket Book, Civil and Criminal, Book A 1869-1886, Cases (some of which are continuances from 1871) 207, 191, 151, 189, 205, 208, 106, 187, 152, 153,157, New Mexico State Records Center and Archive, Santa Fe, New Mexico;. Because at least two of these cases were continuances of cases of 1871, and because there existed no such record for the other cases, I tried to put them in sequential order. Also Tularosa Basin Historical Society, *Otero County Pioneer Family Histories*.

270. *The Borderer, (El Fronterizo)*, May 18 1871.

271. Pablo Melendres, the younger, at this date is Probate Judge of Doña Ana County. He is son of Pablo Melendres, native of San Bartolomé, Chihuahua, Mexico. The younger is around 35 years old here. The elder is one of the first colonists of Doña Ana, being *juez propietario* in 1844 and the prefect with whom the American Officials dealt during the occupation of Doniphan.

272. John Lemon Papers.

273. Tularosa Basin Historical Society, *Otero County Pioneer Family Histories*.

274. Maurice G. Fulton, *History of Lincoln County War*, Chap. II.

275. William Ostic had a large mercantile establishment where Indians were welcome to camp when in town and he was friendly to Mexican and Anglo alike. Tularosa Basin Historical Society, *Otero County Pioneer Family Histories*.

276. District Court Cases. #187, #189, State Records Center and Archive, Santa Fe, New Mexico.

277. District Court Case, #106.

278. Tularosa Basin Historical Society, *Otero County Pioneer Family Histories*.

279. George B. Anderson, *History of New Mexico, Its Resources and People*, Vol II, (Los Angeles, Pacific States Publishing Co., 1907).

280. *The Borderer*, Sept. 20, 1871.

SOURCES

Archives

Archive of the Archdiocese of Santa Fe (AASF), Santa Fe, New Mexico.

Archives of the Diocese of Las Cruces.

Archivos Historícos del Arzobispado de Durango (AHAD), Durango, Mexico:
  "Libro de Sepulturas," San Antonio de Cuencamé, Cuencamé, Durango.

Branigan Library, Las Cruces, NM.
  Herbert W. Yeo manuscripts

Center for Southwest Research, University of New Mexico:
  Fountain-Fall Testimony
  Thomas Catron Papers
  Michael Papers Steck Papers 1839-1882

Church of Saint Genevieve's, Las Cruces, New Mexico:

Baptismal, marriage, and death records

Church of San Albino, Mesilla, New Mexico:
  Libro de Baustismos, Libro de Casamientos, and Libro de Entierros

El Paso Public Library:
  Cleofas Calleros Microfilm

Doña Ana County Courthouse, Las Cruces, New Mexico:
  County Clerk's Office-Record Books; Probate Records; Deed Books

Museum of New Mexico:
  Photograph Collection

National Archives, Washington, D.C.:
  Record Group Number 60, National Archives, Washington, DC.
  Record Group Number 94, Fort Fillmore Post Returns, War Department;
  Records of the Adjutant General's Office 1780-1917.
  Record Group 98, Records of the U.S. Army Commands, Department of New Mexico
  Military records for L.W. Geck

Rio Grande Historical Collections, New Mexico State University:
  United States Department of Indian Affairs Bureau, Microfilm
  Doña Ana Historical Society Photographs
  John Lemon Family Papers
  López Family Photographs
  Pacific Wagon Roads Microfilm
  Carl Schuchard Lithographs

Katherine D. Stoes Papers

State of New Mexico Records Center and Archives, Santa Fe, New Mexico:
  Third Judicial District Court Records, Doña Ana County
  Albert Schroeder Collection
  Executive Records Book, 1851-1855
  Doña Ana County Records: Justice of the Peace Complaints, 1863-1878; Office of the Probate Court, Mesilla, New Mexico; Poll and Tally Books, Doña Ana County; Doña Ana County Docket Book, Civil and Criminal, 1869-1886 Cases

University of Texas at El Paso:
  Archivos del Ayuntamiento de Ciudad Juárez (AACJ), Juárez, Chihuahua.
  Archivos de la Catedral de Ciudad Juárez (ACCJ), Juárez, Chihuahua.
  Father Gerald Decorme, S.J., Manuscript
  Libro de Baustismos of Nuestra Señora de Guadalupe at El Paso del Norte
  Parral Archives Microfilm
  Refugio Colony Grant Land Abstract 1864-1909, ms. 113
  C.L. Sonnichsen Papers

Private Collections

Aureliano and Elizabeth Armendariz Collection, Gadsden Museum, Mesilla, New Mexico.

Gilbert Espinoza Collection, Mesilla, New Mexico.

Fred Lemon Collection, Doña Ana, New Mexico.

Mary D. Taylor, Mesilla, New Mexico

Newspapers

Daily Alta California, San Francisco, California.
Daily National Intelligence.
El Faro, Chihuahua, Mexico.
El Fronterizo, The Borderer, Las Cruces, New Mexico.
El Paso Times, El Paso, Texas.
Evening Bulletin, San Francisco, California.
Mesilla Southwestern Old Times, Mesilla, New Mexico.
Mesilla Times, Mesilla, New Mexico.
Mesilla Valley Independent, Mesilla, New Mexico.
Santa Fe Gazette, Santa Fe, New Mexico.
Santa Fe New Mexican, Santa Fe, New Mexico.
Santa Fe Post, Santa Fe, New Mexico.
Weekly Arizona Miner.

Letters

Dr. Bessie Edsall, October, 1961.

Haydee Noya, Cataloguer, Dept of Manuscripts, Huntington Library, San Marino, Calif.

Dr. Benjamin Sacks, 1963

Interviews

Anastacio Barela descendants, Texas.
Eve Ball, Ruidoso, New Mexico.
Fr. Ernest Burrus, S.J., 1987.
Catalina Butler, Mesilla, New Mexico.
Francisco Butler, Mesilla, New Mexico.
Teresita "Grandma" Fountain, Mesilla, New Mexico.
Myra Ellen Jenkins, Santa Fe, New Mexico, 1965.
Mestas Family, Mesilla, New Mexico.
Pedro Pedraza, Tortugas, New Mexico.
Stith Family, Mesilla, New Mexico, 1965.
Herman Weisner, Las Cruces, New Mexico

Published Works

Albert, James William
  Albert's New Mexico Report 1846-47, Albuquerque, Horn and Wallace Publishers, 1962.

Almada, Francisco R.
  Diccionario de Geographia Y Biographia, Chihuahuenses, Chihuahua, México, Ediciones Universidad de Chihuahua, 1968.
  —*Gobernadores del estado de Chihuahua*, México, Impr. De la H. Cámara de Diputados, 1950.
  —*Resumen de historia del Estado de Chihuahua, Chihuahua, 1986*. Ediciones del Gobierno del estado de Chihuahua.

Anderson, George B.
  History of New Mexico, Its Resources and People, Vol II, Los Angeles, Pacific States Publishing Co., 1907.

Ayer, Mrs. Edward A., Translator
  The Memorial of Fray Alonso de Benavides, 1630, annotated by Fredrick Webb Hodge and Charles Fletcher Lummis, Albuquerque, Horn and Wallace, 1965.

Ball, Larry D.
  United States Marshals of New Mexico and Arizona Territories, 1846-1912, Albuquerque, University of New Mexico Press, 1978.

Bancroft, Hubert Howe
  History of the North Mexican States and Texas, Vol. II, San Francisco, A.L. Bancroft and Co., 1884-89.

Banning, Capt. William and George Hugh Banning
  Six Horses, New York, Century Co., 1928.

Barnes, Thomas C. and Thomas H. Naylor
  Northern New Spain: A Research Guide, Tucson, University of Arizona Press, 1981.

Barrick, Nona A. and Mary Helen Taylor
  "Murder in Mesilla," *New Mexico Magazine*, November 1960.

Beers, Henry Putney
Spanish and Mexican Records of the American Southwest, A Bibliographical Guide to Archive and Manuscript Sources, Tucson, University of Arizona Press, 1979.

Bloom, Lansing
"New Mexico under Mexican Administration, Parts III and IV," *Old Santa Fe*, Vol. I, 1914.

Bolton, H.E.
Coronado, Knight of the Pueblos and Plains, Albuquerque, University of New Mexico Press, 1964.

Bustamante, Adrian Hermino
Los Hispanos: Ethnicity and Social Change. in New Mexico, Ph.D Dissertation, University of New Mexico, 1982.

Butts, Onna Barret Mills
The History of Los Pastores of Las Cruces, New Mexico, Thesis (M.A.), University of Southern California, 1936.

Caloca, Profesor Jesús Ramirez
"Ascensión," *Boletín de la Sociedad Chihuahuense de Estudios Históricos*, Tomo V.

Chávez, Fray Angélico
My Penitente Land, Albuquerque, University of New Mexico Press, 1974.
—"Genízaros," *Handbook of North American Indians*, Vol. 9, Southwest, Washington: Smithsonian Institution, 1979.
—*Tres Macho, He Said, Padre Gallegos of Albuquerque, New Mexico's First Congressman*, Santa Fe, William Gannon Publishers, 1985.

Cotner, Thomas F., editor, Carlos Castañeda, co-editor
Essays in Mexican History; The Charles Wilson Hackett Memorial Edition, Austin, University of Texas, 1958.

Escobar, Romulo
"Las Chuzas ," from the series "Memorias de Paso del Norte," *Boletín de La Sociedad Chihuahuense de Estudios Historicos* , Chapter XXX.
—"Memorias del Paso del Norte, La Cueva del Hermitano," *Boletín de Estudios Chihuahenses*, Vol. 2, Ciudad Chihuaha.

Fulton, Maurice G.
History of The Lincoln County War, edited by Robert N. Mullin, Tucson, University of Arizona Press, 1968.

Griggs, George
History of the Mesilla Valley, Las Cruces, Bronson Printing Co., 1930.

Hart, Herbert
Old Forts of the Southwest, Seattle, Superior Pub. Co., 1964.

Horvath, Steven M.
The Sociological and Political Origins of the Genízaros of the Plaza de Nuestra Señora de los Dolores de Belén, New Mexico 1740-1812, Ph.D. Dissertation, Brown University, 1979.

Horgan, Paul
Lamy of Santa Fe, New York, Farrar, Straus and Giroux, 1975.
—*Great River, The Rio Grande in North American History*, 2 Vols., New York, Rinehart & Company, 1954.

Hunt, Aurora
Kirby Benedict, Glendale, CA, Arthur H. Clark Co., 1961.

Jenkins, Myra Ellen and Albert H. Schroeder
A Brief History of New Mexico, Albuquerque, University of New Mexico Press, 1974.

Lange, Charles H. and Carroll L. Riley
The Southwest Journals of Adolph F. Bandelier, Vol. 1, Albuquerque, University of New Mexico Press, 1966.

Lister, Florence C. and Robert H. Lister
Chihuahua Storehouse of Storms, Albuquerque, University of New Mexico Press, 1966.

McFie, Maude
A History of the Mesilla Valley, M.A. Thesis, New Mexico College of Agriculture and Mechanic Arts, 1903.

Miller, Darlis A.
The California Column in New Mexico, Albuquerque, University of New Mexico Press, 1982.

Moreno, Jimenez and A. Garcia Ruiz
Historia de Mexico-Una Síntesis, Ciudad Mexico, Instituto Nacional de Antropología y Historia, 1962.

Naylor, Thomas H. and Charles W. Polzer
The Presidio and Militia on the Northern Frontier of New Spain, Tucson, University of Arizona Press, 1986.

Padilla, Genaro M.,ed.
The Short Stories of Fray Angélico Chávez, Albuquerque, University of New Mexico Press, 1987.

Ponce de León, José María
Reseñas Historicas del Estado de Chihuahua, 2ed., Tomo I. Chihuahua, Mex., Imprenta del Gobierno, 1910.

Pucket, Fidelia Miller
"Ramón Ortiz: Priest and Patriot," *New Mexico Historical Review*, October, 1950.

Reid, John C.
Reid's Tramp, or a journal of the incidents of ten months travel through Texas, New Mexico, Arizona, Sonora, and California, Austin, Steck Co., 1935.

Riva Palacio, Vicente
México a través de los Siglos, Vol. 2, México, D.F., G.S. López, 1940.

Simmons, Marc
New Mexico, A Bicentennial History, New York, W. W, Norton and Company, Inc., 1977

Sonnichsen, C.L.
Tularosa, Last of the Frontier West, New York, Devin-Adair Co., 1960.

Stoes, Katherine D.
  "Mutiny in Old Mesilla," *New Mexico Magazine*, Feb. 1950.

Strickland, Rex W.
  El Paso in 1854, El Paso, Texas Western Press, 1969.

Tallach, William
  "Tallach Story," *Press Argus*, v. 100, Van Buren, Ark. Centennial Edition.

Taylor, Mary D. and Nona Barrick
  The Mesilla Guard 1851-1861, El Paso, Texas, Texas Western Press, 1976.
  —"Mesilla Entrada," *New Mexico Magazine*, July 1961.

Theisen, Lee Scott
  "Frank Warner Angel's Notes on the New Mexico Territory, 1878," *Arizona and the West*.

Thrapp, Dan L.
  Victorio and the Mimbres Apaches, Norman, University of Oklahoma Press, 1974.

Tularosa Basin Historical Society
  Otero County Pioneer Family Histories, Vol. 1, Alamogordo, New Mexico, 1981.

Twitchell, Ralph E.
  The Leading Facts of New Mexico History, 3 Vols., Cedar Rapids, Iowa, Torch Press, 1911-17.

Velásquez, Mariano
  A New Pronouncing Dictionary of the Spanish and English Languages, New York, Appleton and Company, 1900.

Walz, Vina
  History of the El Paso Area 1680-1692, Ph.D. Dissertation, University of New Mexico, 1951.

War of Rebellion: A Compilation of the Official Records of the Union and Confederate Armies, 128 Vols.,Washington, D.C., 1880-1901.

Way, Phocion R.
  "Overland By 'Jackass Mail," *Arizona and the West*, Spring and Summer, 1960.

Wheat, Carl I.
  Mapping The Transmississippi West, 1540-1861, Parsippany, NJ, Maurizio Martino Publisher, 1995.

Government Documents

34th Congress, 1st session, House of Representatives, Misc. Doc. No. 15, Serial 866: "New Mexico Contested Election. Papers and Testimony in the Case of Miguel A. Otero, contesting the seat of José M. Gallegos, delegate.

Index

Made in the USA
Columbia, SC
07 April 2025

56269314R00096